ALSO BY HELEN NASH

Kosher Cuisine

Helen Nash's Lower-Fat Kosher Kitchen

Healthful and Nutritious Recipes for Everyday Eating and Entertaining

Helen Nash

Random House
New York

Helen Nash's Lower-Fat Kosher Kitchen

All rights reserved under International and Pan-American Copyright Conventions.
Published in the United States by Random House, Inc., New York, and
simultaneously in Canada by Random House of Canada Limited, Toronto.

Originally published in hardcover by Random House, Inc., in 1988.

Library of Congress Cataloging-in-Publication Data

Nash, Helen.
Helen Nash's lower-fat kosher kitchen.
ISBN 0-679-76951-X
Includes index.
1. Cookery, Jewish.   I. Title.
TX724.N355   1988   641.5′676   88-42668

Printed in the United States of America

24689753

FIRST PAPERBACK EDITION

Illustrations by Lilly Langotsky
Book design by Carole Lowenstein

To Jack, Pamela, Joshua and George

Acknowledgments

I would like to thank Jason Epstein for giving me encouragement.
Becky Saletan for her guidance.
Sarah Timberman for her patience.
Carole Lowenstein for her good cheer.
Nilda Fretes for her assistance and pleasant spirit.

Contents

Introduction

When my first book appeared in print I experienced a feeling of great joy intermingled with a feeling of great regret. Joy that finally, after so many years, I could touch and see the work; and regret that there were so many more ideas and dishes that I wanted to share. Would I have another opportunity to present them? I never thought I would. I am so pleased that another opportunity did present itself.

After teaching and lecturing, I realized that what I wanted to share were easy, quick, light, fat-free, nutritious dishes that are also kosher, and visually attractive. To create these dishes I began to experiment with ingredients that were not previously readily available—*shiitake* mushrooms, radicchio, green peppercorns, red and yellow bell peppers, sun-dried tomatoes and many others. I experimented with different ethnic seasonings, such as cumin, coriander, curry, soy sauce, black beans, Japanese horse-radish, ginger, mustard seeds and sesame seeds, among many. I explored many cooking techniques, but concentrated on steaming to enhance the natural flavor of the ingredient. I found that by wrapping fish or poultry in Saran Wrap or foil and steaming it wrapped I was able to preserve the pure flavor of the ingredient and lower the calories. I also reduced the cooking time of most dishes to enhance the flavor and texture. I was able to lighten the sauces, by reducing the stock and by omitting cream, flour, and shortening. I began to substitute lighter, lower in calories ingredients in some of the traditional dishes—for example, substituting turkey for beef in my new cholent recipe. Through such methods I was also able to simplify a few favorite recipes from my first book, *Kosher Cuisine*. I hope that you will find these recipes as enjoyable as their predecessors, but easier to make.

In addition, I included new suggestions that I thought would be helpful. I hope that they will serve as general guides for meal-planning, and also that you will alter them as you see fit. Very often I look for other options than those suggested depending on my mood, the temperature, or the availability of ingredients. There is also a chapter on wines.

The menu suggestions, however, reflect my approach to eating. Most of the time I prefer to begin a meal with a soup. I find soups to be readily digestible, visually attractive and easy to prepare in advance. I like to follow with fish, pasta, poultry or meat. Next a salad, and finally the dessert: homemade sorbet or ice cream; poached fruit; or seasonal fresh fruit accompanied by cake or cookies. You will also find that the individual recipes suggest courses to follow or precede them. These suggestions are only loosely cross-referenced, in order to give you as many alternatives as possible.

Most important, I wanted to give my readers a sense of confidence when composing a menu. I urge you to taste, touch and smell while cooking. Seasonings are a matter of personal taste. Taste everything you cook and take nothing for granted—not even your own palate—for even your own tastes change.

Enjoy the experience.

Kosher

Jewish tradition strives to orient every aspect of our daily life toward holiness. Food is that which gives us the physical sustenance to fulfill God's will. The word *kosher* means "fit" or "proper" in an ethical sense: Prepared in accordance with the laws of *kashruth*, religious dietary laws meant to teach reverence for life.

Consider the prohibition against eating pork. Because pigs were used for sacrifice by heathen cultures, they were deemed ethically unfit for consumption by God-fearing people.

In order to avoid cruelty to animals and underscore the importance of compassion and respect for all living things, special humane methods of slaughter were required. The methods were designed for quick and painless death. Not just anyone could do the slaughtering; it had to be done by someone specially trained for it, one who had the proper spiritual orientation.

There are two important rules regarding meat—in Deut. 14:21 and Ex. 23:19 and 34:26 ("You shall not boil a kid in its mother's milk") and in Lev. 7:26–27 and 17:10–14 ("You must not consume any blood, either, in fowl, or animal, For the life of the flesh is in the blood").

From the first rule has come the separation of meat and milk, not just at meals but in their preparation and even in the cleaning and drying of pots and dishes. Specific time intervals are observed between the eating of meat and the eating of dairy meals. (Some foods are neutral, neither meat nor dairy. These "pareve" foods can be eaten in conjunction with either, but care must be taken in their preparation so that meat utensils are not used for dairy foods or vice versa.)

The second rule about meat, which forbids the consumption of blood, affects the preparation of meat from the moment of slaughter on. First, in addition to the speed and painlessness of the method of slaughter, the law requires complete and rapid draining of the blood. Following this, meat must be "kashered" to remove any remaining blood. While today kashering is generally performed by kosher butchers, it is possible to do it at home by an easy sequence of rinsing and salting the meat.

The rule against consumption of blood also applies to eggs. If you crack open an egg and it has a spot of blood, you must discard it. It is therefore important to open eggs one at a time, over a separate bowl from the one that contains the rest of the eggs.

Only meat from animals with cloven hooves that chew their cud may be eaten. All others are forbidden, such as camel, horse, hare, pig, and donkey, which were often eaten or offered as sacrifice by idolatrous races.

Certain cuts of meat, those taken from the hindquarter, are also forbidden because the sciatic nerve, which runs through the hindquarter, is forbidden. While historically kosher butchers removed this and its accompanying blood vessels (as they do in Israel today), it is too time consuming for the American meat industry, and there are too few butchers skilled enough to do it. Instead, hindquarters are sold to nonkosher butchers.

Kosher rules apply to all foods, not just to meat. Only fish with fins and scales are permitted. All types of shellfish, which are scavengers, are forbidden. But even so, there are at least seventy-five different species of fish allowed, a large enough variety.

Poultry that is permitted include the usual domestic birds—chicken, turkey, duck, goose, dove. Wild birds and birds of prey are not allowed, nor are the eggs from those birds. Anything creeping or crawling is forbidden—insects, snakes, amphibian snails. The prohibition also applies to insects that attack fruits and vegetables. In a kosher kitchen, care is taken to examine all produce for worms and to examine dried beans and peas for weevils. Food that is contaminated in this way is not kosher.

Neutral foods (parve or pareve) include all fruits and vegetables, nuts, spices, sugar, salt, tea, coffee, the permitted fish, and eggs from permitted poultry. These can be eaten with either meat or dairy dishes. When buying packaged foods, look for a symbol that indicates that the contents were prepared under rabbinic supervision. Some symbols are the following:

Ⓤ —the Union of Orthodox Jewish Congregations. New York, New York. (Inasmuch as the Ⓤ is under the aegis of a large communal organization, this is the best known and most widely used symbol of kashruth.)

Ⓚ —O.K. (Organized Kashrut) Laboratories, Brooklyn, New York.

Ⓜ —(K.V.H.) Kashrut Commission of the Vaad Horabanim (Rabbinical Council) of New England, Boston, Massachusetts.

Ⓚ —Rabbi J. H. Ralbag, New York, New York.

ⓑ —Kosher Supervision Service, Hackensack, New Jersey.

Ⓚ —Kosher Overseers Association of America, Beverly Hills, California.

Ⓥ —Vaad Hoeir of St. Louis, St. Louis, Missouri.

Ⓦ —Board of Rabbis, Jersey City, New Jersey.

☆ —Vaad Hakashrus of Baltimore, Baltimore, Maryland.

If you are thinking of setting up a kosher kitchen, you should seek rabbinic advice on how to proceed. You may also wish to consult one of the many excellent books on the subject, such as Blu Greenberg's *How to Run a Traditional Jewish Household* (Simon and Schuster, 1983), through whose courtesy I have reproduced the symbols in the preceding paragraph.

The following is simply a brief overview.

A kosher kitchen can be set up in any space. You will require separate cooking vessels and utensils for meat and dairy foods, as well as separate serving dishes for meat and dairy. Similarly, you will need separate bowls and blades for the food processor, as well as separate blender bowls. If you have two sinks and two dishwashers, you can designate one for meat and one for dairy, as meat and dairy dishes and utensils may not be washed or kept together. Most of us, however, have only one sink and one dishwasher; we use two sets of dish drainers, two sink liners, and two separate dishwasher racks. If you do not want to bother with two separate dishwasher racks, simply use the machine for meat dishes and utensils and wash your dairy set by hand. Use kosher detergents for dishwashing and designate different towels and sponges for dairy and milk dishes. To simplify, use different colored items for meat and dairy.

In addition, Passover requires the use of two completely separate sets of dishes and utensils. Elaborate as all this sounds, keeping kosher becomes quite manageable once you begin living it.

In setting up your kosher kitchen, and when in doubt as to any kashruth-related matter, seek out proper rabbinic advice.

Helen Nash's Lower-Fat Kosher Kitchen

Potato Rounds with Caviar
Tortilla (Vegetable Omelet)
Curried Wontons

Cocktail Food & First Courses

DAIRY
Salmon Pâté
Potato Rounds with Caviar
Strips of Potato Skins with Sour Cream Dip
Spinach Roll
Spinach Strudel
Feta Cheese Strudel

PAREVE
Smoked Whitefish Pâté
Latkes (Potato Pancakes)
Sole in Seaweed Batter
Tortilla (Vegetable Omelet)
Broiled Sweet Peppers
Souffléed Acorn Squash
Baked Spaghetti Squash with Tomato Sauce
Braised Baby Artichokes
Warm Spinach Salad
Stir-fried Shiitake Mushrooms
Marinated Salmon with Green Peppercorns
Salmon Tartare I
Salmon Tartare II
Marinated Salmon
Tuna Seviche
Gefilte Fish
Pasta Salad with Smoked Salmon and Steamed Vegetables

MEAT
Crunchy Chicken Tidbits
Curried Wontons

Salmon Pâté

8 COCKTAIL SERVINGS

The salmon may be steamed in advance, or the entire pâté can be prepared in advance and stored in the refrigerator.

6 ounces skinned salmon fillet
Kosher salt
Freshly ground black pepper
3 tablespoons dry white wine
1½ ounces cream cheese

6 ounces smoked salmon, cut into
  small pieces
1 tablespoon lemon juice
½ teaspoon dry mustard

Place the salmon fillet in the middle of a piece of foil large enough to enclose it. Season with salt and pepper and pour the wine over the fillet. Enclose the fillet by bringing up the edges of the foil and sealing them tightly. Set a steamer basket in a pot, add water to the pot to just below the bottom of the basket and bring to a boil. Place the fish package in the basket, cover and steam over high heat for approximately 7 minutes, or until the inside of the fish turns orange-pink all the way through. Cool, drain the salmon and in a food processor fitted with a steel blade purée with the cream cheese until smooth. Add the smoked salmon and process for a few seconds until just combined.

Transfer the pâté to a serving bowl and season very well with the remaining ingredients. Serve the pâté on endive leaves, whole-wheat triangle toasts or crackers.

Potato Rounds with Caviar

12 SERVINGS

If you are a caviar fan, you will love it with these thin, crisp potato slices. The slices can be baked in advance, wrapped in a towel and refrigerated.

Unsalted butter for greasing cookie sheets
3 medium baking potatoes
Kosher salt
1 tablespoon unsalted butter

2 tablespoons cream cheese mashed with a fork
4 ounces natural salmon caviar
1 teaspoon lemon juice
4 sprigs dill, finely snipped

Preheat the oven to 500° F. Brush 2 or 3 cookie sheets with butter.

Wash and slice the potatoes thin crosswise. Pat them thoroughly dry in a towel and arrange them on the cookie sheets. Sprinkle lightly with salt. Brush with the butter, and bake for 12 to 15 minutes, or until lightly golden and crisp. (Some slices may brown more quickly than others because they are thinner.)

Transfer the slices to paper towels to drain and let cool.

Combine the cream cheese, caviar, lemon juice and dill.

To Serve: Place ¼ teaspoon of the caviar mixture in the center of each potato slice and arrange the rounds on a napkin-lined dish.

Strips of Crisp Potato Skins with Sour Cream Dip

10 SERVINGS

After serving *crudités* for years, I thought I needed a change. These potato strips seemed like a nutritious substitute. If you wish to bake the strips several hours ahead of time, do so, and should they lose their crispness just reheat them for a few minutes in a preheated 450° F. oven before serving.

Unsalted margarine for greasing cookie sheet

DIP

¼ cup sour cream
¼ cup homemade mayonnaise (see page 193)
¼ teaspoon dry mustard
About 1 teaspoon Worcestershire sauce

12 medium to large baking potatoes

5 sprigs dill, finely snipped
Kosher salt
Freshly ground black pepper

Preheat the oven to 450° F. Grease a cookie sheet.

Scrub the potatoes well and dry them. With a paring knife, cut long strips of potato peel 1 inch wide, including a thin layer of the potato. Pat dry. (Steam the peeled potatoes and reserve them for another use.)

Arrange the potato strips skin side down on the cookie sheet. Bake for 8 to 10 minutes. Turn them over and bake for 15 minutes more, or until crisp. Remove from the oven.

While the potatoes are baking, make the dip: Mix together the sour cream, mayonnaise, mustard, Worcestershire sauce and dill. Season with salt and pepper to taste.

To Serve: Place the potato strips in a napkin-lined dish and serve with the dip.

Spinach Roll

This is quite a versatile dish; it can be a festive starter to any meal, as well as a luncheon or brunch course. It is also a very convenient dish: The entire roll can be baked earlier in the day and reheated before serving.

1 tablespoon unsalted butter, melted

1½ tablespoons unseasoned breadcrumbs

Four 10-ounce packages frozen chopped spinach, thawed

5 eggs, separated, at room temperature

Kosher salt

Freshly ground black pepper

Freshly grated nutmeg

FILLING

½ pound firm fresh mushrooms

4 tablespoons unsalted butter

4 medium shallots, minced

8 ounces farmer cheese

3 ounces cream cheese

8 ounces sour cream

About ½ cup freshly grated Parmesan cheese

6 sprigs dill, finely snipped

Kosher salt

Freshly ground black pepper

Preheat the oven to 400° F.

Use half the melted butter to brush the bottom and sides of an 11- by 16-inch jelly-roll pan. Line the pan with a 21-inch sheet of wax paper, so that it extends beyond the short ends of the pan. Brush the paper with the remaining melted butter and dust it evenly with the breadcrumbs. Then, holding the paper, invert the pan and tap it to shake out the excess crumbs.

Squeeze small amounts of the spinach dry with your hands, then wring the spinach in a dish towel, in batches, to dry more. Transfer the spinach in batches to a food processor fitted with a steel blade. With the motor on, add one egg yolk at a time, processing until smooth. Transfer the mixture to a bowl.

In a clean bowl beat the egg whites, at high speed, until stiff. With a rubber spatula, fold ¼ of the whites into the spinach until thoroughly combined. Now reverse the process: Spoon the spinach mixture over the remaining whites. Gently fold the two mixtures together, using a motion like a figure eight, until all the whites have disappeared. Season the mixture with salt, pepper and nutmeg. Spoon it into the prepared pan, spreading evenly and smoothing the top. Bake in the middle of the oven for 10 to 12 minutes, or until the top feels firm and is springy to the touch. Cover the pan with a damp towel and let cool on a rack.

Make the Filling: Wipe the mushrooms clean with a damp paper towel, quarter them and chop them coarse, in batches, in a food processor or by hand. Transfer each batch to a bowl. In a large skillet heat 2 tablespoons of the butter. Add the shallots and sauté, over low heat, until soft. Add the remaining 2 tablespoons butter and the mushrooms and sauté over high heat, stirring with a wooden spoon, until the mushrooms are barely coated with the butter. Let cool.

In a bowl mix together the farmer cheese and the cream cheese. Combine with the sour cream, mushrooms, 6 tablespoons of the Parmesan cheese and the dill. Season to taste with salt and pepper.

To Assemble the Roll: Spread out on a work surface a double layer of wax paper about 2 feet long. Invert the cooled spinach sheet onto the wax paper. Remove the pan, then gently peel off the paper. Trim the edges of the spinach sheet. Spread the filling evenly over the roll. With the help of the wax paper, lift the long edge and loosely roll up the sheet like a jelly roll, rolling it away from you. Press it lightly into a log, shaping with the wax paper. (Don't worry if the roll cracks.) Slide 2 wide spatulas under the ends of the roll and carefully transfer it to a serving platter. Sprinkle with Parmesan cheese, then heat the roll lightly in a food warmer or in a preheated 200° F. oven for 10 to 15 minutes. You may also heat the spinach roll by placing the serving platter over a pot of boiling water. If you are not serving the roll right away, cover it with foil and refrigerate it. Heat lightly before serving. Slice into approximately 1-inch pieces.

SERVING SUGGESTIONS: As an appetizer, follow with Fish Soup with Vegetables or any broiled fish. As a luncheon course, precede by a green salad, Chilled Cucumber Soup or Puréed Romaine and Watercress Soup.

Spinach Strudel

2 STRUDELS, EACH SERVING 8 TO 10

Both this strudel and the one that follows are extremely versatile and convenient dishes to prepare. They can be served as first courses, or as brunch or luncheon dishes. They can be prepared in advance, refrigerated, and baked when needed.

FILLING

Two 10-ounce packages frozen chopped spinach, thawed

2 tablespoons unsalted butter

4 scallions, including green parts, thinly sliced

¼ pound feta cheese, crumbled

10 tablespoons unsalted butter, melted

¾ cup unseasoned breadcrumbs

A 15-ounce container ricotta

4 eggs, lightly beaten

1¼ cups freshly grated Parmesan cheese

Kosher salt

Freshly ground black pepper

1 pound fresh or frozen *phyllo* dough

Make the Filling: Squeeze small batches of the spinach dry with your hands, then wring the spinach out in a dish towel, in batches, to dry more. Place in a large bowl. In a small skillet heat 2 tablespoons of the butter. Add the scallions and sauté them until they are wilted. Add to the spinach with the feta, ricotta, eggs and Parmesan cheese. Season the filling well with salt and pepper.

Preheat the oven to 375° F. Butter a cookie sheet or jelly-roll pan. Have the melted butter, a pastry brush, the breadcrumbs and 2 damp (not wet) dish towels ready. (*Phyllo* dough dries out very quickly, so it is important that you have everything ready before you start using it.)

Spread 1 of the damp towels out on a clean surface. Unwrap 2 of the *phyllo* sheets, and lay them one on top of the other on the towel with the longest side nearest you. (Keep the remaining sheets covered with the other towel.) Brush the sheets lightly with butter and sprinkle very lightly with the breadcrumbs. Place 1 more *phyllo* sheet on top, brush with butter and sprinkle with crumbs. Continue layering, brushing and sprinkling, 3 more sheets. Spread ½ of the spinach filling along the edge closest to you, leaving about 1½ inches of dough uncovered at each short end. Fold the short ends in and brush with melted butter. Using the towel, lift the *phyllo* and carefully roll it away from you, jelly-roll fashion. (You will have a 13- to 14-inch strudel.)

Place the strudel seam side down on the cookie sheet. Brush generously with butter and score the top of the dough with a serrated knife into portions. Form the second strudel in the same fashion. Bake the strudels for approximately 35 minutes, or until light golden. Let rest for a few minutes before slicing and serving.

NOTE: *Phyllo* sheets come in 1-pound packages, so you will have some left over. Very often, however, the sheets are not very fresh, which means that they will crack and tear. It's best to always have extra on hand.

SERVING SUGGESTIONS: As an appetizer, follow with any broiled fish. As a luncheon course, precede by a salad, Sweet Potato Soup or Souffléed Acorn Squash.

Feta Cheese Strudel

FILLING

1 pound feta cheese, crumbled
1 pound farmer cheese
3 ounces cream cheese
4 eggs, slightly beaten
¼ cup freshly grated Parmesan
  cheese

4 tablespoons finely snipped dill
Kosher salt
Freshly ground black pepper

10 tablespoons unsalted butter,
  melted
¾ cup unseasoned breadcrumbs

1 pound fresh or frozen *phyllo*
  dough

Combine the ingredients for the filling and season to taste with salt and pepper. Form and bake the strudels following the directions in the preceding recipe.

SERVING SUGGESTIONS: As an appetizer, follow with Fish Soup with Vegetables, Fillet of Grey Sole en Papillote or any broiled fish. As a luncheon course, precede by a green salad, Tuna Seviche or Carrot Soup.

Pareve

Smoked Whitefish Pâté

This is another pâté that can be made in advance and stored in the refrigerator.

4 scallions, including green parts, quartered
1 smoked whitefish (approximately 2 pounds)
About 4 tablespoons homemade mayonnaise (see page 193)

About 2 tablespoons drained bottled horseradish
About 4 tablespoons lemon juice
Freshly ground black pepper
Capers for garnish

Chop the scallions in a food processor fitted with a steel blade. Fillet the whitefish, making sure to remove all the small bones. Add the fish to the processor with the mayonnaise, horseradish, and lemon juice and purée until smooth. Transfer the pâté to a bowl, and season very well with the pepper.

Serve the pâté on endive leaves, whole-wheat triangle toasts or crackers and garnish with the capers.

Latkes (Potato Pancakes)

Although potato pancakes are usually associated with Hanukkah, I love to serve these dainty, crisp pancakes on a cloth napkin for cocktails as well. You may serve them with sour cream or applesauce if you like.

4 large baking potatoes	**2 tablespoons unbleached flour**
1 medium onion	**Kosher salt**
1 teaspoon lemon juice	**Freshly ground black pepper**
2 eggs	**Vegetable oil for frying**

Peel the potatoes, quarter them and place in a bowl of cold water to cover. Finely grate the potatoes and the onion in a food processor or by hand. Immediately sprinkle with the lemon juice to prevent the potatoes from turning dark. Empty the potato pulp into a mesh sieve set over a bowl and press the pulp with a spoon to extract all the liquid. Set the liquid aside for a few minutes to allow a starchy sediment to settle at the bottom. Carefully pour off the clear liquid and reserve the sediment. Transfer the potato pulp to a large bowl, add the eggs, flour and the sediment. Combine thoroughly and season well.

In one or two 12-inch nonstick skillets heat oil to a depth of approximately ¼ inch. Drop full tablespoons of potato mixture (without the accumulated liquid) into the oil. Flatten each mound slightly and fry in batches over medium-high heat, until golden brown on both sides. Drain the potato pancakes on paper towels, changing the towels frequently as they absorb the oil. To keep the finished pancakes warm and crisp while you fry the rest (or to reheat them if they were fried in advance), place them on a rack set over a cookie sheet in a preheated 300° F. oven. Between batches add more oil to the skillet if needed, and make sure that it is hot enough before dropping in more potato mixture.

Sole in Seaweed Batter

This is one of my favorite hors d'oeuvres. Little pieces of sole are dipped in light batter, deep-fried and served immediately with a pepper-salt dip. The pieces look like tiny green speckled packages.

1¼ to 1½ pounds grey sole fillets
1 tablespoon dry white wine
BATTER
¾ cup unbleached flour
⅓ cup plus 1 tablespoon
  cornstarch
½ teaspoon kosher salt
3 teaspoons baking powder
1 cup plus 2 tablespoons cold
  water
PEPPER-SALT DIP
1 teaspoon black peppercorns
2 tablespoons dried Szechuan
  peppercorns

¼ teaspoon freshly ground white
  pepper

4½ tablespoons dried seaweed,
  such as Chinese *tai tiao* or Japa-
  nese *aonoriko*
2 cups peanut oil

¼ cup kosher salt

Pat the fillets dry and remove the center cartilages. Cut the fillets into 1½-inch pieces. Place them in a small bowl and coat with the wine and pepper. Cover and set aside.

Whisk together the flour, cornstarch, salt, baking powder and water until the batter is smooth. Refrigerate it for approximately 1 hour. Just before you are ready to fry the fish, stir in the seaweed.

To Deep-Fry the Fish: Place a wok over high heat, add the oil and heat until it reaches 350° F. on a frying thermometer. (To test if the oil is hot enough without a frying thermometer, dip a chopstick into the batter, then dip it into the oil: If it sizzles immediately the oil is ready; if it burns, then the oil is too hot.) Dip the pieces of fish into the batter and deep-fry them, a few at a time, turning frequently until lightly golden. The packages will be puffed and crisp on the outside, and just cooked on the inside. Remove the pieces with a mesh strainer to drain on a cookie sheet lined with several layers of paper towels. Change the towels frequently.

Make the Dip: Place the peppercorns and the salt in a skillet and cook over medium heat, shaking the pan from time to time, until the salt turns light brown; do not let it burn. The peppercorns will open and release a strong fragrance. Grind the mixture fine in a blender. Strain through a mesh sieve. The dip will keep indefinitely, stored in a small jar.

To Serve: Arrange the fish on a dish lined with a cloth napkin and serve the dip on the side.

NOTE: The frying oil can be reused if you strain it and refrigerate it in a glass jar.

Tortilla (Vegetable Omelet)

This is a very attractive and light dish that looks like a small crustless pizza. It is equally good served hot or at room temperature.

4 tablespoons olive oil

6 scallions, including green parts, sliced into thin rounds

3 cloves garlic, minced

1 red bell pepper, diced

2 medium tomatoes (approximately ¾ pound), peeled, seeded and diced

4 medium mushrooms, wiped with a damp paper towel and thinly sliced

¼ cup tightly packed fresh basil, finely chopped

Kosher salt

Freshly ground black pepper

6 eggs, lightly beaten

Preheat the oven to 400° F.

In a 10-inch silverstone skillet heat the oil. Add the scallions and the garlic and sauté over low heat until the scallions are wilted. Add the pepper, tomatoes and mushrooms and sauté over medium-high heat, stirring, for 3 minutes. Stir in the basil and season the mixture with salt and pepper. Season the eggs with salt and pepper and add them to the skillet. Cook the mixture over low heat for 3 to 5 minutes, without stirring, or until the mixture is set on the bottom and still runny on top.

Transfer the tortilla to the oven for 4 to 6 minutes, or until the top is set. Loosen the edges with a knife and invert the tortilla onto a platter. (The bottom will look like a red mosaic.) Cut into wedges.

SERVING SUGGESTIONS: As an appetizer, follow with Bow Ties with Green Beans and Basil, Whole Steamed Salmon in Foil with Ginger Vinaigrette or Barbecued Tuna Steaks. As a light main luncheon course, precede by a green salad, Puréed Beet Soup, or Chilled Cucumber Soup.

Broiled Sweet Peppers

8 SERVINGS

I have a special fondness for simple, low-calorie vegetable dishes, especially in the summer. This is a convenient and colorful dish that must be prepared in advance. What a pleasure it is to leave the kitchen cool.

4 medium yellow bell peppers
4 medium red bell peppers
Olive oil
Wine vinegar
Kosher salt

Freshly ground black pepper
2 tablespoons drained capers,
   rinsed, patted dry, and coarsely
   chopped (optional)

Line the rack of a broiler pan with foil and place the peppers in it. Broil the peppers close to the heat (approximately 6 inches) for 15 to 20 minutes, turning them from time to time until they are blistered and charred on all sides. Place the peppers in a plastic bag. This will steam them slightly and loosen the skins. When the peppers are cool enough to handle, peel them, starting at the stem ends. Discard the stems, seeds and ribs. Quarter the peppers.

Arrange the peppers on individual plates or on a serving dish. Drizzle with the oil and vinegar, season with salt and pepper, and sprinkle with the capers, if you like.

SERVING SUGGESTIONS: Follow with Broiled Salmon Steaks, Broiled Fillets of Red Snapper with Pine Nut Coating, or Broiled Veal Chops with Mustard and Mustard Seeds.

Souffléed Acorn Squash

Acorn squash shells serve as containers for this delicate soufflé, which makes an interesting, unusual and light first course. It is important that you use small squash so as not to overpower the individual plates.

3 small acorn squash (¾ to 1 pound each)
2 tablespoons unsalted margarine, melted
2½ tablespoons brown sugar

½ teaspoon ground cinnamon
1 egg, separated
Kosher salt
Freshly ground black pepper

Preheat the oven to 400° F.

Halve the squash with a sharp knife, cut a very thin slice from the bottom of each half so that it will stand up on a plate. With a spoon, scoop out the seeds and fiber and discard. Place the squash cut side down in a baking pan and add ½ inch water. Cover the pan with heavy foil and bake for 30 to 45 minutes, or until the flesh is tender. Pour off the water from the pan, turn the squash over and let cool. Carefully scoop the cooked flesh into a bowl, leaving approximately ⅛ inch layer all around the cavity. Be careful not to pierce the shells. Purée the flesh with the margarine, brown sugar, cinnamon and egg yolk in a food processor fitted with a steel blade. Transfer to a bowl. (You may prepare in advance up to this point.)

In a clean dry bowl beat the egg white until stiff. Fold it into the puréed squash mixture and season with salt and pepper. Divide the purée evenly among the squash shells and bake on a cookie sheet in the upper third of the oven for approximately 25 minutes, or until the tops are lightly golden.

SERVING SUGGESTIONS: Follow with any of the duck, Cornish hen or veal recipes.

Baked Spaghetti Squash with Tomato Sauce

4 SERVINGS

Think of this dish as low-calorie pasta. It's interesting to prepare and very light.

1 medium spaghetti squash (approximately 3½ pounds)
1 cup tomato sauce (see page 192)
Kosher salt

Freshly ground black pepper
Freshly grated Parmesan cheese for garnish

Preheat the oven to 375° F.

Place the whole squash in a pan and bake for 45 minutes to 1 hour, turning once, until the flesh feels tender when pressed. Remove from the oven and halve at once. (Otherwise the squash will continue cooking.) Let cool briefly, then scoop out and discard the seeds. With a fork "comb" the strands from each half until only the shell remains.

Heat the tomato sauce in a medium saucepan and stir in the squash; mix well and season to taste with salt and pepper. Serve hot, garnished with the Parmesan cheese.

SERVING SUGGESTIONS: Follow with Chicken with Capers and Olives, Stir-fried Chopped Meat and Rice or Fillet of Grey Sole en Papillote.

Braised Baby Artichokes

6 SERVINGS

This is a simple way to prepare artichokes that are small enough so that the whole choke can be eaten. The artichokes can be cooked in advance and reheated before serving.

18 baby artichokes, approximately
   2 inches in diameter
Juice of 1½ lemons
1 cup tightly packed Italian parsley
   (discard the lower halves of the
   stems), coarsely chopped

3 cloves garlic, minced
⅓ cup olive oil
¾ tablespoon kosher salt
¼ cup water

Discard the hard outer leaves of the artichokes (3 to 4 layers) and peel the stems lightly. Trim off the ends and rinse well. Arrange the artichokes on their sides in a saucepan large enough to hold them in a single layer.

In a small bowl mix together the lemon juice, parsley, garlic, olive oil and salt. Pour this mixture over the artichokes along with the water. Bring to a boil, reduce the heat, cover, and cook slowly, braise, for 10 minutes. Turn the artichokes and braise them for another 5 to 10 minutes, or until crisply tender. Serve the artichokes in bowls with the braising liquid.

SERVING SUGGESTIONS: Follow with Millie Chan's Lion's Head, Chicken with Capers and Olives or Chicken Breasts in Tomato Mushroom Sauce.

Warm Spinach Salad

4 SERVINGS

If you enjoy salads as much as I do, I think that you will like this unusual and nutritious starter.

1 pound fresh young spinach	**6 tablespoons olive oil**
1½ teaspoons Dijon-type mustard	**1 clove garlic, minced**
1½ tablespoons lemon juice	**Freshly ground black pepper**
1 tablespoon water	

Discard the spinach stems, wash the leaves very thoroughly and dry in a salad spinner. Cut the leaves into manageable pieces. Combine mustard, lemon juice and water. Set aside. In a wok or a large skillet heat the oil. Add the garlic and sauté over low heat (it burns easily) for a minute. Pour in the mustard, lemon and water. Raise the heat to high, add the spinach at once and toss it as you would a salad until it is just heated through, not really wilted. Serve at once.

(For a more elaborate salad, add very thinly sliced fresh mushrooms.)

SERVING SUGGESTIONS: Follow with any baked Cornish hen recipe, Chicken with Dried and Fresh Mushrooms or Veal Chops with Mustard and Mustard Seeds.

Stir-fried *Shiitake* Mushrooms

6 SERVINGS

Shiitake mushrooms are Oriental mushrooms that are cultivated, among other places, in California and Vermont. They have a woodsy flavor and are available, in season, in select supermarkets. They are as common in the Orient as our commercially grown mushrooms. You can prepare other varieties of mushrooms—chanterelles, oyster or regular mushrooms—in the same way.

1½ pounds fresh *shiitake* mushrooms	½ cup loosely packed Italian parsley (discard the lower halves of the stems), finely chopped
4 tablespoons vegetable oil	Kosher salt
3 cloves garlic, thinly sliced	Freshly ground black pepper
3 to 4 tablespoons dry white wine	

Discard the mushroom stems. Wipe the mushrooms with a damp paper towel and slice them thin.

Heat a wok or skillet, add the oil and heat well. Add the garlic and stir-fry until golden over low heat; remove the garlic with a slotted spoon and discard. Add the mushrooms and stir-fry over medium-high heat for a minute. Add the wine and continue to stir until the mushrooms are crisply tender, about a minute more. Stir in the chopped parsley and season to taste with salt and pepper.

SERVING SUGGESTIONS: Follow with Baked Chicken Breasts with Lemon and Mustard, Braised Soy Sauce Duck or Steamed Salmon Steaks with Black Beans.

Marinated Salmon with Green Peppercorns

6 SERVINGS

Once you have purchased very fresh salmon, the remainder of this recipe is simplicity itself. No lengthy preparations are necessary, but the dish must be prepared a day in advance. This is an elegant first course.

1½ pounds salmon fillet, center cut, skinned
3 tablespoons lime juice
3 tablespoons dry white wine
2 tablespoons rice vinegar
1 teaspoon dry mustard

⅓ cup olive oil
3 tablespoons drained green peppercorns
1 tablespoon kosher salt
Freshly ground black pepper

Cut the salmon, following the grain, into ¼-inch-wide slices. (The length of the slices will be determined by the width of the fish; they may be 5 to 6 inches long.)

In a small bowl mix together the lime juice, white wine, vinegar and mustard. Pouring in a slow stream, whisk in the olive oil until the marinade is emulsified. Add the peppercorns, salt and pepper. Place the salmon in a glass or ceramic dish, pour the marinade over it, and mix well. Cover and refrigerate overnight, turning the fish once. The lime juice will "cook" the salmon.

To Serve: Arrange the salmon on plates decorated sparingly with shredded French chicory (*frisé*) or other bitter greens, and drizzle a little of the marinade over the fish.

SERVING SUGGESTIONS: Follow with Braised Curried Veal, any baked or broiled Cornish hen recipe or Baked Chicken Breasts with Lemon and Mustard.

Salmon Tartare I

This salmon tartare and the following one are my favorite cocktail foods or first courses. They are easy to prepare, elegant, and attractive to serve. The only essential is that the fish be very fresh; frozen won't do. Toasted bread triangles are a nice accompaniment. The dish may be prepared several hours in advance and refrigerated.

1¾ pounds very fresh salmon fillet, skinned
4 shallots
2 scallions, including green parts, finely chopped
1 tablespoon olive oil
1 tablespoon pure Oriental sesame oil
About 2 tablespoons thin Chinese soy sauce

¼ cup loosely packed Italian parsley, finely chopped
8 sprigs fresh dill, finely snipped
Kosher salt
Freshly ground black pepper
2 medium cucumbers
White vinegar

12 thin slices whole-wheat bread

4 tablespoons unsalted margarine, melted

Carefully pick over the salmon and remove all bones. (Tweezers are good for this.) Cut the salmon into small pieces, then chop it coarse and place in a bowl. Chop the shallots fine, place in a strainer and rinse. Wring the shallots dry in a dish towel. Add them to the salmon with the scallions, olive and sesame oils, soy sauce, parsley, dill, and salt and pepper to taste. Mix well. Taste the tartare and adjust ingredients; it should be well seasoned.

Peel the cucumbers and trim the ends. Halve them lengthwise, scoop out the seeds with a spoon, and slice the halves into very thin half rounds. Season with the vinegar and sprinkle lightly with salt.

Preheat the oven to 425° F.

Stack the slices of bread and cut off the crusts. Cut the bread diagonally into small triangles. Place the triangles on a baking dish and brush them with the melted margarine. Bake for about 5 minutes, or until lightly browned.

To Serve: Spoon a portion of the salmon tartare into the center of each plate and arrange the sliced cucumbers in a half-moon pattern on either side of the salmon. Pass the toasted bread triangles. If you wish, you can also serve the salmon tartare as a cocktail food with crackers, bread triangles, or endive leaves.

SERVING SUGGESTIONS: Follow with Chicken Breasts and Tomato Mushroom Sauce, Broiled Cornish Hens or Braised Soy Sauce Duck.

Salmon Tartare II

8 SERVINGS

This tartare has a paler tone and is seasoned more delicately than the one that precedes it.

1¾ pounds very fresh salmon fillet, skinned

1½ to 2 tablespoons Japanese powdered horseradish or freshly grated horseradish

4 scallions, including green parts, finely chopped

2 tablespoons drained capers, coarsely chopped

¼ cup loosely packed Italian parsley, finely chopped

Juice of 1 lemon

Kosher salt

Freshly ground black pepper

1 *daikon* (Japanese white radish), approximately 13 inches long

Carefully pick over the salmon to remove all bones. (Tweezers are good for this.) Cut the salmon into small pieces, then chop it coarse. Place the salmon in a bowl, add the remaining ingredients, except the *daikon*, and mix thoroughly. Be sure to season the salmon tartare very well.

Peel the *daikon* and slice it in half crosswise. Slice ½ into paper-thin rounds and coarsely grate the other.

To Serve: Spoon some of the salmon tartare onto the center of each plate; arrange the sliced radish in a half-moon pattern on one side of the plate, and the grated radish on the other. Pass toasted bread triangles (see preceding recipe). If you wish you can also serve this salmon tartare as cocktail food, on ¼-inch-thick radish rounds or on endive leaves.

NOTE: You may prepare the salmon several hours in advance, but do not add the lemon juice. Incorporate the lemon juice just before serving; otherwise it will "cook" the salmon.

SERVING SUGGESTIONS: Follow with Steamed Chicken Breasts with Tomato, Basil and Vinegar, Duck with *Hoisin* Sauce or Braised Curried Veal.

Marinated Salmon

This is an adaptation of a popular pickled salmon dish that I find to be spongy and vinegary. To avoid that, I steam the fish first, then marinate it for a few days. The onions become soft and the fish gains a wonderful texture and flavor. Marinated salmon makes an excellent first course or a summertime main course.

3 salmon steaks, approximately 1 inch thick, skinned and halved, center bone removed (each steak weighing approximately 9 ounces before boning and skinning)
Kosher salt
Freshly ground white pepper
2 tablespoons dry white wine

2 small onions, halved and very thinly sliced
¼ cup olive oil
¼ cup wine vinegar
2 bay leaves
15 sprigs fresh dill, finely snipped, plus additional for garnish

Fold in the ends of the salmon steaks if they are long and place the pieces in an oiled heatproof glass or ceramic dish large enough to hold them in a single layer, with a little room to spare. Season the fish with salt and pepper and sprinkle with the wine.

Fill a large pot with water to a depth of 1½ to 2 inches, place a trivet in the pot and bring the water to a boil. Set the dish of salmon on the trivet, cover and steam over high heat for about 7 minutes, or just before the fish turns orange pink all the way through. (It will continue cooking a bit after you remove it from the heat and while it is marinating.) Pour off the accumulated juices in the dish, and let stand to cool.

Scatter the onions over the fish. Whisk together the oil, vinegar, bay leaves, 2 teaspoons of salt and pepper to taste; the marinade should be well seasoned. Pour the marinade over the salmon and sprinkle with dill. Cover the dish with wax paper, then foil, and refrigerate for 3 to 5 days.

Serve the salmon at room temperature, garnished with the onions and additional snipped dill.

NOTE: You may also steam the fish in a steamer basket lined with foil, but be sure to oil the foil and pull up the edges so that the juices do not spill out. The steaming time will be shorter, approximately 4 minutes. After steaming, remove the basket from the heat and let stand to cool before transferring the fish to a dish to marinate.

SERVING SUGGESTIONS: As an appetizer, follow with Roast Breast of Veal, Curried Veal or Baked Chicken with Soy Sauce and Ginger. As a luncheon course, precede by Pasta Shells with Cheese Filling, Bow Ties with Green Beans and Basil or Gazpacho.

Tuna Seviche

8 SERVINGS AS A FIRST COURSE, 4 TO 6 SERVINGS AS A MAIN COURSE

This dish is traditionally prepared with scallops. Never having tasted the original, I invented this piquant version. The lemon juice, vermouth and vinegar do not heat but "cook" the fish. You can serve it either as a first course or a summer luncheon main course.

3 pounds very fresh tuna fillet, center cut, skinned
¾ cup wine vinegar
½ cup dry vermouth
Juice of 1 lemon
1 tablespoon dark Chinese soy sauce
2 tablespoons olive oil
1 tablespoon superfine sugar
3 cloves garlic, halved

A 2-inch piece fresh ginger, peeled and thinly sliced
About 1 tablespoon kosher salt
Freshly ground white pepper
¼ cup loosely packed coriander (Chinese parsley), coarsely chopped
Extra sprigs of coriander for garnish

Cut away and discard any dark flesh from the tuna, then cut the fish into 1-inch cubes. Place in a glass or ceramic bowl. Mix the remaining ingredients, except for the coriander, thoroughly. Pour over the tuna and mix well. Cover the dish and refrigerate for 12 to 24 hours, depending on how well you like your fish "cooked," stirring several times.

Before serving, remove and discard the garlic and ginger and pour off the liquid. Toss the seviche with the coriander and adjust the seasonings. (It should be spicy.) Serve while the seviche is still chilled.

To Serve: Arrange the seviche on individual plates garnished with sprigs of coriander, if you like.

SERVING SUGGESTIONS: Follow with Bow Ties with Peppers and Basil, Rigatoni Puttanesca or Spinach Spaghetti Primavera. As a main luncheon dish, precede by Gazpacho, Chilled Cucumber Soup or Puréed Romaine and Watercress Soup.

Gefilte Fish

This is a simpler version of Gefilte Fish than the one in my previous book. Make it a day before to allow it to chill. I suggest serving the gefilte fish with freshly grated horseradish.

FISH OVALS

One approximately 3-pound whitefish
One approximately 3-pound pike
2 medium onions, finely grated
3 egg yolks beaten well with a fork
3 tablespoons matzoh meal

About 1 tablespoon sugar
About 2½ tablespoons kosher salt
Freshly ground white pepper
½ teaspoon almond extract
½ cup ice water

STOCK

Heads, skin and bones from whitefish and pike
2 medium onions, quartered
1 carrot, quartered

7 cups cold water
1 tablespoon kosher salt
2 teaspoons sugar
10 peppercorns

SAUCE

2 medium onions, coarsely cubed
3 carrots, sliced into thin rounds
About 2 teaspoons kosher salt

About 2 teaspoons sugar
Freshly ground white pepper

12-inch piece fresh horseradish root

2—3 lemons

To Make the Fish Ovals: Have the fishmonger fillet the fish and grind it together twice so that the combination has a smooth texture. Reserve the heads, bones and skin for stock. Place the fish in a large bowl. Add the onions, eggs, matzoh meal, sugar, salt, pepper and almond extract. Mix the fish with your hands or a wooden spoon and gradually add the ice water. Be thorough and patient. Season the fish to taste with salt and pepper and refrigerate it while you are preparing the stock.

To Make the Stock: In a large enameled pot, approximately 12 by 17 inches, place all the fish trimmings, onions, carrot, water and seasoning. Bring to a boil over high heat. Reduce the heat and boil gently, covered, for 45 minutes. Let stock cool a bit. Wet a cotton cloth with cold water, wring it dry and drape it over a large bowl. Strain the stock through the cloth. Wring the cloth to obtain all the liquid and flavor from the bones and vegetables. (This stock will be cloudy; do not worry about it.) Rinse the pan and return the stock to it.

To Make the Sauce and Fish: Add the onions, carrots and seasonings to the stock. Bring to a boil.
  Mix the ground fish again.
  Have a bowl of cold water nearby. Wet your hands well. Place 2 heaping tablespoons

of fish in your hands and shape a smooth oval. Place it in the gently boiling stock and continue with the remainder. Be sure to wet your hands each time.

Cover the pan and bring the fish to a gentle boil. Cook slowly for 45 minutes, turning the fish once. Season the sauce to taste with salt and pepper. Let the fish cool completely, then transfer to a tight-fitting container and chill overnight.

To Make the Horseradish: Peel the horseradish root and grate it finely by hand. Moisten it frequently with lemon juice to prevent it from turning gray. Mix well and refrigerate in a tight-fitting container.

To Serve: Serve the gefilte fish with the sauce and place horseradish on the side.

NOTE: If you have an electric mixer, use the flat beater to gradually add water to make the fish ovals.

SERVING SUGGESTIONS: Follow with Chicken Breasts in Tomato Mushroom Sauce, Roast Chicken or Roast Breast of Veal.

Pasta Salad with Smoked Salmon and Steamed Vegetables

12 SERVINGS AS A FIRST COURSE, 6 TO 8 SERVINGS AS A MAIN COURSE

Gnocchi are generally thought of as little dumplings made of boiled mashed potatoes and flour. These gnocchi are small shell-like noodles. If you cannot find these, use any other small pasta, such as squares, bow ties or even penne. I prefer to make this dish early in the day to allow for chilling.

⅓ cup virgin olive oil
Juice of 2 limes

A 10-ounce package frozen lima beans, thawed
1 pound tiny green beans
5 scallions, including green parts, cut into 3-inch thin matchstick pieces
¾ cup pitted and slivered black Gaeta oil-cured olives
10 ounces smoked salmon, cut into ¾-inch-wide strips
1 bunch arugula, stems discarded and cut into ¾-inch-wide strips, plus additional whole leaves for garnish

About 2 teaspoons Dijon-style mustard

¼ cup loosely packed fresh coriander (cilantro or Chinese parsley), finely chopped
Kosher salt
1½ pounds gnocchi (or any other small pasta)
Freshly ground black pepper

In a small bowl whisk together the olive oil, lime juice and mustard and set aside.

Place the beans in a large bowl, add the scallions, olives, smoked salmon, arugula and cilantro.

Meanwhile, bring 5 quarts of water to a rolling boil in a large covered pot. Add 2 tablespoons salt and all the pasta at once; stir well. Boil briskly, uncovered, for about 7 minutes, or until the pasta is al dente, tender but still firm to the bite. Pour into a colander and shake vigorously to drain well. Transfer to a bowl. Toss the pasta with about ¼ of the dressing (just to coat it lightly) and allow it to cool for a few minutes. Add the beans, scallions, olives, salmon, arugula, and coriander and toss with some more dressing. Season the salad to taste with salt and pepper. Chill thoroughly.

To Serve: I like to serve this dish on a bed of arugula lightly dressed with Vinaigrette Dressing (see page 189).

SERVING SUGGESTIONS: As an appetizer, follow with Steamed Chicken Breasts with Tomato, Basil and Vinegar, Baked Chicken Breasts with Lemon and Mustard or Duck with *Hoisin* Sauce. As a luncheon dish, precede by Tortilla Tomato Soup or Cold Carrot Soup.

Meat

Crunchy Chicken Tidbits

6 TO 8 SERVINGS (ABOUT 24 PIECES)

These delectable little tidbits of crunchy chicken make a wonderful hors d'oeuvre. The chicken pieces are marinated first, then dipped in an almond-sesame mixture, quickly deep-fried and served with a piquant dip.

1 pound boned, skinned chicken breasts (approximately 3 half breasts)

MARINADE

1 clove garlic, crushed to a paste with ¼ teaspoon salt

A 1-inch piece fresh ginger, peeled and finely minced

1 tablespoon lemon juice

1 teaspoon grated lemon rind

1 tablespoon thin Chinese soy sauce

DIP

½ cup apricot preserves

1 teaspoon dry mustard dissolved in 1 teaspoon warm water

2 teaspoons lemon juice

¾ cup finely ground blanched almonds combined with 2 tablespoons hulled sesame seeds

2 cups vegetable oil

Freeze the chicken for about 15 minutes, then slice it into 1-inch strips. (It is easier to slice the chicken when it is semifrozen.)

Make the Marinade: In a small dish combine the marinade ingredients.

Place a plastic food storage bag inside another and put the chicken inside. Pour in the marinade and turn to coat evenly. Seal both bags well and refrigerate for 4 to 8 hours.

Make the Dip: Place the apricot preserves in a small saucepan and warm over low heat. Strain through a mesh sieve, pushing the solids through with the back of a spoon. Place in a serving bowl and mix in the mustard mixture and the lemon juice.

To Deep-Fry the Chicken: Heat 2 inches of the oil in a wok or a large skillet to 350° F. on a frying thermometer. (To test if the oil is hot enough without a frying thermometer, drop a pinch of the almond-sesame mixture into the oil; if it sizzles immediately, the oil is ready; if it burns, the oil is too hot.) Dip the chicken pieces in the almond-sesame mixture to coat them, and deep-fry a few at a time until lightly golden, approximately 1 minute. Remove with tongs to a cookie sheet lined with paper towels, changing the towels as needed.

To Serve: Arrange the tidbits on a dish lined with a cloth napkin and serve the dip on the side.

Curried Wontons

A crisp well-seasoned finger food that is easy to make, delightful to serve and freezes very well.

FILLING

1 small potato	1½ to 2 teaspoons kosher salt
¼ cup peanut oil	½ teaspoon sugar
1 pound lean ground meat (½ pound veal ground together with ½ pound chuck)	1 medium onion, finely chopped
	1 tablespoon curry powder
1½ to 2 tablespoons dark Chinese soy sauce	

1 pound thin wonton skins (for frying not boiling)	2 cups peanut oil

Make the Filling: Wash the potato, place it in a small saucepan with water to cover and bring to a boil. Reduce heat, cover and simmer until tender. Pour off the water and let the potato cool, then peel and mash it until smooth.

Heat a wok or skillet over high heat, add 3 tablespoons of the oil and heat well. Add the meat and stir-fry over high heat, stirring constantly until the meat changes color and separates. Mix in the soy sauce, salt and sugar. Remove to a bowl.

Return the wok to the heat and add the remaining oil. When the oil is hot, add the onion and stir-fry over medium heat until soft. Add the curry powder, the chopped meat and the potato. Raise the heat to high and mix thoroughly. Season to taste with soy sauce and salt. It should be well seasoned. Remove to a bowl and let cool thoroughly.

Fill the Wontons: Have a glass of water nearby. Unwrap the skins and keep them covered with a damp paper towel. Working with one skin at a time, place it at an angle on a sheet of wax paper. Put 1 teaspoon of the filling at the corner nearest to you. Fold the corner over the filling and roll to the center, but leaving ½ inch of the opposite corner unrolled. (You will have a triangle.) Lightly moisten the left corner of the triangle with cold water, then fold backward toward the center and pinch the two ends together to seal well. Place the wontons on a cookie sheet with wax paper between the layers. Cover with a damp towel and refrigerate until ready to fry. (If the towel dries out in the refrigerator, moisten it again.)

Deep-Fry the Wontons: Heat a wok over high heat, add 2 cups of oil and heat until the oil reaches 350° F. on a frying thermometer. (To test if the oil is hot enough without a frying thermometer, drop a piece of wonton wrapper into the hot oil: if it sizzles immediately, the oil is ready; if it burns, the oil is too hot.) Deep-fry 4 wontons at a time, turning them frequently so that they brown evenly. Fry them till golden, about 1 minute. Remove with a mesh hand strainer to a cookie sheet lined with several layers of paper towels, changing the towels as needed.

Keep the wontons warm on a rack set over a cookie sheet in a preheated 300° F. oven as you finish frying the rest.

NOTES: Wontons may be deep-fried earlier in the day and reheated in a preheated 300° F. oven for approximately 10 minutes. You may also freeze the uncooked wontons on trays. After they are frozen remove them and wrap them first in foil and then in a plastic bag to save space. Return to the freezer. Before deep-frying, defrost them in the refrigerator for 30 minutes. The frying oil can be reused if you strain it and refrigerate it in a glass jar.

Beet Consommé with Piroshki

Soups

DAIRY
Sweet Potato Soup
Puréed Romaine and Watercress Soup
Carrot Soup
Chilled Cucumber Soup
Puréed Vegetable Soup

PAREVE
Minestrone
Puréed Beet Soup
Tomato Soup
Gazpacho
Fish Soup with Vegetables

MEAT
Puréed Butternut Squash Soup
Cold Carrot Soup
Leek and Lettuce Soup
Arugula, Leek and Potato Soup
Sherry's Jerusalem Artichoke Soup
Puréed Broccoli Soup
Hearty Vegetable Soup
Chicken Soup with Arugula or Watercress
Chicken Soup with Ginger, Tree Ears and Peas
Beet Consommé
Chicken Soup

Sweet Potato Soup

4 TO 5 SERVINGS

1 medium onion, coarsely chopped
2 medium sweet potatoes (approximately 1¼ pounds), peeled and diced
4 teaspoons (2 packets) instant vegetable broth such as MBT, dissolved in 4 cups boiling water, or homemade vegetable stock (see page 191)

About ¾ cup half-and-half or milk
Freshly ground nutmeg
Kosher salt
Freshly ground black pepper
About 1 teaspoon lemon juice

Place the onion, potatoes and vegetable broth in a large saucepan and bring to a boil. Reduce the heat, cover and cook slowly, until the potatoes are tender, approximately 25 minutes. Cool slightly. Purée until smooth, in batches, in a blender. Return the soup to the saucepan, add the half-and-half and heat through. Season to taste with nutmeg, salt, pepper and lemon juice. Adjust the consistency with more half-and-half as desired.

SERVING SUGGESTIONS: Follow with Broiled Red Snapper with Pine Nut Coating, Fillet of Grey Sole en Papillote, Steamed Salmon with Tomato Sauce and Julienne Vegetables, Spinach Strudel, Linguine with Mushroom Sauce, Penne with Mushroom Sauce or Potato Cheese *Piroshki.*

Puréed Romaine and Watercress Soup

8 SERVINGS

This is a lovely summer soup. The buttermilk gives it a mildly tart flavor.

2 tablespoons unsalted butter
6 scallions, including green parts, sliced
1 large potato (approximately 8 ounces), peeled and sliced
2 teaspoons (2 packets) instant vegetable broth, such as MBT, dissolved in 5 cups boiling water, or 5 cups homemade vegetable stock (see page 191)

1 head Romaine lettuce (approximately 1 pound)
1 bunch watercress
About 1½ cups buttermilk
Kosher salt
Freshly ground black pepper
Finely snipped dill or chives for garnish

In a large saucepan heat the butter. Add the scallions and sauté over low heat until they are soft. Add the potato and the vegetable broth. Wash the lettuce, shake off as much water as possible and add the lettuce to the saucepan. Discard the lower halves of the watercress stems, wash and remove excess water and add the watercress as well. Bring the soup to a boil, reduce the heat, cover and cook until the potato is soft. Cool slightly. Purée until smooth, in batches, in a blender. Chill the soup. Stir in the buttermilk and season to taste with salt and pepper.

Serve the soup garnished with the dill or chives.

SERVING SUGGESTIONS: Follow with Tuna Seviche, Marinated Salmon, Spaghetti with Uncooked Tomato Sauce, Pasta Shell Salad with Vegetables, Fusilli with Uncooked Tomato Olive Sauce or Bow Ties with Green Beans and Basil.

Carrot Soup

This soup is delicious served hot or cold. It has a beautiful orange color and, as the ingredients are not seasonal, is delightful to serve and to eat all year round. Do make it a day in advance to give the flavors time to blend.

2 tablespoons unsalted butter
1 medium onion, coarsely chopped
1 clove garlic, coarsely chopped
10 medium carrots (approximately 1½ pounds), sliced
1 small potato, peeled and sliced
1½ cups freshly squeezed orange juice
6 teaspoons (3 packets) instant vegetable broth such as MBT, dissolved in 5 cups boiling water, or homemade vegetable stock (see page 191)

¾ to 1 cup half-and-half or milk
Kosher salt
Freshly ground black pepper
¼ cup loosely packed coriander (cilantro or Chinese parsley), finely chopped, for garnish

In a large saucepan heat the butter, add the onion and garlic and sauté over low heat until soft. Add the carrots, potato, orange juice, and broth. Bring the soup to a boil, reduce the heat, cover and cook slowly until the vegetables are tender. Cool slightly. Purée until smooth, in batches, in a blender. Return the soup to the saucepan, and heat it through. Thin it as desired with the half-and-half and season to taste with salt and pepper. If you wish to serve the soup cold, chill it overnight.

Serve the soup garnished with the coriander.

SERVING SUGGESTIONS: Follow with Steamed Salmon with Tomato Sauce and Julienne Vegetables, Broiled Halibut Steaks with Tomato Coulis, Pasta Shells with Cheese Filling, Spaghettini with Fresh Vegetables or Pasta Shell Salad with Vegetables.

Chilled Cucumber Soup

6 TO 8 SERVINGS

This is a pleasing soup to make on hot summer days. It is refreshing, piquant and requires no cooking. Refrigerate it overnight to chill well.

2 cups plain yogurt
2 cups half-and-half
4 to 5 tablespoons lemon juice
4 medium cucumbers
1 clove garlic crushed to a paste
    with ½ teaspoon salt

10 chives, finely snipped
20 mint leaves, finely chopped
Kosher salt
Freshly ground black pepper

In a large bowl mix together the yogurt, half-and-half and 4 tablespoons lemon juice. Peel the cucumbers, trim the ends, and halve the cucumbers lengthwise. Scoop out the seeds with a spoon and then chop the cucumbers coarsely. Add the cucumbers to the soup with the garlic and chives. Chill the soup. Before serving, stir in the mint and season the soup to taste with lemon juice and salt and pepper.

SERVING SUGGESTIONS: Follow with Tuna Seviche, Marinated Salmon, Bow Ties with Peppers and Basil, Fusilli with Uncooked Tomato Olive Sauce or Bow Ties with Green Beans and Basil.

Puréed Vegetable Soup

No single vegetable predominates in this unusual soup, and the cheese added at the end enhances the combined vegetable flavors. It may easily be made several days in advance.

2 tablespoons unsalted butter
1 medium onion, coarsely chopped
2 cloves garlic, coarsely chopped
2 carrots, quartered
1 medium potato, sliced
½ pound string beans, cut into small pieces
1 head broccoli, stems peeled and cut into small pieces along with the florets
¼ cup dry white wine

6 teaspoons (3 packets) instant vegetable broth, such as MBT, dissolved in 7 cups boiling water, or homemade vegetable stock (see page 191)
About 1 cup buttermilk
Kosher salt
Freshly ground black pepper
Finely snipped dill for garnish
Freshly grated Parmesan cheese for garnish

In a large saucepan heat the butter. Add the onion and garlic and sauté over low heat until soft. Add the carrots, potato, string beans, broccoli and wine. Raise the heat and cook, stirring, until the excess liquid has evaporated. Add the vegetable broth and bring to a boil. Reduce the heat, cover, and cook slowly until the vegetables are tender. Cool slightly. Purée until smooth, in batches, in a blender. Return the soup to the saucepan and heat it through. Thin it as desired with the buttermilk and season to taste with salt and pepper. Serve in heated soup bowls and garnish with the dill and Parmesan cheese.

SERVING SUGGESTIONS: Follow with Broiled Halibut Steaks with Tomato Coulis, Broiled Salmon Steaks, Broiled or Barbecued Tuna Steaks, Spinach Roll, Feta Cheese Strudel, Spaghetti with Tomato Ricotta Sauce or Spaghettini with Arugula.

Pareve

Minestrone

8 TO 10 SERVINGS

Cumin is not a spice that I frequently use, because I associate it mostly with Middle Eastern dishes. After one of my trips to Israel I decided to try it in this low-calorie, light vegetable soup. I think it works very well. This soup freezes nicely.

2 tablespoons vegetable oil
6 scallions, including green parts, thinly sliced
4 cloves garlic, coarsely chopped
2 carrots, coarsely chopped
2 medium potatoes, peeled and coarsely chopped
4 medium-ripe tomatoes, peeled, seeded and coarsely chopped
1 bunch broccoli, stems peeled, coarsely chopped

½ cup tightly packed Italian parsley, coarsely chopped
8 cups cold water
A 10-ounce package frozen sweet corn, thawed
About 1 teaspoon ground cumin
Kosher salt
Freshly ground black pepper

In a large saucepan heat the vegetable oil. Add the scallions and garlic and sauté over low heat until soft. Add the carrots, potatoes, tomatoes, broccoli, parsley and water. Bring to a boil, reduce the heat, cover and cook for 20 minutes. Add the corn, cumin, salt and pepper, and cook 10 minutes more.

SERVING SUGGESTIONS: Follow with Roast Chicken, Meat Loaf, Chicken Loaf, Broiled Salmon Steaks, Spaghetti with Peppers, Eggplant and Ricotta, Spaghetti with Tomato and Crushed Red Pepper Flakes or Tortilla.

Puréed Beet Soup

This is a versatile soup with the wonderful taste and color of beets. You can serve it hot, or add yogurt and serve it at room temperature. It is delicious either way. (Note that the addition of yogurt makes this a dairy soup.)

8 medium beets, peeled and sliced
2 medium onions, sliced
1 clove garlic, sliced
3 carrots, sliced
1 medium potato, peeled and sliced
1 cup tightly packed Italian parsley
Few sprigs of dill
6 teaspoons (3 packets) instant vegetable broth such as MBT, dissolved in 8 cups boiling water, or homemade vegetable stock (see page 191)

About 2 tablespoons white vinegar
Kosher salt
Freshly ground black pepper
Finely snipped dill for garnish
1 cup plain yogurt (optional)

In a large saucepan combine the first 8 ingredients and bring to a boil. Reduce the heat, cover and cook slowly until all the vegetables are tender, about 30 minutes. Cool slightly, then purée until smooth, in batches, in a blender. Return to the saucepan, reheat, add the vinegar and season to taste with salt and pepper. Serve garnished with the dill. (Or, if you like, purée the soup, add the vinegar, then whisk the yogurt to loosen it a bit and mix it into the soup. Season to taste with salt and pepper and serve at room temperature, garnished with dill.)

SERVING SUGGESTIONS: If you are serving the soup hot, you may wish to follow it with Roast Turkey, Meat Loaf or Roast Chicken. If you are serving it at room temperature, as a dairy soup, follow it with Tuna Seviche, Marinated Salmon, Pasta Shell Salad with Vegetables, Bow Ties with Green Beans and Basil or Feta Cheese Strudel.

Tomato Soup

7 OR 8 SERVINGS

This soup may be served hot or cold. It has a beautiful orange-red color and a wonderful, smooth texture.

½ cup dried kidney beans
2 tablespoons olive oil
2 medium onions, coarsely
  chopped
2 cloves garlic, coarsely chopped
3 pounds ripe tomatoes, cored and
  cut into large pieces
½ cup loosely packed Italian
  parsley
1 cup tomato juice
2 teaspoons (1 packet) instant vegetable broth such as MBT, dissolved in 1 cup boiling water, or
  homemade vegetable stock (see
  page 191)

1 teaspoon tomato paste
1 to 2 teaspoons balsamic vinegar
Kosher salt
Freshly ground black pepper
Finely chopped chives or basil for
  garnish

Place the beans in a small bowl and cover them with cold water. Let soak overnight. Drain them and pick over. Place the beans in a small pot and again cover them with cold water. Bring to a boil, reduce the heat and cook them, partially covered, until tender, approximately 1 hour. Drain.

In a large saucepan heat the oil, add the onions and garlic and sauté over low heat until soft. Add the beans, the tomatoes, the parsley, tomato juice, the broth, and the tomato paste. Bring the soup to a boil, reduce the heat, cover and cook slowly until the tomatoes are soft. Cool slightly, then purée until smooth, in batches, in a blender. Strain the soup in batches through a mesh sieve, pushing it through with the back of a wooden spoon to obtain as much purée as possible. Return the soup to the saucepan and heat it through. Season to taste with vinegar and salt and pepper. If you wish to serve the soup cold, chill it overnight. Serve the soup garnished with basil or chives.

SERVING SUGGESTIONS: Follow with Whole Steamed Salmon in foil with Ginger Vinaigrette, Roast Capon with Olives or Penne with Mushroom Sauce.

Gazpacho

I love to serve chilled soups in the summer. They are generally easy to prepare, and they can be made in advance. Gazpacho is an uncooked soup that must be prepared a day in advance to permit the seasonings to blend and to allow for chilling. This soup has a beautiful color and looks lovely served in glass bowls or goblets with pita triangles (recipe follows).

2 medium cucumbers
2 cloves garlic, quartered
6 to 7 cups tomato juice
3 tablespoons olive oil
About 3 tablespoons balsamic
   vinegar
1 small hot red pepper
1 small jalapeño pepper

2 pounds ripe tomatoes, peeled,
   seeded and finely chopped
5 scallions, including green parts,
   finely chopped
½ cup tightly packed fresh basil
   leaves, finely chopped
Kosher salt
Freshly ground black pepper

Peel the cucumbers and trim the ends. Halve the cucumbers lengthwise and scoop out the seeds with a spoon. Quarter one cucumber and reserve the other. Place the quartered cucumber in a blender with the garlic, 5 cups of the tomato juice, the olive oil and vinegar. Purée until smooth and transfer to a bowl. Finely chop the remaining cucumber and add it to the soup. Wearing rubber gloves for protection, seed and finely mince both the red and the jalapeño pepper. Add to the soup with the tomatoes, scallions and basil. Refrigerate the gazpacho overnight. Before serving, adjust the consistency of the soup as desired with the remaining tomato juice and season to taste with vinegar and salt and pepper. (Gazpacho should be fairly thick and rather highly seasoned.)

SERVING SUGGESTIONS: Follow with Roast Capon with Olives, Baked Chicken Breasts with Lemon and Mustard, Whole Steamed Salmon in Foil with Ginger Vinaigrette Sauce, any broiled poultry or fish, any chicken salad, Cold Chinese-Style Linguine with Chicken and Vegetables or Chinese-Style Pasta with Vegetables.

Pita Triangles

4 tablespoons unsalted margarine
4 cloves garlic, finely minced

6 small rounds (6 inches in diameter) whole-wheat pita bread
Kosher salt

Preheat the oven to 400° F.

In a small saucepan melt the margarine, add the garlic and sauté over low heat until soft. Cut each pita round into 4 wedges and separate each wedge into 2 triangles. Arrange the triangles rough side up in a single layer on jelly-roll pans or cookie sheets. Brush with the garlic margarine and sprinkle lightly with salt. Bake the triangles for approximately 8 minutes, or until crisp and lightly golden. The triangles may be made a day in advance and refrigerated in a plastic bag. Reheat on a cookie sheet in a preheated 200° F. oven for a few minutes.

SERVING SUGGESTIONS: Follow with Broiled Salmon Steaks, Broiled or Barbecued Tuna Steaks or Chicken with Capers and Olives.

Fish Soup with Vegetables

This soup is a light meal in itself. The crisp vegetables and delicate texture of the fish are offset by the wonderful flavors of garlic and saffron.

FISH STOCK

6 pounds fresh fishbones, heads and trimmings, or 4 pounds bony fish
1 carrot, quartered
1 medium onion, quartered
3 cloves garlic
3 leeks
1 small bulb fennel, quartered
6 cups water
1 cup dry white wine
2 bay leaves
5 sprigs Italian parsley
7 black peppercorns
2 medium ripe tomatoes, peeled, seeded and coarsely chopped
1 large baking potato, peeled and cut into 1-inch cubes
¼ teaspoon saffron threads
1¼ pounds fish fillets (red snapper, flounder or halibut), cut into 1-inch cubes
Kosher salt
Freshly ground black pepper

Make the Fish Stock: Rinse the fish or bones well. Place them in a large stockpot with the carrot, onion, 1 clove of garlic, the green parts of the leeks (rinse and cube the white parts and reserve), rinsed well, the fennel, water and wine. Bring to a boil over high heat. Skim the foam as it rises to the surface, then add the bay leaves, parsley and whole peppercorns. Reduce the heat and cook slowly, partially covered, for 45 minutes. Remove from heat and let cool slightly. Rinse a clean cotton cloth in cold water and wring well. Drape the cloth over a large bowl and strain the contents of the pot through it. Gather the cloth around the solids and squeeze them very lightly to extract additional juices. Rinse the stockpot and return the strained stock to it. Boil briskly, uncovered, until the stock is reduced by half, approximately 45 minutes. The stock should be very concentrated. Mince the remaining 2 cloves of garlic and add to the stock, with the white cubed leeks (rinsed very well), tomatoes, potato and saffron. Bring to a simmer and cook, covered, until the potato is tender. While the soup is cooking, sprinkle the fish with 2 teaspoons of the salt and set aside. (The soup can be made in advance up to this point.)

Just before serving, bring the soup to a brisk boil, drop the fish in, stir it and return to a boil. Continue to boil until the fish is barely firm and white inside; it will continue cooking in the hot soup after it is removed from heat. Season the soup to taste with salt and pepper.

SERVING SUGGESTIONS: When serving this soup as a light main course, precede it with Spinach Strudel, Spinach Roll, Tortilla, Pasta Shells with Cheese Filling, Penne with Mushroom Sauce or Bow Ties with Peppers and Basil.

Puréed Butternut Squash Soup

8 SERVINGS

I don't like to use my food processor for puréeing soups: the texture is rarely as smooth as it should be and the liquid tends to spill out. Instead I prefer the blender. This is a wonderful soup to serve in the fall and winter when butternut squash is plentiful and delicious.

1 tablespoon vegetable oil
1 medium onion, coarsely chopped
1 clove garlic, coarsely chopped
1 carrot, quartered
2 medium butternut squash (3 to 3½ pounds)
5½ cups light chicken stock (see page 194)

A ¾-inch piece fresh ginger, peeled and minced
¼ teaspoon cinnamon
Freshly grated nutmeg
Kosher salt
Freshly ground black pepper
Fresh lemon juice

In a large saucepan heat the oil. Add the onion, garlic and carrot and sauté over low heat for 2 minutes. Trim thin slices from each squash end. Peel the squash, seed it and cut it into large cubes. Add to the saucepan with 5 cups of the stock, the ginger, the cinnamon and a few grindings of nutmeg. Bring to a boil, reduce the heat, cover and cook slowly until all the vegetables are tender, approximately 15 minutes. Cool slightly, then purée until smooth, in batches, in a blender. Return the soup to the saucepan and heat it through. Thin the soup as desired with the additional remaining stock and season to taste with ginger, nutmeg, salt and pepper and lemon juice.

SERVING SUGGESTIONS: Follow with Chicken with Dried and Fresh Mushrooms, Braised Soy Sauce Duck, Roast Turkey or Baked or Broiled Cornish Hens.

Cold Carrot Soup

8 TO 10 SERVINGS

The flavor of the apples in this recipe, although not readily discernible when combined with carrots and curry, adds a splendid tartness to this refreshing soup. It must be made a day in advance to allow for chilling.

2 tablespoons unsalted margarine
1 tablespoon olive oil
3 medium onions, coarsely
  chopped
8 medium carrots (approximately
  1¼ pounds), sliced
2 Granny Smith apples, peeled,
  cored and sliced

About 2 teaspoons curry powder
6½ to 7 cups light chicken stock
  (see page 194)
2 whole cloves
2 teaspoons lemon juice
Kosher salt
Freshly ground black pepper
Finely snipped chives for garnish

In a large saucepan heat the margarine and olive oil. Add the onions and sauté over low heat until soft. Add the carrots, apples and curry and cook for a few minutes, stirring well. Add 6½ cups of the stock and the cloves. Bring to a boil, reduce the heat, cover and cook slowly until the carrots are tender, approximately 45 minutes. Cool slightly and discard the cloves. Purée until smooth, in batches, in a blender. Thin the soup as desired with the additional remaining stock and season to taste with lemon juice and salt and pepper. Serve garnished with the chives.

SERVING SUGGESTIONS: Follow with Baked Chicken Breasts with Lemon and Mustard, Steamed Chicken Breasts with Tomato, Basil and Vinegar, Chicken Salad with Fresh Herbs or Broiled or Barbecued Tuna Steaks.

Leek and Lettuce Soup

If you like delicately flavored puréed soups, you will enjoy this one.

4 medium leeks

1 pound red-skinned potatoes,
  peeled and cubed

6½ cups light chicken stock (see
  page 194)

1 head Boston lettuce

Kosher salt

Freshly ground black pepper

Finely snipped dill or chives for
  garnish

Cut off the bottoms and all but 1 inch of the green parts of the leeks and discard. Discard the tough outer leaves. Cube the trimmed leeks, place in a sieve and rinse well under cold running water. Let drain.

Place the leeks in a large saucepan with the potatoes and 6 cups of the stock. Bring to a boil. Reduce the heat, cover and cook until the potatoes are tender.

Wash the lettuce and shake off as much water as possible. Add to the soup, return to a boil and cook slowly, covered, until the lettuce is wilted, approximately 5 minutes. Cool slightly and purée until smooth, in batches, in a blender. Adjust the consistency as desired with the additional remaining stock and season to taste with salt and pepper. Serve garnished with the dill or chives.

SERVING SUGGESTIONS: Follow with Chicken with Capers and Olives, Duck with *Hoisin* Sauce or Lettuce Packages Filled with Chicken.

Arugula, Leek and Potato Soup

3 medium leeks
1 tablespoon unsalted margarine
1 tablespoon olive oil
¾ pound red-skinned potatoes,
  peeled and cubed
6 cups light chicken stock (see
  page 194)

1 bunch arugula
Kosher salt
Freshly ground black pepper
Finely snipped chives for garnish

Cut off the bottoms and most of the green tops of the leeks and discard. Discard tough outer leaves. Cube the trimmed leeks, place in a sieve and rinse well under cold running water. Let drain.

In a large saucepan heat the margarine and the olive oil. Add the leeks and sauté over low heat, stirring from time to time, until they are soft. Add the potatoes and the stock and bring to a boil. Reduce the heat, cover, and cook slowly until the potatoes are tender. Discard the lower halves of the arugula stems. Wash the arugula and shake off as much water as possible. Add to the soup and cook until it is wilted. Let the soup cool slightly, then purée until smooth, in batches, in a blender. Return the soup to the saucepan and heat it through. Season to taste with salt and pepper. Serve garnished with the chives.

SERVING SUGGESTIONS: Follow with Baked Chicken with Sun-Dried Tomatoes, Braised Curried Veal or Stir-fried Chopped Meat and Rice.

Sherry's Jerusalem Artichoke Soup

10 TO 12 SERVINGS

Sherry Beltramini-Pincus is a talented and innovative professional cook. I am grateful to her for sharing this very fine recipe with me.

3 pounds Jerusalem artichokes (sun chokes)
2 tablespoons unsalted margarine
2 medium onions, coarsely chopped
6 cloves garlic, coarsely chopped
2 pounds ripe tomatoes, peeled, seeded and coarsely chopped

6 to 6½ cups light chicken stock (see page 194)
Rind of 1 orange
1 bay leaf
About 1 tablespoon tomato paste
Kosher salt
Freshly ground black pepper

Peel the artichokes carefully. (They are not difficult to peel, but there is a considerable amount of waste.) Slice them thick and rinse. In a large saucepan heat the margarine and add the artichokes. Cover and cook over low heat, stirring from time to time, for 10 minutes. (Do not let them brown.) Add the onions, garlic, tomatoes, 6 cups of the stock, the orange rind and the bay leaf tied together in a piece of cheesecloth. Bring the soup to a boil, reduce the heat, cover and cook slowly until the artichokes are tender, approximately 30 minutes. Cool the soup slightly and discard the cheesecloth bag. Purée the soup until smooth, in batches, in a blender. Return the soup to the saucepan and heat it through. Thin it with the additional remaining stock, if necessary, and season to taste with the tomato paste and salt and pepper.

SERVING SUGGESTIONS: Follow with Baked Chicken with Soy Sauce and Ginger, Braised Soy Sauce Duck, any of the Cornish hens or Braised Curried Veal.

Puréed Broccoli Soup

2 tablespoons olive oil
1 medium onion, coarsely chopped
2 cloves garlic, coarsely chopped
1 bunch broccoli (3 to 4 stalks),
    stems peeled and cut into small
    pieces with the florets

5 cups light chicken stock (see
    page 194)
About 2 teaspoons lemon juice
Freshly ground black pepper
3 scallions, green parts only, sliced
    into thin rounds for garnish

In a large saucepan heat the oil. Add the onion and garlic and sauté over low heat until soft. Add the broccoli and 4½ cups of the stock. Bring to a boil, reduce the heat, cover, and cook slowly until the broccoli is tender, approximately 20 minutes. Cool slightly, then purée the soup until smooth, in batches, in a blender. Return the soup to the saucepan and heat it through. Thin it as desired with the additional remaining stock and season to taste with the lemon juice and salt and pepper.

Serve garnished with the scallions.

SERVING SUGGESTIONS: Follow with Braised Veal Shanks, Millie Chan's Lion's Head or Broiled Chicken Breasts with Mustard and Thyme.

Hearty Vegetable Soup

This is a nourishing soup that I like to serve on chilly winter days. You can be as adventurous as you like in substituting other vegetables. Do make the soup even several days in advance to let the flavors blend, stored in the refrigerator. This soup also freezes very well.

½ cup dried chick peas
½ cup dried baby lima beans
1 ounce dried imported mushrooms (*cépes* or *porcini*)
1 cup boiling water
10 cups strong chicken stock (see
  page 193)
2 medium onions, finely chopped
4 cloves garlic, finely chopped
3 carrots, finely chopped
A 28-ounce can peeled tomatoes,
  coarsely chopped, with their
  juice
2 bay leaves, crushed
½ pound green beans, ends
  trimmed and cut into ½-inch
  lengths

1 medium zucchini, diced
5 ounces (approximately 1 cup),
  frozen sweet peas, thawed
About 2 pounds chicory lettuce,
  washed, drained and coarsely
  chopped
1 cup tightly packed Italian parsley
  with stems, coarsely chopped
1 to 2 teaspoons dried thyme
  (rubbed to release extra flavor)
Kosher salt
Freshly ground black pepper

Place the beans in separate medium bowls, cover them with cold water and let soak overnight. Drain and pick them over. Set aside.

Place the dried mushrooms in a bowl and pour 1 cup boiling water over them. Let stand for approximately ½ hour. Strain the soaking liquid through a sieve lined with a paper towel, squeezing the mushrooms over the sieve to extract as much liquid as possible. Set aside. Rinse the mushrooms to remove any remaining dirt, then squeeze them dry and chop coarse.

In a large stockpot bring to a boil over high heat the stock, beans, mushroom liquid, chopped mushrooms, onions, garlic, carrots, tomatoes with their juice and bay leaves. Reduce the heat, cover and cook slowly, for approximately 1 hour, or until the beans are tender. Add the green beans, zucchini, peas, chicory, parsley and thyme. Bring to a boil over high heat, reduce the heat and cook over low heat, covered, for ½ hour. Season the soup to taste with salt and pepper.

SERVING SUGGESTIONS: Follow with Roast Breast of Veal, Veal Stew or Beef Stew.

Chicken Soup with Arugula or Watercress

Once you have prepared the stock, this soup requires minimal preparation, and it has an intriguing flavor.

2 bunches arugula or watercress
7 cups strong chicken stock (see page 193)
1 clove garlic crushed to a paste with ¼ teaspoon salt

3 tablespoons couscous
Kosher salt
Freshly ground black pepper

Discard the lower halves of the arugula or watercress stems. Wash, spin dry and chop the leaves coarse. Set aside.

In a large saucepan bring the stock, garlic and couscous to a boil. Add the chopped arugula or watercress and bring to a boil. Season to taste with salt and pepper and serve at once.

SERVING SUGGESTIONS: Follow with Chicken with Dried and Fresh Mushrooms, Stir-fried Chicken with Broccoli or Stir-fried Chopped Meat and Rice.

Chicken Soup with Ginger, Tree Ears and Peas

8 SERVINGS

This is a superb basic chicken soup with the extra twist of soy sauce and ginger, as well as a pretty appearance. You can make the broth up to a few days in advance.

½ pound chicken breasts, skinned and boned
½ cup tree ears (about 1 ounce)
2 tablespoons peanut oil
A ½-inch piece fresh ginger, peeled and cut into thin matchstick pieces
7 cups strong chicken stock (see page 193)

1 tablespoon dry white wine
About 1 tablespoon thin Chinese soy sauce
5 ounces (approximately 1 cup) frozen sweet peas, thawed
4 scallions, including green parts, sliced into thin rounds
Kosher salt
Freshly ground black pepper

Freeze the chicken for a few minutes. (It is easier to slice if semifrozen.) Cut the chicken against the grain into thin matchstick pieces. Set aside.

Place the tree ears in a large bowl and pour boiling water over them. Let stand for a few minutes. (They will soak up the water and expand.) Drain, rinse well, squeeze dry and tear into bite-size pieces. Set aside.

Heat a wok or skillet, add the oil and heat. Add the ginger and stir-fry over medium-high heat for a few seconds. Add the chicken and the tree ears and stir-fry for 1 minute. Transfer to a dish. Bring the stock to a boil in a large saucepan. Add the wine, soy sauce, and the ginger, chicken and tree ears mixture. (The soup can be made in advance up to this point.) Just before serving, return the soup to a boil, stir in the peas and scallions and season to taste with soy sauce and salt and pepper.

SERVING SUGGESTIONS: Follow with any of the duck recipes, any of the Cornish hen recipes or Steamed Salmon Steaks with Black Beans.

Beet Consommé

This light Polish winter soup is traditionally served with *piroshki*, but you can also serve it as a clear broth or garnish it with baked shredded beets. The flavor is enhanced if this soup is made in advance. (I allow 3 to 5 *piroshki* per person.)

9 cups strong chicken stock (see page 193)
8 medium beets, peeled and cubed
2 cloves garlic crushed to a paste with ½ teaspoon salt
2 bay leaves

2 cloves
½ teaspoon sugar
About 2 tablespoons white vinegar
Kosher salt
Freshly ground black pepper

Dilled Chicken and Beef *Piroshki* (see page 94)

Finely snipped dill for garnish

In a large saucepan bring the stock, beets, garlic, bay leaves, cloves and sugar to a boil. Reduce the heat, cover and cook slowly until the beets are tender, approximately 30 minutes. Strain the soup, discarding the vegetables, and return the broth to the saucepan. Bring to a simmer and season to taste with the vinegar and salt and pepper.

To Serve: Divide the hot *piroshki* among heated soup bowls, ladle the beet consommé over and garnish with dill. (You may substitute grated baked beets (see page 178) for the *piroshki* or you may even serve the consommé plain.)

SERVING SUGGESTIONS: Follow with Roast Breast of Veal, Roast Turkey or Beef Stew.

Chicken Soup

When I think of Friday nights or holidays I immediately think of this glorious fat-free, crystal-clear, delicately toned soup. Serve it with square noodles, or Dilled Chicken or Meat *Piroshki* (see page 94) and garnish it with finely snipped fresh dill.

**A 6-pound boiling chicken, quart-
ered, or an equivalent amount of
chicken parts (carcasses, necks,
wings, legs and gizzards)**
4 ice cubes
1 carrot, quartered
1 onion, quartered

Several parsley sprigs
Several fresh dill sprigs
Kosher salt
Freshly ground black pepper
**Extra sprigs of fresh dill, finely
snipped, for garnish**

Rinse the chicken very well to get rid of any salt, and discard the excess fat. Place in a large stockpot with enough cold water to almost cover the chicken. Bring to a boil over high heat. Add the ice cubes, reduce the heat to low, and skim the scum as it rises to the surface. Add the vegetables and herbs and simmer the stock, partially covered, for approximately 2 hours. Remove the chicken and the vegetables to a bowl. Reserve the soup, then rinse the stockpot.

Wet a clean cotton cloth (such as an old pillowcase) with cold water and wring it dry. Drape it over a large bowl and pour the stock through it. Do not wring the cloth at the end, or droplets of fat will get through. (Unlike cheesecloth, the cotton strains the stock fat free and particle free.) Return the soup to the rinsed pot and gently bring to a boil. Season to taste with salt and pepper. Garnish with dill.

NOTE: You may eat the chicken and vegetables.

SERVING SUGGESTIONS: Follow with Roast Breast of Veal, Braised Veal Shanks or Roast Chicken.

Pasta Shell Salad with Vegetables
Bow Ties with Green Beans and Basil
Potato Cheese Piroshki

Pasta & Grains

DAIRY
Spaghettini with Fresh Vegetables
Linguine with Mushroom Sauce
Bow Ties with Green Beans and Basil
Spaghetti with Eggplant, Peppers and Ricotta
Spaghetti with Tomato Ricotta Sauce
Penne with Mushroom Sauce
Pasta Shells with Cheese Filling
Potato Cheese Piroshki
Pasta Shell Salad with Vegetables
Fusilli with Uncooked Tomato Olive Sauce
Fusilli with Radicchio

PAREVE
Spaghetti with Tomato and Crushed Red Pepper Flakes
Spaghettini with Arugula
Bow Ties with Peppers and Basil
Rigatoni with Red Pepper Tomato Sauce
Spaghetti with Uncooked Tomato Sauce
Rigatoni Puttanesca
Spinach Spaghetti Primavera
Chinese-Style Pasta with Vegetables
Orzo with Parsley
Boiled Rice Chinese Style
Plain Boiled Rice
Stir-fried Rice
Rice Pilaf
Rice with Saffron and Pine Nuts
Bulghur Pilaf
Kasha

MEAT
Cold Chinese-Style Linguine with Chicken and Vegetables
Dilled Chicken and Beef Piroshki
Cholent

Spaghettini with Fresh Vegetables

6 TO 8 SERVINGS AS A FIRST COURSE, 4 TO 6 SERVINGS AS A MAIN COURSE

If you are a vegetable and pasta lover, you will enjoy this delightful dish, which combines the two.

2 tablespoons unsalted butter	1 cup tightly packed Italian parsley, finely chopped
2 tablespoons olive oil	½ cup tightly packed fresh basil leaves, finely chopped
2 cloves garlic, minced	
4 scallions, including green parts, sliced into thin rounds	A 10-ounce package frozen peas, thawed and drained
3 medium ripe tomatoes, peeled, seeded and coarsely chopped	½ to 1 cup half-and-half
About ¾ teaspoon crushed red pepper flakes	Kosher salt
	Freshly ground black pepper
½ pound firm fresh mushrooms	1 pound spaghettini
1 bunch broccoli	1½ cups freshly grated Parmesan cheese
2 small zucchini	
2 small yellow squash	

In a very large saucepan heat 1 tablespoon of the butter and 1 tablespoon of the olive oil. Add the garlic and the scallions and sauté over low heat until the scallions are wilted. Add the tomatoes and the red pepper flakes and cook, covered, over low heat for 5 minutes. Remove this mixture to a dish.

Wipe the mushrooms with a damp paper towel and slice them thin. Heat the remaining butter and oil in the saucepan and sauté the mushrooms over high heat until they are just coated with the butter. Set aside.

Separate the broccoli tops into bite-size florets and peel and dice the stems. Steam the broccoli for 2 minutes, or until crisply tender (see page 253). Transfer the broccoli to the saucepan.

Steam both the zucchini and the squash (whole) for 2 minutes, or until crisply tender, then trim off the ends and dice the vegetables. Add to the saucepan with parsley, basil, peas and half-and-half. Bring the sauce to a boil and season with salt and pepper.

Meanwhile, bring 5 quarts of water to a rolling boil in a large covered pot. Add 2 tablespoons salt and all the pasta at once; stir well. Boil briskly, uncovered, for about 5 minutes, or until the pasta is al dente, tender but still firm to the bite. Pour into a colander and shake vigorously to drain well. Toss the pasta with the hot sauce and 1 cup of the Parmesan cheese. Season to taste with crushed red pepper flakes, salt, and pepper and Parmesan cheese. Serve with the remaining Parmesan cheese.

SERVING SUGGESTIONS: As a first course, follow with Whole Steamed Salmon in Foil with Ginger Vinaigrette, Broiled Salmon Steaks or Broiled Halibut Steaks with Tomato Coulis. As a main course, precede by Sweet Potato Soup, Marinated Salmon with Green Peppercorns or Tuna Seviche.

Linguine with Mushroom Sauce

6 TO 8 SERVINGS AS A FIRST COURSE, 4 TO 6 SERVINGS AS A MAIN COURSE

When I combined dried wild mushrooms with fresh cultivated ones, I came astonishingly close to that wonderfully musky flavor of fresh wild mushrooms. It was a lovely discovery because fresh wild mushrooms are not only very expensive and hard to find, but seasonal as well.

1 ounce dried Polish mushrooms (or substitute a mixture of ½ ounce dried *porcini* and ½ ounce dried morels)
¼ cup olive oil
1 medium onion, finely chopped
2 cloves garlic, minced
¾ pound firm fresh mushrooms

¼ cup dry white wine
About ¼ cup heavy cream
¼ cup tightly packed Italian parsley, finely chopped
Kosher salt
Freshly ground black pepper
1 pound linguine
Freshly grated Parmesan cheese

Place the dried mushrooms in a small bowl and pour ¾ cup boiling water over them. Let stand for about ½ hour. Strain the soaking liquid through a sieve lined with a paper towel, squeezing the mushrooms over the sieve to extract more liquid. Set the liquid aside. Wash the soaked mushrooms carefully to remove any dirt, pat them dry with paper towels and cut them into matchstick pieces. Set aside.

In a large enameled saucepan heat the olive oil. Add the onion and garlic and sauté them over low heat until soft. With a damp paper towel wipe the fresh mushrooms, slice them thinly without detaching the stem and cut them into matchsticks. Set aside.

Add the dried mushrooms, half of the mushroom liquid and the wine to the saucepan and stir over high heat until the mushrooms are dry. Add the fresh mushrooms, the remaining mushroom liquid and the cream. Bring the sauce to a boil. Lower the heat and cook, covered, for 10 minutes. Stir in parsley and season with salt and pepper.

Meanwhile, bring 5 quarts of water to a rolling boil in a large covered pot. Add 2 tablespoons kosher salt and all the pasta at once; stir well. Boil briskly, uncovered, for about 7 minutes, or until the pasta is al dente, tender but still firm to the bite. Pour into a colander and shake vigorously to drain well. Toss the pasta with the hot sauce and season to taste with salt and pepper. Serve with the Parmesan cheese.

SERVING SUGGESTIONS: As a first course, follow with Fish Soup with Vegetables, Fillet of Grey Sole en Papillote, or Steamed Salmon with Tomato Sauce and Steamed Vegetables. As a main course, precede by Tomato Soup, Broiled Sweet Peppers or either of the salmon tartare recipes.

Bow Ties with Green Beans and Basil

6 TO 8 SERVINGS AS A FIRST COURSE, 4 TO 6 SERVINGS AS A MAIN COURSE

When I think of summer, this colorful pasta comes to mind. Young beans, wonderful basil and almost no cooking. Serve it at room temperature or hot, if you wish.

1 pound young green beans
1 cup tightly packed fresh basil
    leaves
2 cloves garlic, quartered
⅓ cup olive oil
1 pound bow ties, or any other
    small pasta

¾ to 1 cup freshly grated Parme-
    san cheese
Kosher salt
Freshly ground black pepper

Trim the beans if needed (if they are young they will not need it), and steam them for 2 minutes, or until they are crisply tender (see page 253). Transfer them to a large bowl and set aside. Place the basil and garlic in a food processor fitted with a steel blade. With the motor on add the oil through the feed tube and process until smooth. Add to the beans and mix thoroughly.

Meanwhile, bring 5 quarts of water to a rolling boil in a large covered pot. Add 2 tablespoons salt and all the pasta at once; stir well. Boil briskly, uncovered, for about 7 minutes, or until the pasta is al dente, tender but still firm to the bite. Pour into a colander and shake vigorously to drain. Toss the pasta with the string bean mixture and the Parmesan cheese. Season to taste with salt and pepper.

SERVING SUGGESTIONS: As a first course, follow with Steamed Salmon Steaks with Black Beans, Whole Steamed Salmon in Foil with Ginger Vinaigrette or Broiled Halibut Steaks with Tomato Coulis. As a main course, precede by Chilled Cucumber Soup, Tomato Soup or Broiled Sweet Peppers.

Spaghetti with Eggplant, Peppers and Ricotta

6 TO 8 SERVINGS AS A FIRST COURSE, 4 TO 6 SERVINGS AS A MAIN COURSE

This combination of eggplant, peppers, tomato and ricotta makes for a hearty, filling dish that I prefer to make in the fall or winter.

1 medium eggplant, approximately 1 pound
⅓ cup olive oil
1 onion, finely chopped
3 cloves garlic, finely chopped
¼ teaspoon crushed red pepper
1 medium red bell pepper, diced
1 medium yellow bell pepper, diced
A 28-ounce can peeled tomatoes, drained and coarsely chopped

A 15-ounce container part-skim ricotta
½ cup tightly packed Italian parsley, coarsely chopped
½ cup tightly packed fresh basil leaves, coarsely chopped
Kosher salt
Freshly ground black pepper
1 pound spaghetti

Peel the eggplant and cut it into ½-inch cubes. Place the cubes in a large bowl of ice water. Add 2 tablespoons of salt and let stand for ½ hour. Drain the eggplant, then squeeze it dry in a dish towel. Set aside.

In a large saucepan heat the oil. Add the onion and garlic and sauté over low heat, covered, until soft. Add the crushed peppers, the eggplant and the pepper and sauté over medium heat, uncovered, for approximately 5 minutes. Add the tomatoes, bring to a boil, reduce the heat and cook the sauce for 5 minutes. Stir in the ricotta, parsley and basil. Season with salt and pepper.

Meanwhile, bring 5 quarts of water to a rolling boil in a large covered pot. Add 2 tablespoons salt and all the pasta at once; stir well. Boil briskly, uncovered, for about 7 minutes, or until the pasta is al dente, tender but still firm to the bite. Pour into a colander and shake vigorously to drain well. Toss with the hot sauce and season the pasta to taste with salt and pepper.

SERVING SUGGESTIONS: As a first course, follow with Puréed Vegetable Soup, Fish Soup with Vegetables or Broiled Salmon Steaks. As a main course, precede by Tortilla, Minestrone or Warm Spinach Salad.

Spaghetti with Tomato Ricotta Sauce

6 TO 8 SERVINGS AS A FIRST COURSE, 4 TO 6 SERVINGS AS A MAIN COURSE

Mushrooms, ricotta, tomatoes and basil blend wonderfully in this hearty sauce.

4 tablespoons olive oil
1 medium onion, finely chopped
3 cloves garlic, minced
¾ pound firm fresh mushrooms
A 28-ounce can peeled tomatoes, drained and coarsely chopped
A 15-ounce container part-skim ricotta
½ cup tightly packed Italian parsley, finely chopped

½ cup tightly packed fresh basil leaves, finely chopped
Kosher salt
Freshly ground black pepper
1 pound spaghetti
½ cup freshly grated Parmesan cheese

In a large saucepan heat the olive oil. Add the onion and garlic and sauté over low heat, covered, until soft. Wipe the mushrooms clean with a damp paper towel and slice them thin. Add the mushrooms to the saucepan, and stir continuously, over high heat, until they are well coated with the olive oil, about 1 minute. Add the tomatoes, bring to a boil and cook, uncovered, for a few minutes more. Stir in the ricotta, parsley, basil and salt and pepper.

Meanwhile, bring 5 quarts of water to a rolling boil in a large covered pot. Add 2 tablespoons salt and all the pasta at once; stir well. Boil briskly for about 7 minutes, or until the pasta is al dente, tender but still firm to the bite. Pour into a colander and shake vigorously to drain. Toss with the hot sauce and season the pasta to taste with salt and pepper. Serve with the Parmesan cheese.

SERVING SUGGESTIONS: As a first course, follow with Fish Soup with Vegetables, Tortilla or Gazpacho. As a main course, precede by Puréed Vegetable Soup, Minestrone or Braised Baby Artichokes.

Penne with Mushroom Sauce

6 TO 8 SERVINGS AS A FIRST COURSE, 4 TO 6 SERVINGS AS A MAIN COURSE

Cultivated mushrooms with snowy-white caps are available year round. This sauce uses them but has a deep musky flavor like that of the harder-to-find and much more expensive *porcini* mushroom.

3 tablespoons unsalted butter
3 tablespoons olive oil
2 medium onions, finely chopped
2 cloves garlic, minced
1 pound firm fresh mushrooms
Juice of ½ to 1 lemon
1 cup tightly packed Italian parsley, coarsely chopped

Kosher salt
Freshly ground black pepper
1 pound penne
1 cup freshly grated Parmesan
cheese

In a large saucepan heat 1 tablespoon of the butter and 1 tablespoon of the olive oil. Add the onions and garlic and sauté over low heat, covered, until the onions are soft. Remove to a dish.

Wipe the mushrooms clean with a damp paper towel and chop them coarse. Heat the remaining butter and oil in the same saucepan. Add the mushrooms and sauté over high heat, uncovered, stirring all the time, until the mushrooms are hot. Add the juice of ½ lemon, the onion and garlic mixture and the parsley. Cook, uncovered, over low heat for a minute. Season with salt and pepper.

Meanwhile, bring 5 quarts of water to a rolling boil in a large covered pot. Add 2 tablespoons salt and all the pasta at once; stir well. Boil briskly, uncovered, for about 7 minutes, or until the pasta is al dente, tender but still firm to the bite. Pour into a colander and shake vigorously to drain. Toss with the hot sauce and the Parmesan cheese. Season to taste with more lemon juice and salt and pepper.

SERVING SUGGESTIONS: As a first course, follow with Whole Steamed Salmon in Foil with Ginger Vinaigrette, Fillet of Grey Sole en Papillote or Broiled Fillet of Red Snapper with Pine Nut Coating. As a main course, precede by Tomato Soup, Marinated Salmon or Tortilla.

Pasta Shells with Cheese Filling

This is a pretty dish that can be served hot or at room temperature. It can also be assembled in the morning, refrigerated, and baked before serving.

The pasta shells usually come in 14-ounce boxes, and I suggest cooking 2 boxes as some of the shells will be broken and others may tear when boiled. (The broken shells may be prepared with the leftover tomato sauce.)

**Two 14-ounce boxes jumbo or
king-size pasta shells**
FILLING
1½ pounds farmer cheese
**A 15-ounce container part-skim
ricotta**
**1½ cups freshly grated Parmesan
cheese**
2 eggs, lightly beaten
SAUCE
1 cup heavy cream

**½ cup tightly packed Italian pars-
ley, finely chopped**
**½ cup tightly packed fresh basil
leaves, finely chopped**
Kosher salt
Freshly ground black pepper

**1 cup Fresh Tomato Sauce (see
page 192)**

Preheat the oven to 325° F.

Bring 5 quarts of water to a rolling boil in a large covered pot. Add 2 tablespoons salt and all the pasta at once; stir well. Boil briskly, uncovered, for 12 or 13 minutes, or until the pasta is al dente, tender but still firm to the bite. Pour into a colander, refresh the shells with cold water, drain and pat dry in a dish towel.

Make the Filling: In a large bowl thoroughly combine the farmer cheese, ricotta, 1 cup of the Parmesan cheese, eggs, parsley and basil. Season the filling well with salt and pepper. Set aside.

Make the Sauce: Bring the heavy cream to a boil in an enameled or glass saucepan over medium heat and reduce it, uncovered, to ½ cup. Stir in the tomato sauce and season with salt and pepper. Use the sauce to coat the bottom of an ovenproof dish large enough to hold the shells tightly in a single layer. Use a flat knife to fill the shells with the cheese mixture and place them in the dish. Sprinkle with Parmesan cheese. Cover the dish with heavy foil and bake for 20 to 30 minutes, or until the shells are heated through.

To Serve: Arrange the shells in a serving dish and drizzle the sauce over them.

SERVING SUGGESTIONS: Follow with Steamed Salmon with Tomato Sauce and Julienne Vegetables, Broiled Fillet of Red Snapper with Pine Nut Coating or Whole Steamed Salmon in Foil with Ginger Vinaigrette. As a main course precede by Puréed Vegetable Soup, Carrot Soup or Broiled Sweet Peppers.

Potato Cheese *Piroshki*

ABOUT 100 MINIATURE *PIROSHKI*, 6 TO 8 SERVINGS AS A FIRST COURSE, 4 SERVINGS AS A MAIN COURSE

Piroshki (also known as *kreplach*) are small half-moon-shaped dumplings of Polish origin into which one can put a variety of stuffings. These *piroshki* are stuffed with a potato and cheese mixture. The dough is quite easy to make. Just remember that the moister you make it, the lighter and softer it will be. This is another splendid dish that freezes very well.

FILLING

¾ pound all-purpose potatoes
3 tablespoons vegetable oil
1 medium onion, finely chopped

½ pound farmer cheese
Kosher salt
Freshly ground black pepper

DOUGH

2¼ cups unbleached flour
¼ teaspoon salt
1 egg yolk
⅔ cup plus 3 to 4 tablespoons very
   warm water (115° F.–120° F.)

Unsalted butter
Freshly grated Parmesan cheese

Make the Filling: Boil the potatoes in their jackets until they are tender, approximately 30 minutes. Peel and quarter them. Heat the oil in a small skillet and sauté the onion over medium heat until light brown. Strain the potatoes, onion, and farmer cheese through the medium blade of a food mill. Season the filling to taste with salt and pepper. Set aside.

Make the Dough: Mix the flour and salt in a large bowl. Add the egg yolk and gradually pour the water over the flour mixture, working it well with a pastry blender until you can gather the dough into a ball. Turn out the dough on a pastry board. Knead it lightly, dusting it from time to time with flour, until the dough no longer sticks to your hands and is smooth. Divide the dough into 4 pieces. Work with ¼ at a time and keep the rest of the dough covered with plastic wrap. Roll out the dough, rolling it on both sides, on a floured pastry board, as thinly as you can. Cut out 2½-inch rounds with a cookie cutter or a glass.

Place ½ teaspoon of the filling in the center of each round and fold it over to make a half moon, then pinch the edges very tightly to seal. (Sometimes you may have to moisten the inside edge with water.) Dust the *piroshki* generously with flour, place them on a generously floured cookie sheet with floured paper between the layers, and repeat with the remaining dough, using the scraps as well. (Flouring the *piroshki* well prevents them from sticking to each other, and the flour dissolves when they are boiled.) Cover the *piroshki* with a towel and refrigerate them until you are ready to boil them.

Bring a large pot of salted water to a boil. Carefully drop in a batch of *piroshki*, only as many as your pot will comfortably hold. Return the water to a slow boil and cook the *piroshki* slowly, uncovered, until they rise to the surface, approximately 3 minutes. Pour into a sieve and drain well. Repeat with the remaining *piroshki*.

Melt a little butter in a skillet, add the *piroshki*, toss, and season to taste with salt and pepper. Serve right away, sprinkled with the Parmesan cheese, if you like.

NOTE: If you wish to freeze uncooked *piroshki*, cover the cookie sheet with foil and place in a freezer. Once the *piroshki* are frozen, remove them, wrap them in foil and place in a plastic bag. When needed, take them straight from the freezer and cook as above.

SERVING SUGGESTIONS: Follow with Broiled Halibut Steaks with Tomato Coulis, Whole Steamed Salmon in Foil with Ginger Vinaigrette or Fillet of Grey Sole en Papillote. As a main course, precede by Marinated Salmon, Gazpacho or Puréed Vegetable Soup.

Pasta Shell Salad with Vegetables

This salad is a luscious combination of colors, flavors and textures. It is substantial enough to serve as a summer luncheon main course. Prepare the entire dish 2 to 3 hours in advance and refrigerate it, then remove a few minutes before serving to return it to room temperature.

4 medium zucchini
1 cup sun-dried tomatoes
1 cup tightly packed Italian parsley, finely chopped
¾ pound feta cheese, diced
2 cloves garlic, crushed to a paste with ¼ teaspoon salt
2 teaspoons Dijon-style mustard

2 teaspoons Worcestershire sauce
¼ cup olive oil
3 to 4 tablespoons wine vinegar
Kosher salt
Freshly ground black pepper
1 pound conchiglie (pasta shells), or any other small pasta

Rinse the zucchini, trim the ends and steam them whole for 2 minutes (see page 254). Allow the zucchini to cool, then dice them. Place in a large bowl.

Place the sun-dried tomatoes in a bowl and cover them with boiling water. Let soak for 5 minutes, then squeeze them dry and dice them. Add to the zucchini along with the parsley and feta.

In a small bowl whisk together the garlic, mustard, Worcestershire sauce, olive oil, vinegar and salt and pepper. Set aside.

Bring 5 quarts of water to a rolling boil in a large covered pot. Add 2 tablespoons salt and all the pasta at once and stir well. Boil briskly, uncovered, for about 7 minutes, or until the pasta is al dente, tender but still firm to the bite. Pour into a colander, refresh with cold water, and shake vigorously to drain well. Toss the pasta with the vegetable-cheese mixture and the dressing.

SERVING SUGGESTIONS: As a first course, follow with Tortilla, Marinated Salmon or Broiled or Barbecued Tuna Steaks. As a main course, precede by Gazpacho, Puréed Romaine and Watercress Soup or Tuna Seviche.

Fusilli with Uncooked Tomato Olive Sauce

6 TO 8 SERVINGS AS A FIRST COURSE, 4 TO 6 SERVINGS AS A MAIN COURSE

I love to serve this dish on hot, lazy summer days, when tomatoes and basil are at their best and when the less cooking required, the more inviting the dish.

1 pound mozzarella
4 large ripe tomatoes, peeled, seeded and diced
10 black olives, pitted and coarsely chopped
2 cloves garlic, crushed to a paste with ¼ teaspoon salt

1 cup tightly packed fresh basil leaves, coarsely chopped
¼ cup olive oil
Kosher salt
Freshly ground black pepper
1 pound fusilli (spiral-shaped pasta)

Freeze the mozzarella for 15 minutes to make it easier to handle, then dice it. Combine the mozzarella, tomatoes, olives, garlic, basil, and olive oil. Season with salt and pepper.

Bring 5 quarts of water to a rolling boil in a large covered pot. Add 2 tablespoons salt and all the pasta at once; stir well. Boil briskly, uncovered, for about 7 minutes, or until the pasta is al dente, tender but still firm to the bite. Pour into a colander, refresh with cold water and shake vigorously to drain. Toss with the sauce and season to taste with salt and pepper.

SERVING SUGGESTIONS: As a first course, follow with Tortilla, Whole Steamed Salmon in Foil with Ginger Vinaigrette, Carrot Soup or Marinated Salmon. As a main course, precede by Gazpacho, Chilled Cucumber Soup or Tuna Seviche.

Fusilli with Radicchio

Radicchio, which in the United States generally looks like a small red cabbage, is lettuce with a slightly bitter taste. (There is a second variety, more popular in Italy, which looks like a slender Romaine with purplish red leaves and white striations.) I find that American radicchio makes an interesting sauce (that very few can identify). With cooking the red color turns dark brown and some of the bitterness disappears. I know that it is expensive, but it makes for a nice change of pace.

3 tablespoons olive oil	Kosher salt
2 medium onions, finely chopped	Freshly ground black pepper
½ pound radicchio, shredded	1 pound fusilli (spiral-shaped pasta)
A 14-ounce can peeled plum toma-	or penne, or other tubular pasta
toes, coarsely chopped	1¼ cups freshly grated Parmesan
½ cup heavy cream	cheese

In a large saucepan heat the olive oil. Add the onions and sauté over low heat, covered, until they are soft. Add the radicchio and cook over medium heat, uncovered, stirring, until the radicchio has turned dark. Add the tomatoes and cream and bring to a boil. Season with salt and pepper.

Meanwhile, bring 5 quarts of water to a rolling boil in a large covered pot. Add 2 tablespoons salt and all the pasta at once; stir well. Boil briskly, uncovered, for about 7 minutes, or until the pasta is al dente, tender but still firm to the bite. Pour into a colander and shake vigorously to drain well. Toss the pasta with the hot sauce and ¾ to 1 cup of the Parmesan cheese. Season to taste with salt and pepper. Serve with the remaining Parmesan cheese.

SERVING SUGGESTIONS: As a first course, follow with Broiled Fillet of Red Snapper with Pine Nut Coating, Puréed Vegetable Soup or Tomato Soup. As a main course, precede by Tomato Soup, Stir-fried *Shiitake* Mushrooms or Tortilla.

Spaghetti with Tomato and Crushed Red Pepper Flakes

6 TO 8 SERVINGS AS A FIRST COURSE, 4 TO 6 SERVINGS AS A MAIN COURSE

¼ cup olive oil
5 medium shallots, finely chopped
3 cloves garlic, minced
5 medium ripe tomatoes, peeled, seeded and cut into large pieces
½ teaspoon crushed red pepper flakes

1 cup tightly packed fresh basil leaves, cut into very narrow strips
Kosher salt
Freshly ground black pepper
1 pound spaghetti

In a large saucepan heat the oil. Add the shallots and garlic and sauté over low heat until soft. Add the tomatoes and the crushed red pepper flakes and cook gently, covered, for approximately 10 minutes. Add the basil and season the sauce well.

Meanwhile, bring 5 quarts of water to a rolling boil in a large covered pot. Add 2 tablespoons salt and all the pasta at once; stir well. Boil briskly for about 7 minutes, or until the pasta is al dente, tender but still firm to the bite. Pour into a colander and shake vigorously to drain. Toss with the hot sauce and season the pasta to taste with salt and pepper.

SERVING SUGGESTIONS: As a first course, follow with Meat Loaf, Chicken Loaf or Steamed Chicken Salad. As a main course, precede by Tuna Seviche, Tortilla or Gazpacho.

Spaghettini with Arugula

Arugula, or rugula, is a green lettuce with a small, flat leaf and a bitter, slightly peppery, flavor. It is generally used for salads, but I love it in this pasta dish.

⅓ cup olive oil
3 cloves garlic, crushed to a paste with ¼ teaspoon salt
½ teaspoon crushed red pepper flakes
2 pounds ripe plum tomatoes, peeled, seeded and coarsely chopped
1 ounce sun-dried tomatoes packed in oil, coarsely chopped

1 pound spaghettini
1 bunch arugula, stems discarded, coarsely chopped
1 tablespoon (approximately) lemon juice
Kosher salt
Freshly ground black pepper

In a large saucepan heat the oil. Add the garlic and sauté over low heat for 1 minute. Add the crushed pepper flakes, the fresh tomatoes and the sun-dried tomatoes and cook gently, covered, for 5 minutes.

Meanwhile, bring 5 quarts of water to a rolling boil in a large covered pot. Add 2 tablespoons salt and all the pasta at once; stir well. Boil briskly, uncovered, for about 7 minutes, or until the pasta is al dente, tender but firm to the bite. Pour into a colander and shake vigorously to drain well. Add the arugula to the hot sauce, then toss with the pasta. Season to taste with the lemon juice and salt and pepper. Serve right away.

SERVING SUGGESTIONS: As a first course, follow with Broiled Veal Chops with Mustard and Mustard Seed, Braised Curried Veal or Chicken Loaf. As a main course, precede by Stir-fried *Shiitake* Mushrooms, Tuna Seviche or Puréed Broccoli Soup.

Bow Ties with Peppers and Basil

6 TO 8 SERVINGS AS A FIRST COURSE, 4 TO 6 SERVINGS AS A MAIN COURSE

The combination of peppers, sun-dried tomatoes, basil and vinegar makes for a delightfully colorful and light pasta. This dish is equally delicious served hot or at room temperature.

1 medium yellow bell pepper	A few drops of Tabasco
1 medium red bell pepper	1 to 2 tablespoons balsamic
1 ounce sun-dried tomatoes	vinegar
¼ cup olive oil	Kosher salt
2 cloves garlic, minced	Freshly ground black pepper
1 cup tightly packed fresh basil	1 pound bow ties, or other small
leaves, coarsely chopped	pasta

Broil the peppers (see page 16) and dice them. Set aside. Place the sun-dried tomatoes in a small bowl and cover them with boiling water. Let soften for approximately 5 minutes. Squeeze them dry, dice them and add them to the peppers.

In a large saucepan heat the oil. Add the garlic and sauté over low heat until soft. Add the diced peppers and the tomatoes, cover, and cook gently for 2 minutes. Stir in the basil, Tabasco, and vinegar and cook, uncovered, for 1 minute. Season with salt and pepper.

Meanwhile, bring 5 quarts of water to a rolling boil in a large covered pot. Add 2 tablespoons salt and all the pasta at once; stir well. Boil briskly, uncovered, for about 7 minutes, or until the pasta is al dente, tender but still firm to the bite. Pour into a colander and shake lightly. Add 3 tablespoons of the cooking water to the sauce and toss with the pasta. Season to taste with the vinegar, Tabasco, and salt and pepper.

SERVING SUGGESTIONS: As a first course, follow with Broiled or Barbecued Tuna, Broiled Salmon Steaks or Steamed Chicken Salad with Fresh Herbs. As a main course, precede by Chilled Cucumber Soup, Carrot Soup or Tuna Seviche.

Rigatoni with Red Pepper Tomato Sauce

6 TO 8 SERVINGS AS A FIRST COURSE, 4 TO 6 SERVINGS AS A MAIN COURSE

The combination of lemon juice, garlic, crushed red pepper and Tabasco gives this pasta a tangy taste.

2 medium red bell peppers
3 tablespoons olive oil
3 cloves garlic, crushed to a paste
with ¼ teaspoon salt
A 14-ounce can peeled plum toma-
toes, drained and coarsely
chopped

¼ teaspoon crushed red pepper
flakes
A few drops of Tabasco
1 to 2 tablespoons lemon juice
Kosher salt
Freshly ground black pepper
1 pound rigatoni

Broil the peppers, then peel them and remove the ribs and seeds (see pages 16, 254). Purée them in a blender or food processor and set aside.

In a large saucepan heat the oil. Add the garlic and sauté over low heat until soft. (Be careful; garlic burns very quickly.) Add the pepper purée, the tomatoes and the crushed red pepper. Bring to a boil, reduce the heat and cook gently, uncovered, for 2 minutes. Season the sauce to taste with the Tabasco, lemon juice, and salt and pepper.

Meanwhile, bring 5 quarts of water to a rolling boil in a large covered pot. Add 2 tablespoons salt and all the pasta at once; stir well. Boil briskly, uncovered, for about 7 minutes, or until the pasta is al dente, tender but still firm to the bite. Pour into a colander and shake vigorously to drain. Toss the pasta with the hot sauce and season to taste with more lemon juice, Tabasco, and salt and pepper.

SERVING SUGGESTIONS: As a first course, follow with Meat Loaf, Chicken Loaf or Chicken with Capers and Olives. As a main course, precede by Feta Cheese Strudel, Tortilla or Braised Baby Artichokes.

Spaghetti with Uncooked Tomato Sauce

6 TO 8 SERVINGS AS A FIRST COURSE, 4 TO 6 SERVINGS AS A MAIN COURSE

This is a well-seasoned dish that is perfect for hot summer days, as the sauce requires no cooking. The peppers can be peeled a day before and refrigerated. Serve the pasta at room temperature.

2 medium green bell peppers
3 large ripe tomatoes
8 pitted green olives, cut into thin strips
1 cup tightly packed Italian parsley, coarsely chopped
2 ounces sun-dried tomatoes packed in oil, cut into thin strips
2 tablespoons drained capers, coarsely chopped

¼ cup olive oil
2 to 3 tablespoons wine vinegar
½ teaspoon crushed red pepper flakes
Kosher salt
Freshly ground black pepper
1 pound spaghetti

Broil the peppers, then peel them, and remove the ribs and seeds (see pages 16, 254). Cut the peppers into ¼-inch strips. Place in a large bowl. Halve the tomatoes and cut them into thin strips (the seeds will fall out); add them to the peppers. Add the olives, parsley, sun-dried tomatoes, capers, olive oil, vinegar, and crushed pepper. Season with salt and pepper.

Bring 5 quarts of water to a rolling boil in a large covered pot. Add 2 tablespoons salt and all the pasta at once; stir well. Boil briskly, uncovered, for about 7 minutes, or until the pasta is al dente, tender but still firm to the bite. Pour into a colander, refresh with cold water and shake vigorously to drain well. Toss the pasta with the sauce and season to taste with more vinegar and salt and pepper.

SERVING SUGGESTIONS: As a first course, follow with any of the chicken salads, Chicken Loaf or Tuna Seviche. As a main course, precede by Tortilla, Spinach Roll or Puréed Romaine and Watercress Soup.

Rigatoni Puttanesca

If you like piquant pasta sauces, you will love this one, which combines tomatoes, capers, anchovies, garlic and olives. It is one of my favorites.

3 tablespoons olive oil
5 anchovy fillets, drained and minced
3 cloves garlic, minced
2 tablespoons drained capers
A 35-ounce can peeled tomatoes, coarsely chopped (discard ¾ cup of the juice; reserve the rest)

1 teaspoon tomato paste
½ cup pitted and slivered black olives
1 cup tightly packed Italian parsley, coarsely chopped
Kosher salt
Freshly ground black pepper
1½ pounds rigatoni

In a large saucepan heat the olive oil. Add the anchovies, garlic and capers and cook over low heat for 1 minute. Add the tomatoes with the juice, the tomato paste and the olives. Bring to a boil, reduce the heat, cover and cook slowly for 10 minutes. Stir in the parsley.

Meanwhile, bring 5 quarts of water to a rolling boil in a large covered pot. Add 2 tablespoons salt and all the pasta at once; stir well. Boil briskly, uncovered, for about 7 minutes, or until the pasta is al dente, tender but still firm to the bite. Pour into a colander and shake vigorously to drain. Toss with the hot sauce and season to taste with salt and pepper.

SERVING SUGGESTIONS: As a first course, follow with Broiled Salmon Steaks, Tortilla or Gazpacho. As a main course, precede by Minestrone or Marinated Salmon.

Spinach Spaghetti Primavera

12 SERVINGS AS A FIRST COURSE, 6 TO 8 SERVINGS AS A MAIN COURSE

This is a colorful summer dish that may be prepared 4 to 5 hours in advance, refrigerated and served at room temperature. If you own a Mouli Julienne (such a time-saver!), use the number 3 blade to julienne the zucchini and the carrots.

DRESSING

A 1-inch piece fresh ginger, peeled and minced

2 cloves garlic, crushed to a paste with 1 teaspoon salt

½ cup vegetable oil

5 tablespoons thin Chinese soy sauce

4 tablespoons pure Oriental sesame oil

¼ cup rice vinegar

¼ cup wine vinegar

1 teaspoon kosher salt

Freshly ground black pepper

1 bunch broccoli, cut into bite-size florets (discard stems)

1 small head cauliflower, cut into bite-size florets (discard stems)

1 small red bell pepper

1 small yellow bell pepper

2 small zucchini, cut into 2-inch matchstick pieces

2 carrots, cut into 2-inch matchstick pieces

A 10-ounce package frozen sweet peas, thawed and drained

1½ pounds spinach spaghetti

Make the Dressing: In a blender or food processor combine the dressing ingredients thoroughly. Set aside.

Steam the broccoli and the cauliflower separately until crisply tender, approximately 2 minutes (see page 253). Refresh with cold water and pat dry in a dish towel. Place both vegetables in a large bowl.

Cut off the tops and bottoms of the peppers. Halve, seed, and remove the ribs. Cut the peppers into thin matchstick pieces, pat dry and add to the bowl with the zucchini, carrots and peas. Toss with ½ of the dressing and refrigerate for several hours.

Bring 5 quarts of water to a rolling boil in a large covered pot. Add 2 tablespoons salt and all the pasta at once and stir well. Boil briskly, uncovered, for about 7 minutes, or until the pasta is al dente, tender but still firm to the bite. Pour into a colander, refresh with cold water, and shake vigorously to drain well. Transfer the pasta to a large bowl, toss with another ¼ of the dressing and refrigerate it as well.

To Serve: Pour off and discard the liquid that has accumulated around the vegetables. Add the vegetables to the pasta. Toss with 2 to 3 tablespoons of the remaining dressing and season to taste with salt and pepper.

SERVING SUGGESTIONS: As a first course, follow with Baked Chicken with Soy Sauce and Ginger, Duck with *Hoisin* Sauce or any of the Cornish hen recipes. As a main course, precede by either Salmon Tartare, Marinated Salmon or Tomato Soup.

Chinese-Style Pasta with Vegetables

6 TO 8 SERVINGS AS A FIRST COURSE, 4 TO 6 SERVINGS AS A MAIN COURSE

Peanut butter, soy sauce and vinegar give this lovely summer dish an unusual flavor, and the vegetables lend it a wonderful texture. Serve at room temperature.

DRESSING

¼ cup vegetable oil

6 scallions, including green parts, cut into thick 2-inch long matchstick pieces

3 cloves garlic, minced

5 tablespoons thin Chinese soy sauce

2 to 3 tablespoons creamy peanut butter

2 to 3 tablespoons wine vinegar

2 tablespoons pure Oriental sesame oil

8 dried Chinese mushrooms

¼ pound snow peas

¼ pound green beans

2 medium zucchini

A 10-ounce package frozen sweet peas, thawed and drained

Olive oil

Kosher salt

Freshly ground black pepper

1 pound spaghettini or fusilli (spiral-shaped pasta)

Make the Dressing: In a large skillet heat the oil. Add the scallions and the garlic and sauté over low heat until the scallions are wilted. Stir in the soy sauce, peanut butter, vinegar and sesame oil. Set aside.

Place the dried mushrooms in a small bowl and pour boiling water over them. Let stand for approximately 10 minutes. Squeeze the mushrooms dry, cut off and discard the stems and quarter the tops. Place in a bowl.

Steam the snow peas, the string beans and the zucchini separately until crisply tender, each for approximately 2 minutes (see page 253). Refresh with cold water and pat dry in a dish towel. Cut the vegetables diagonally into ½-inch pieces and add them to the mushrooms. Toss all the vegetables with a few drops of olive oil and season lightly with salt and pepper.

Meanwhile, bring 5 quarts of water to a rolling boil in a large covered pot. Add 2 tablespoons salt and all the pasta at once; stir well. Boil briskly, uncovered, for about 7 minutes, or until the pasta is al dente, tender but firm to the bite. Pour into a colander, refresh with cold water and shake vigorously to drain. Toss with the dressing and the vegetables. Season to taste with salt and pepper.

NOTE: If you wish to prepare this dish a day in advance, toss the pasta with the dressing and refrigerate it. Refrigerate the vegetables without adding any salt or dressing to them. (Salt will make them soggy, and the dressings will discolor them.) Before serving, toss the pasta with the vegetables and the extra dressing. Season to taste with salt and pepper and serve at room temperature.

SERVING SUGGESTIONS: Precede by Gazpacho, Cold Carrot Soup or Marinated Salmon.

Orzo with Parsley

3 TO 4 SERVINGS

Orzo is a rice-shaped pasta which I like to serve, at times, instead of rice. It makes for a lovely accompaniment to fish dishes. If you make the orzo earlier in the day, stir in the parsley just before serving.

1 cup orzo
1 tablespoon unsalted margarine

½ cup loosely packed Italian parsley, coarsely chopped
Kosher salt

In a medium saucepan bring 2 quarts of water to a boil. Add the orzo and boil briskly, uncovered, for approximately 7 minutes, or until it is al dente, tender but still firm to the bite. Pour into a colander and shake vigorously to drain well. Heat the margarine in a small saucepan. Add the orzo and the parsley, stirring with a fork to fluff the grains, until hot. Season with salt.

SERVING SUGGESTIONS: Follow with Steamed Salmon with Black Beans, Broiled Halibut Steaks with Tomato Coulis or any Cornish hen recipe.

Boiled Rice Chinese Style

6 SERVINGS

This plain rice is served mainly with Chinese dishes and is, therefore, cooked until it is very tender so that it can be handled with chopsticks.

1½ cups extra long-grain white rice (enriched Carolina brand)   **2 cups cold water**

Place the rice in a strainer and rinse under cold running water until the water runs clear. Drain well and place the rice in a small heavy-bottomed saucepan with a tight-fitting lid. Add the water, bring to a boil over high heat, and cook, uncovered, for 1 minute. Cover the pan and cook over very low heat for 20 minutes. Remove the pan from the heat and let stand, covered, for 10 minutes more. Fluff the rice with a fork.

SERVING SUGGESTIONS: Serve alongside Millie Chan's Lion's Head, Stir-fried Chicken with Broccoli or Lettuce Packages Filled with Chicken.

Plain Boiled Rice

4 SERVINGS

1 cup long-grain rice (Uncle Ben's
   converted brand)
1 cup cold water

1 tablespoon unsalted margarine
About 1 teaspoon kosher salt

Place all the ingredients in a heavy-bottomed medium suacepan. Cover tightly and cook over very low heat until all the water is absorbed and the grains are tender, approximately 45 minutes. If the rice is undercooked add 1 to 2 tablespoons boiling water and cook for another few minutes. Fluff the rice with a fork right away to separate the grains.

SERVING SUGGESTIONS: Serve alongside Chicken with Capers and Olives, Roast Capon with Olives or Braised Veal Shanks

6 SERVINGS

This recipe makes for a lovely rice variation. It is a perfect accompaniment to roasted or broiled meat or fowl.

Cold Boiled Rice Chinese Style (see page 85)

2 tablespoons peanut or vegetable oil

3 scallions, including green parts, sliced into thin rounds

1 cup raw shelled sweet peas, or 1 cup frozen peas, thawed

2 tablespoons dark Chinese soy sauce

Heat a wok or a skillet, add the oil and heat well. Add the rice, scallions and peas. Lower the heat to medium, add the soy sauce and toss constantly until the rice is hot through.

NOTE: This dish can be made in advance and reheated. However, if you used a wok for stir-frying, transfer the rice to a skillet and then reheat it. (A wok's tempered steel will change the flavor of food made with soy sauce if the food is left in the wok for too long.)

SERVING SUGGESTIONS: Serve alongside Roast Chicken, Meat Loaf or Veal Chops with Mustard and Mustard Seeds.

Rice Pilaf

I have recently developed a fondness for brown rice, a delicious, nutritious grain. I like it best when it is prepared this way.

1¾ cups water
1½ cups brown rice
⅓ cup vegetable oil
2 medium onions, finely chopped
2 cloves garlic, minced
A 1½-inch piece fresh ginger,
   peeled and minced
¼ teaspoon cinnamon

12 mushrooms, wiped with a damp
   towel and thinly sliced
½ cup golden raisins
4 to 6 ounces unsalted roasted ca-
   shews, very coarsely chopped
Kosher salt
Freshly ground black pepper

Combine the water and rice in a heavy-bottomed medium saucepan. Place over very low heat, cover tightly and cook until all the water is absorbed and the grains are tender, 45 minutes to 1 hour.

Heat 3 tablespoons of the oil in a large skillet. Add the onions and garlic, cover and sauté over low heat until the onions are soft. Increase the heat and stir in the ginger and the cinnamon. Add the remaining oil and the mushrooms and stir until the mushrooms are slightly wilted, approximately 1 minute. Stir in the raisins, nuts and rice and mix thoroughly. Remove the pan from heat and season to taste with salt and pepper. Make the pilaf in advance if you like and reheat it over low heat.

SERVING SUGGESTIONS: Serve alongside Roast Turkey, Roast Chicken or Chicken Loaf.

Rice with Saffron and Pine Nuts

4 SERVINGS

Pine nuts and saffron make this a wonderful dish with a subtle flavor and texture. You may prepare it in advance.

⅓ cup pine nuts
1 tablespoon unsalted margarine
1 small onion, finely chopped
1 clove garlic, minced
½ teaspoon loosely packed saffron
    threads
1 cup long-grain rice (Uncle Ben's
    converted brand)

1 teaspoon (½ packet) instant veg-
    etable broth such as MBT, dis-
    solved in 1¼ cups boiling water,
    or 1¼ cups homemade vegetable
    stock (see page 191)
Kosher salt

In a heavy-bottomed saucepan sauté the pine nuts over medium heat, stirring constantly until lightly golden. Remove from the pan and set aside. Add the margarine, onion and garlic and sauté over low heat until soft. Add the saffron and rice and stir well. Stir in the broth, cover and cook over very low heat until all the water is absorbed and the grains are tender, approximately 30 minutes (If the rice is not tender and all the water is absorbed add 1 to 2 tablespoons boiling water and cook for a few minutes more.) Stir in the pine nuts and season to taste with salt.

Make the pilaf in advance if you like and reheat it over low heat.

SERVING SUGGESTIONS: Serve alongside Broiled Chicken Breasts with Mustard and Thyme, Chicken with Dried and Fresh Mushrooms or Roast Breast of Veal.

Bulghur Pilaf

8 SERVINGS

This is one of my favorite accompaniments to broiled or roasted meat or poultry. The spices and fruits offer an interesting variety of flavors and textures in this delightful, crunchy dish. This pilaf may be made in advance and reheated.

1¾ cups water
1 teaspoon salt
1¾ cups medium-size bulghur
¼ cup vegetable oil
1 medium onion, finely chopped
¾ teaspoon ground coriander
½ teaspoon ground cumin

¾ cup slivered blanched almonds
¾ cup coarsely chopped apricots
¾ cup golden raisins
½ teaspoon ground cinnamon
Kosher salt
Freshly ground black pepper

Bring the water and salt to a boil in a small saucepan. Add the bulghur, cover, and cook over very low heat for approximately 10 minutes, or until the water is absorbed. Uncover and fluff the grains with a fork.

In a large skillet heat the oil. Add the onion and sauté over low heat until soft. Add the coriander, cumin, almonds, apricots and raisins and stir over medium heat until the almonds are golden. Add the bulghur and cinnamon and combine well. Season to taste with salt and pepper.

Make the pilaf in advance if you like and reheat it over low heat.

SERVING SUGGESTIONS: Serve alongside Roast Chicken, Roast Turkey or Meat Loaf.

Kasha

I am very fond of this nutritious staple so popular in Russian and Eastern European cuisines. You can make it as simple or elaborate as you like, by adding sautéed sliced mushrooms, sautéed finely chopped onions, cooked bow tie noodles, chopped parsley, snipped dill, or any combination of the above. Kasha can be cooked in advance and gently reheated.

1 egg

About ¾ tablespoon kosher salt

1 cup medium-grain kasha (buckwheat groats)

1 tablespoon unsalted margarine

2 to 3 tablespoons vegetable oil

1¼ cups boiling water

In a small bowl, beat the egg with a fork, add the salt and kasha and mix. In a small saucepan heat the margarine and the oil and add the kasha mixture, stirring with a wooden spoon until the grains separate. Add the boiling water, lower the heat, cover the pan and cook for approximately 15 minutes, or until all the water is absorbed and the grains are soft. Stir with a fork at once to fluff the grains. (If you wish you can now add any of the suggested garnishes in the note preceding this recipe and season the kasha to taste with salt.)

SERVING SUGGESTIONS: Serve alongside Roast Breast of Veal, Turkey Meat Loaf, Braised Veal Shanks, Beef Stew or Braised Curried Veal.

Meat

Cold Chinese-Style Linguine
with Chicken and Vegetables

If you wish to prepare this dish for the Sabbath, you may cook the linguine on Friday, dress it with sesame oil and refrigerate it. Steam the chicken and the string beans, mix the dressing, and refrigerate them as well. You may prepare the cucumbers and the scallions on Saturday. Toss all of the ingredients together a few hours before serving. This dish can be a meal in itself.

**4 medium chicken breast halves,
  skinned and boned**
Kosher salt

½ pound small young green beans
4 medium Kirby cucumbers
**4 scallions, including green parts,
  cut into thin 2-inch matchstick
  pieces**
DRESSING
**About 2 tablespoons thin Chinese
  soy sauce**
2 tablespoons sesame oil
1 tablespoon chili paste with garlic
4 tablespoons dry white wine
About 5 tablespoons rice vinegar

Freshly ground black pepper
¼ cup dry white wine

1 pound linguine
**1 tablespoon pure Oriental sesame
  oil**

**A 1-inch piece fresh ginger, peeled
  and finely minced**
**5 tablespoons creamy peanut
  butter**
**2 tablespoons hulled sesame seeds,
  lightly toasted**

Place the breasts in a single layer on a piece of aluminum foil. Season them lightly with salt and pepper and sprinkle over the wine. Seal the foil and steam the packet, tightly covered, over high heat for 5 to 6 minutes, or until the outside of the chicken has turned white and the inside still has a touch of pink (see page 253). Allow to cool. Pour off the juices and reserve. Cut the chicken with the grain into ¼-inch strips. Place in a bowl.

Steam the string beans until crisply tender, about 2 minutes (see page 253), and add to the chicken. Peel the cucumbers, trim the ends, halve them lengthwise and scoop out the seeds with a spoon. Cut them into thick 2-inch matchstick pieces. Place them in a strainer, sprinkle lightly with salt and let drain for a few minutes. Pat dry and add to the chicken and the beans with the scallions.

Meanwhile, bring 5 quarts of water to a rolling boil in a large covered pot. Add 2 tablespoons salt and all the pasta at once; stir well. Boil briskly, uncovered, for 7 minutes, or until the pasta is al dente, tender but still firm to the bite. Pour into a colander and rinse immediately with cold water to stop the cooking and to prevent the strands from sticking to each other. Shake vigorously to drain well. Transfer the pasta to a large bowl and toss with the sesame oil.

Make the Dressing: In a small bowl thoroughly mix the soy sauce, sesame oil, chili paste, wine, vinegar, ginger and the reserved liquid from steaming the chicken. Cream the peanut butter with a spoon and gradually add to the dressing until thoroughly combined.

Toss the vegetables and the pasta with the dressing. Season to taste with more soy sauce, vinegar and salt and pepper and sprinkle the top with sesame seeds.

SERVING SUGGESTIONS: Precede by Gazpacho, Cold Carrot Soup or Tomato Soup.

Dilled Chicken or Beef *Piroshki*

ABOUT 100 MINIATURE *PIROSHKI*, 6 TO 8 SERVINGS AS A FIRST COURSE, 4 SERVINGS AS A MAIN COURSE

These *piroshki* are filled with a dilled chicken or beef mixture and are quite light. Serve them in piping hot chicken stock or other soups, approximately 5 to a person.

3 tablespoons vegetable oil
1 medium onion, finely chopped
1¼ pounds boiled chicken, or
   cooked and boned lean chuck,
   finely chopped

10 sprigs dill, finely snipped
Kosher salt
Freshly ground black pepper

1 recipe *piroshki* dough (see page
71)

Heat the oil in a small skillet and in it sauté the onion over medium-high heat until golden. Remove from heat and add the chicken or beef and dill. Season the filling with salt and pepper and set aside.

Form the *piroshki* following the directions on page 71.

Bring a large pot of salted water to a boil. Carefully drop in a batch of *piroshki*, only as many as your pot can comfortably hold. Return the water to a slow boil and cook the *piroshki* slowly, uncovered, until they rise to the surface, approximately 3 minutes. Drain the *piroshki* and repeat with the remainder. To serve with soup, place 5 *piroshki* in each bowl and ladle soup over them. Or, sauté the *piroshki* until golden in vegetable oil. Season with salt and pepper and garnish with snipped dill. Serve sautéed *piroshki* without soup.

SERVING SUGGESTIONS: As a first course, follow with Chicken with Dried and Fresh Mushrooms, Chicken with Capers and Olives or Braised Curried Veal. As a main course, precede by Hearty Vegetable Soup, Warm Spinach Salad or Braised Baby Artichokes.

Cholent

This popular Eastern European Sabbath luncheon stew, usually a winter dish, cooks slowly over the night before it is served. There are many versions, but traditionally it is made with beef bones, flanken, barley and beans. After a bit of experimentation I decided to make it with dark turkey meat. I find it much lighter and, of course, less caloric.

2 tablespoons vegetable oil
1 large onion, finely chopped
3 cloves garlic, finely chopped
½ cup barley
¾ cup dried baby lima beans or
   Great Northern beans
¾ cup dried red kidney beans

½ cup dried chick peas
2 pounds boned dark turkey meat,
   with a bit of fat left on, cut into
   2-inch pieces
5 cups cold water
Kosher salt
Freshly ground black pepper

Heat the vegetable oil in a 3-quart enameled cast-iron saucepan or any other heavy pot with a tight-fitting lid. Add the onion and garlic and sauté for a few minutes. Rinse the barley and add to the onion. Pick over the beans and the chick peas, rinse them and add to the pan with the turkey and water. Season with a little salt and pepper and bring the cholent to a boil over high heat. Reduce the heat, cover, and cook the cholent slowly for 15 minutes. Before lighting the Sabbath candles on Friday night, place the cholent in a preheated 200° F. oven and leave it to cook until the following day.

Cholent can also be cooked in an electric crockpot overnight. Follow the manufacturer's instructions.

SERVING SUGGESTIONS: As a first course, follow with Meat Loaf, Chicken Loaf or Roast Chicken. As a main course, precede by Marinated Salmon, Smoked Whitefish Pâté or Hearty Vegetable Soup.

Steamed Salmon Fillets with Black Beans

Fish

DAIRY

Broiled Fillets of Red Snapper with Pine Nut Coating
Fillet of Grey Sole en Papillote
Steamed Salmon with Tomato Sauce and Julienne Vegetables

PAREVE

Broiled Salmon Steaks
Broiled or Barbecued Tuna Steaks
Broiled Halibut Steaks with Tomato Coulis
Steamed Salmon Fillets with Black Beans
Steamed Salmon Steaks with Black Beans
Whole Steamed Salmon in Foil with Ginger Vinaigrette

Broiled Fillets of Red Snapper with Pine Nut Coating

2 SERVINGS

Red snapper is a delicate fish that is nicely enhanced by the flavor of pine nuts.

A 2-pound red snapper, filleted and
  skinned
Kosher salt
Juice of ½ lemon

¼ cup finely ground pine nuts
Freshly ground black pepper
1 tablespoon unsalted butter, cut
  into small bits

Place the fillets in a glass or ceramic dish. Season them lightly with salt and sprinkle with lemon juice. Cover and refrigerate for several hours.

Preheat the broiler. Line the rack of the broiling pan with foil.

Spread the pine nuts, mixed with a few grindings of pepper, on a piece of wax paper. Press the pine nuts onto both sides of the snapper and transfer the fish to the broiling pan. Dot the fish with butter. Broil the fillets 4 to 6 inches from the heat for approximately 6 minutes, without turning. The fish should be barely firm and white; it will continue cooking a bit after you remove it from the broiler.

SERVING SUGGESTIONS: Start with Sweet Potato Soup, Tortilla or Spaghettini with Fresh Vegetables. Serve accompanied by Broiled Cherry Tomatoes, Grated Carrots or Yellow Squash au Gratin.

Fillets of Grey Sole en Papillote

4 SERVINGS

Fish cooked in this closed-casing method at very high heat remains moist and delicious. Try it with other kinds of fish, vegetables and seasonings.

4 skinned grey sole fillets (approximately 8 ounces each)
Juice of 1 lemon
Kosher salt
Freshly ground black pepper
2 small zucchini
6 mushrooms

3 tablespoons unsalted butter
4 scallions, including green parts, sliced into thin rounds
½ teaspoon saffron threads
2 small tomatoes, peeled, seeded and cut into large pieces

Preheat the oven to 500° F.

Cut 4 sheets of heavy foil, each large enough to enclose a portion of fish. Place each fillet on a piece of foil, sprinkle it with lemon juice, and season lightly with salt and pepper. Fold both ends of each fillet under, to form a small rectangular packet.

Rinse the zucchini and pat dry. Trim off the ends and cut the zucchini into thick 2-inch-long matchstick pieces. Wipe the mushrooms with a damp paper towel and slice thin. Heat the butter in a large skillet, add the scallions and sauté over low heat until soft. Add the zucchini and the mushrooms and sauté over high heat for ½ minute; they should still be very crisp. Stir in the saffron and remove from heat. Add the tomatoes and season with salt and pepper. Spoon equal amounts of the vegetables over each fillet. Enclose the fish and vegetables in the foil, crimping the edges to seal securely.

Place the foil packages on a cookie sheet and bake for 9 or 10 minutes, or until the fish is barely firm and white inside; it will continue cooking a bit after you remove it from the oven. Unwrap the packages and with a wide spatula transfer the fish, topped with vegetables, to heated plates. Spoon the accumulated juices over and serve at once.

SERVING SUGGESTIONS: Start with Spinach Roll, Bow Ties with Green Beans and Basil or Linguine with Mushroom Sauce. Follow with a green salad.

Steamed Salmon with Tomato Sauce and Julienne Vegetables

6 SERVINGS

I wanted to create a fish dish that would be low in calories, well seasoned, pretty, and easy to prepare. This is what I came up with. The vegetables are steamed in advance, the fillets are steamed in plastic wrap. Then the sauce (which can also be cooked in advance) is cooked briefly. You may substitute other vegetables if you wish.

3 medium zucchini
2 tablespoons unsalted butter
18 medium asparagus
1 small white cabbage (approximately 1½ pounds)
6 skinned center-cut salmon fillets, approximately 6 ounces each (the fillets should be approximately 3 inches wide and 5 inches long; if they are longer trim them)

Juice of 1 lemon
Kosher salt
Freshly ground black pepper

SAUCE

4 tablespoons olive oil
4 medium ripe tomatoes, peeled, seeded and coarsely chopped
About ¼ teaspoon crushed red pepper flakes

¾ cup tightly packed fresh basil leaves, coarsely chopped, plus extra whole leaves for garnish
Kosher salt
Freshly ground black pepper

Rinse the zucchini, trim the ends and steam them whole for 2 minutes (see page 253). Allow to cool, then cut them into thick, 3-inch-long matchstick pieces. Pat dry and place in a piece of foil large enough to enclose the vegetables. Add ½ tablespoon butter and seal well. Set aside.

Snap each asparagus spear at the point where it breaks naturally and discard the ends. Trim the spears to make them even. Rinse, then steam for 3 minutes, or until crisply tender. Allow to cool and cut them into thick 3-inch matchstick pieces. Pat dry and place in another piece of foil. Add ½ tablespoon butter and seal well. Set aside.

Cut the cabbage into quarters, core it and steam for 3 minutes, or until crisply tender. Allow to cool and shred thin. Pat dry and place in another piece of foil. Add the remaining tablespoon of butter and seal well. Set aside.

Make the Sauce: In a small saucepan heat the olive oil. Add the tomatoes, crushed red pepper flakes and chopped basil. Bring to a boil, reduce the heat, cover and cook slowly for 1 minute. Season the sauce to taste with more crushed red pepper flakes and salt and pepper. Remove from heat.

Lightly butter 6 pieces of plastic wrap large enough to enclose each piece of salmon. Place a fillet in the center of each. Season with the lemon juice and salt and pepper.

Fold in the ends of the plastic wrap and roll them to seal. Set a steamer basket in a pot, add water to a depth below the bottom of the basket and bring to a boil. Place the fish packages in the basket in a single layer. Cover and steam over high heat for 6 to 7 minutes, or until the salmon just turns orange-pink all the way through; it will continue cooking a bit after it is removed from the heat.

To Serve: Warm the foil-wrapped vegetables in a preheated 325° F. oven. Heat the tomato sauce. Place the fish on a serving dish or on individual plates and top with the tomato sauce. Unwrap the vegetables and season them with salt and pepper. Arrange them around the fish. Garnish with the reserved basil.

SERVING SUGGESTIONS: Start with Carrot Soup, Pasta Shells with Cheese Filling or Linguine with Mushroom Sauce. Serve accompanied by Orzo with Parsley, Plain Boiled Rice or Potato and Celery Root Pie.

Broiled Salmon Steaks

2 SERVINGS

What gives this fish its special flavor is the combination of lemon juice and soy sauce. I find that no other seasonings are necessary.

2 skinned salmon steaks, approxi-
   mately ¾ inch thick
Juice of ½ lemon
1 tablespoon thin Chinese soy
   sauce

1 tablespoon olive oil
Lime wedges and watercress sprigs
   for garnish

Place the salmon steaks in a glass or ceramic dish. Combine the remaining ingredients, except the garnishes, and coat the fish with the mixture. Cover and refrigerate for several hours.

Preheat the broiler and line the rack of the broiling pan with foil. Place the salmon on the rack and broil it 4 inches from the heat, without turning, for 6 to 8 minutes, or until the fish has barely turned orange pink all the way through; it will continue cooking a bit after you remove it from the broiler. Serve garnished with the lime wedges and sprigs of watercress.

SERVING SUGGESTIONS: Start with Gazpacho, Chilled Cucumber Soup or Spinach Strudel. Serve accompanied by Broiled Cherry Tomatoes, Yellow Squash au Gratin or Broiled Zucchini Strips.

Broiled or Barbecued Tuna Steaks

8 SERVINGS

Broiling is my favorite quick way of cooking fish; it retains all of its natural flavor and its pretty appearance. But in the summer, when tuna is at its best, barbecuing is an equally delicious method.

8 boned and skinned tuna steaks,
¾ to 1 inch thick (approximately
8 ounces each)
Juice of 3 limes
3 tablespoons dark Chinese soy
sauce

1 teaspoon kosher salt
A 1-inch piece fresh ginger, peeled
and minced
Lime wedges for garnish

Cut away and discard any dark flesh from the tuna and place it in a glass or ceramic dish. Combine the lime juice, soy sauce, salt and ginger and coat the fish with it. Cover and refrigerate for several hours.

Preheat the broiler and line the rack of a broiling pan with foil.

Place the tuna on the prepared pan and broil it 4 inches from the heat for about 3 minutes on each side, or until the fish has barely changed color all the way through. It will continue cooking a bit after you remove it from the broiler. Or, barbecue the fish on a preheated grill for approximately the same amount of time.

SERVING SUGGESTIONS: Start with Puréed Beet Soup (add yogurt and serve it cold), Puréed Romaine and Watercress Soup or Pasta Shell Salad with Vegetables. Serve accompanied by Broiled Cherry Tomatoes, Crisp Potato Skins or Acorn Squash Purée.

Broiled Halibut Steaks with Tomato Coulis

4 SERVINGS

Halibut is a rather delicate-flavored white-fleshed fish that, to my mind, requires strong flavoring. This simple sauce complements the fish very well.

2 pounds skinned halibut steaks, ¾ to 1 inch thick, with the middle bones removed to make 4 equal pieces

TOMATO COULIS

4 medium ripe tomatoes, peeled, seeded and finely chopped
3 tablespoons olive oil
1 small onion, finely chopped
2 cloves garlic, minced
3 tablespoons wine vinegar

Juice of 1 lemon
2 tablespoons olive oil
Kosher salt
Freshly ground black pepper

3 tablespoons dry red wine
2 sprigs fresh thyme or 1 teaspoon dried
Kosher salt
Freshly ground black pepper

Place the halibut steaks in a glass or ceramic dish. Coat them well with the lemon juice and olive oil. Season lightly with salt and pepper. Cover and refrigerate for several hours, turning the fish once.

Make the Tomato Coulis: Place the tomatoes in a strainer and set aside to drain for 10 minutes. In a small saucepan heat the olive oil. Add the onion and garlic and cook, covered, over low heat until the onion is very soft. Add the tomatoes, vinegar, wine and thyme and cook, uncovered, over medium heat for 5 minutes. Season to taste with salt and pepper.

Preheat the broiler and line the rack of a broiler pan with foil. Place the halibut on the pan and broil the fish about 6 inches from the heat without turning, for 4 to 6 minutes. The fish should be barely firm and white; it will continue cooking a bit after you remove it from the broiler.

To Serve: Coat a heated serving dish or plates with the tomato coulis and top with the fish.

SERVING SUGGESTIONS: Start with Sweet Potato Soup, Feta Cheese Strudel or Spinach Spaghettini Primavera. Serve accompanied by Potato and Celery Root Pie, Orzo with Parsley or Steamed Asparagus.

Steamed Salmon Fillets with Black Beans

4 SERVINGS

The salmon and the vegetables are steamed together in this well-seasoned dish. It makes for a beautiful, elegant entrée.

4 skinned center-cut salmon fillets, approximately 6 ounces each (the fillets should be approximately 3 inches wide and 5 inches long; if they are longer, trim them)
Kosher salt
Freshly ground black pepper
4 teaspoons fermented black beans
1 medium red bell pepper
1 medium green bell pepper
1 medium yellow bell pepper

6 scallions, white parts only, cut into 3-inch-long, thin matchstick pieces
A 1-inch piece fresh ginger, peeled, cut into very thin matchstick pieces
4 tablespoons thin Chinese soy sauce
2 teaspoons pure Oriental sesame oil
2 teaspoons vegetable oil
2 tablespoons lemon juice

Place the fish in a lightly oiled heatproof dish and season it lightly with salt and pepper. Scatter the black beans on top. Remove the tops and bottoms from the peppers and cut them in half. Seed them, remove the ribs, and cut them into thin matchstick pieces. Scatter the peppers, scallions and ginger over the fish. Whisk together the soy sauce, oils and lemon juice and pour over the vegetables.

Fill a wok or pot with water to a depth of 1½ to 2 inches. Place a trivet in the pot and bring the water to a boil. Set the dish of fish on the trivet, cover, and steam over high heat for 5 to 6 minutes, or just until the fish turns orange-pink all the way through; it will continue cooking a bit after it is removed from the heat. Serve topped with the vegetables drained of their juices.

SERVING SUGGESTIONS: Start with Sherry's Jerusalem Artichoke Soup, Chicken Soup with Arugula or Watercress or Fusilli with Radicchio. Serve accompanied by Orzo with Parsley, any stir-fried mushroom recipe or Steamed Asparagus.

Steamed Salmon Steaks with Black Beans

2 SERVINGS

Fermented black beans are whole soybeans preserved in salt and ginger. Refrigerated, they keep for months and lend a delicious flavor to many dishes, including this one.

2 skinned salmon steaks, approximately ¾ inch thick
Juice of ½ lemon
2 teaspoons fermented black beans
1 clove garlic, minced
½ teaspoon sugar
1 tablespoon thin Chinese soy sauce

¼ teaspoon pure Oriental sesame oil
4 scallions, including green parts, cut into 3-inch-long, thick matchstick pieces

Place the salmon steaks in an ovenproof dish. Coat them well with the lemon juice. Cover and refrigerate for approximately 1 hour.

In a small bowl combine the beans, garlic, sugar, soy sauce and sesame oil. Coat the steaks with this mixture and place the scallions over them.

Fill a wok or a large pot with water to a depth of 1½ to 2 inches, place a trivet in the wok or pot and bring the water to a boil. Set the dish of salmon steaks on the trivet, cover and steam over high heat for approximately 8 minutes, or until the fish just turns orange-pink all the way through; it will continue cooking a bit after it is removed from the heat. Serve with, or without, the accumulated juices.

SERVING SUGGESTIONS: Start with Spinach Spaghetti Primavera, Chinese-Style Pasta with Vegetables or Baked Spaghetti Squash with Tomato Sauce. Serve accompanied by Steamed Cabbage, any stir-fried mushroom recipe or Orzo with Parsley.

Whole Salmon Steamed in Foil with Ginger Vinaigrette

8 SERVINGS AS A FIRST COURSE, 6 SERVINGS AS A MAIN COURSE

The classic Western method of poaching fish is in a *court bouillon*; I prefer this easy method of steaming, where the fish cooks in its own juices and therefore retains its natural flavor and moistness. You can apply this method of steaming to any fish. This makes a beautiful buffet or summer dinner dish.

A 5-pound whole salmon, spine removed and cleaned but with head and tail left on
Vegetable oil
Juice of ½ lemon
VINAIGRETTE
A 1-inch piece fresh ginger, peeled and minced
2 medium shallots, minced
¾ cup rice vinegar
Juice of 2 limes
2 tablespoons dark Chinese soy sauce

Kosher salt
Freshly ground black pepper
¼ cup dry white wine
Boiling water

1 tablespoon pure Oriental sesame oil
½ cup olive oil
¼ cup tightly packed Italian parsley, finely chopped
Kosher salt
Freshly ground black pepper

Preheat the oven to 375° F.

Pat the salmon dry with paper towels. Cut a sheet of heavy foil long enough to enclose the fish and grease it lightly with oil. Arrange the fish in the center of the foil and sprinkle it inside and out with lemon juice and salt and pepper. Grease the head and tail with oil, and wrap them in 2 separate small pieces of oiled foil. (The oil prevents them from sticking to the foil.) Place the fish on its belly and bend it so that it will look pretty when the packet is opened. Bring up the edges of the foil, pour the wine over the fish, and seal the edges of the foil tightly. Place the foil-enclosed salmon in a baking pan approximately 18 by 12 by 2 inches. Pour boiling water into the pan to a depth of approximately 1 inch. Steam the salmon in the oven for about 30 minutes. Loosen the foil and test the center of the fish with the tip of a knife. It should have barely turned orange-pink all the way through. Don't worry if the fish seems slightly undercooked; it will continue cooking as it cools. The steaming time should be approximately 6 minutes per pound.

Reseal the edges of the foil, pour out the water in the pan and let the fish cool a bit. While the fish is still warm, open the top of the packet, fold in both foil edges and pour off the accumulated liquid. Skin the fish while it is still warm, starting at the tail end (it is easier that way). Flip the fish onto a platter and wipe off any juices that accumulate on the platter.

Make the Vinaigrette: Place all the ingredients except for the oils, parsley and salt and pepper in a blender. With the motor running, pour in the oils through the opening in the lid. Pour the sauce into a bowl, add the parsley and season to taste with salt and pepper.

Serve the fish at room temperature, decorated with watercress, chives or arugula, and serve the sauce separately.

SERVING SUGGESTIONS: Start with Gazpacho, Cold Carrot Soup or Spaghetti with Uncooked Tomato Sauce. Serve accompanied by Orzo Salad, Couscous Salad, any green salad or Potato Salad.

Broiled Cornish Hens
Stir-fried Chicken with Broccoli

Poultry

Roast Capon with Olives
Roast Turkey
Roast Chicken
Chicken with Dried and Fresh Mushrooms
Chicken with Capers and Olives
Baked Chicken with Sun-Dried Tomatoes
Baked Chicken with Soy Sauce and Ginger
Broiled Chicken Breasts with Mustard and Thyme
Baked Chicken Breasts with Lemon and Mustard
Steamed Chicken Breasts with Tomato, Basil and Vinegar
Chicken Breasts in Tomato Mushroom Sauce
Chicken Breasts with Lemon and Raisins
Stir-fried Chicken with Broccoli
Lettuce Packages Filled with Chicken
Chicken Loaf
Baked Cornish Hens
Baked Cornish Hens with Chinese Flavorings
Broiled Cornish Hens
Braised Soy Sauce Duck
Broiled Duck Breasts with Ginger Sauce
Duck with Hoisin Sauce

Roast Capon with Olives

Olives give this dish an interesting spicy flavor.

1 capon, approximately 6 pounds	3 small onions
Juice of 1 lemon	½ cup pitted and quartered black
Kosher salt	olives (Kalamata)
Freshly ground black pepper	3 tablespoons vegetable oil
¼ cup tightly packed Italian pars-	½ cup dry white wine
ley with stems, coarsely chopped	

Preheat the oven to 350° F.

Wash the capon and pat it dry inside and out with paper towels. Pull off and discard any excess fat and skin. Place the capon in a roasting pan just large enough to hold it. Season it inside and out with the lemon juice and salt and pepper. Place the parsley in the cavity. Quarter 1 of the onions and place it in the cavity with the olives. Thinly slice the remaining 2 onions and scatter them around the bird. Brush the capon with oil. Put the capon on its side and place the pan on the middle rack of the oven. Roast for 30 minutes. Baste with the wine. Turn bird to other side and roast for another 30 minutes, basting frequently. Turn the capon breast side up and roast for 15 minutes more, again basting frequently, then turn it breast side down for a final 15 minutes. The total roasting time should be approximately 1½ to 1¾ hours, or about 15 minutes per pound. The capon is ready when the drumsticks move easily in their sockets and the juices run clear. Remove the bird from the oven and cover the pan tightly with heavy foil. Let stand for 20 minutes before carving to permit the juices to flow back into the meat.

To Serve: Carve the capon into serving pieces and arrange on a serving dish. Skim the pan juices and serve them alongside.

SERVING SUGGESTIONS: Start with Sherry's Jerusalem Artichoke Soup, Puréed Broccoli Soup or Tuna Seviche. Serve accompanied by Plain Boiled Rice, Stir-fried Red Radishes or Roasted Shallots.

12 TO 14 SERVINGS

Since most kosher turkeys are sold frozen, find a reliable butcher and ask for young turkeys. Thaw them slowly in the refrigerator. I prefer turkey unstuffed, but you can always make the stuffing and bake it in a separate dish. I allow approximately 1 pound of uncooked turkey per person. Since I don't like my poultry overdone, I calculate 15 minutes of roasting time per pound and 30 minutes of resting time before carving, but do keep your own record as to how you like it.

A 14-pound young turkey
Juice of 1 lemon
2 to 3 tablespoons dark Chinese
   soy sauce
Freshly ground black pepper
5 sprigs fresh tarragon or 1 tablespoon dried

2 medium onions
5 tablespoons unsalted margarine,
   melted
½ cup prepared orange juice
½ cup dry white wine

Preheat the oven to 325° F.

Wash the turkey and pat it dry inside and out with paper towels. Pull off and discard any excess fat and skin. Place the turkey in a roasting pan and season it inside and out with the lemon juice, soy sauce, and pepper. Place the tarragon in the cavity. Quarter 1 onion and place it in the cavity. Thinly slice the remaining onion and scatter it around the bird. Brush the turkey with the margarine. Combine the orange juice and the wine. Place the turkey on its side and roast it for 30 minutes on each side, basting it frequently with the orange juice–wine mixture. Turn the turkey breast side up and roast it for 30 minutes, again basting frequently. Turn the turkey breast side down for a final 30 minutes. (If the drumsticks begin to brown excessively, cover the ends with foil.) The turkey is ready when the drumsticks move easily in their sockets and the juices run clear, or when a meat thermometer inserted in the thickest part reads 180° to 185° F. Remove the turkey from the oven and cover the pan with heavy foil. Let stand for 30 minutes before carving, to permit the juices to flow back into the meat. The total roasting and resting time should be approximately 1½ to 2 hours.

To Serve: Carve the turkey into serving pieces and arrange on a serving dish. Skim the pan juices and serve them alongside.

NOTE: If you are making turkey on Passover, omit the soy sauce and use kosher salt instead.

SERVING SUGGESTIONS: Start with Puréed Butternut Squash Soup, Puréed Beet Soup or Vegetable Medley. Serve accompanied by Rice Pilaf, Roasted Shallots or Potato and Celery Root Pie.

Roast Chicken

3 OR 4 SERVINGS

I find that simple roasting at high heat is the best way to obtain a juicy, crispy-skinned chicken.

**1 roasting chicken, approximately
  3 pounds**
2 cloves garlic, with skins left on
**2 sprigs fresh tarragon or thyme or
  1 teaspoon dried**

1 tablespoon vegetable oil
Kosher salt
Freshly ground black pepper
¼ cup dry white wine

Preheat the oven to 450° F.

Wash the chicken and pat it dry inside and out with paper towels. Pull off and discard any excess fat and skin. Place the chicken in a roasting pan just large enough to hold it. Place the garlic cloves and tarragon in the cavity. Brush the chicken with oil and season it lightly with salt and pepper.

Place the chicken on the middle rack of the oven and roast it breast side down for 25 minutes, basting it with the wine. Turn the chicken breast side up for 20 to 25 minutes more, basting again. The chicken should be golden brown and the juices should run clear.

To Serve: Cut the chicken into serving pieces and arrange on a serving dish.

SERVING SUGGESTIONS: Start with Beet Consommé, Puréed Butternut Squash Soup or Braised Baby Artichokes. Serve accompanied by Rice with Saffron and Pine Nuts, Steamed Brussels Sprouts or Grated Carrots.

Chicken with Dried and Fresh Mushrooms

6 TO 8 SERVINGS

The combination of dried and fresh mushrooms adds a distinct taste to this simple but wonderful dish.

2 ounces dried imported mush-
    rooms (*cépes* or *porcini*)
1½ cups boiling water
¾ pound fresh mushrooms
¼ cup olive oil
3 cloves garlic, minced
½ cup loosely packed Italian pars-
    ley (discard the lower half of the
    stems), finely chopped

Kosher salt
Freshly ground black pepper
2 roasting chickens (approximately
    3 pounds each)
Juice of 1 lemon

Place the dried mushrooms in a bowl and pour the water over them. Let stand for approximately ½ hour. Strain the soaking liquid through a sieve lined with a paper towel, squeezing the mushrooms over the sieve to extract more liquid. Pour the liquid into a small saucepan and boil it for 5 minutes. Set aside. Rinse the mushrooms to remove any remaining dirt, squeeze them dry and chop them coarse. Wipe the fresh mushrooms with a damp paper towel, chop them coarse, and add to the dried mushrooms.

In a large skillet heat 3 tablespoons olive oil. Add the garlic and all the mushrooms and sauté over high heat stirring continuously for 1 minute. Remove the skillet from the heat, stir in the parsley and season the mixture very well with salt and pepper.

Preheat the oven to 400° F.

Wash the chickens and pat them dry inside and out with paper towels. Gently loosen the skin around the breasts and thighs, taking care not to tear the skin. Stuff the mushroom mixture between the loosened skin and the meat. Brush the chickens with the remaining oil and sprinkle lightly with salt and pepper.

Place the chickens breast side down on a rack in a roasting pan and roast them on the middle rack of the oven for 30 minutes. Turn them over and roast them for 20 to 25 minutes more, or until the chickens are golden brown and the juices run clear.

To Serve: Cut the chicken into serving pieces, arrange them on a serving dish and keep them warm. Add the juices from the roasting pan and the carving board to the reserved mushroom liquid and bring to a boil. Boil the sauce for a few minutes and skim off the surface fat, if necessary. Season to taste with salt and pepper and lemon juice. Spoon some of the sauce over the chicken and serve the rest alongside.

SERVING SUGGESTIONS: Start with Sherry's Jerusalem Artichoke Soup, Chicken Soup with Ginger, Tree Ears and Peas or Souffléed Acorn Squash. Serve accompanied by Roasted Shallots, Potato and Celery Root Pie or Steamed Cabbage.

Chicken with Capers and Olives

4 SERVINGS

I prefer to serve chicken in small serving pieces. I usually ask the butcher to cut each chicken into 10 pieces, removing the backbone, wing tips, gizzards and neck (I save these for stock). Remove the wings, then split the breasts and halve them again cross-wise. Lastly, cut the thighs from the drumsticks.

1 chicken (approximately 3 pounds), cut into 10 small serving pieces
2 tablespoons unsalted margarine
1 tablespoon olive oil
Kosher salt
Freshly ground black pepper
1 large onion, finely chopped
2 cloves garlic, minced
2 to 3 tablespoons wine vinegar

A 28-ounce can peeled tomatoes, drained and coarsely chopped
¼ cup capers, drained and coarsely chopped
10 green olives, pitted and coarsely chopped
3 sprigs fresh thyme or 1 teaspoon dried
1 cup tightly packed Italian parsley, coarsely chopped

Preheat the oven to 400° F.

Pat the chicken pieces dry with paper towels and discard excess fat and skin. In a large skillet heat 1 tablespoon of the margarine and the olive oil and in it sauté the chicken pieces over medium heat a few at a time, until lightly golden on both sides. Season lightly with salt and pepper. Transfer the pieces, except the breasts, skin side down, as they are browned to a roasting pan large enough to hold them in a single layer.

Heat the remaining margarine in the same skillet. Add the onion and the garlic and sauté them over low heat until soft. Stir in the vinegar, the tomatoes, capers, olives, thyme and parsley. Coat the chicken with half of the sauce. Cover the pan with heavy foil and bake for 20 minutes. Turn the chicken, add the chicken breasts, skin side up, and coat with the remaining sauce. Cover and bake for 25 to 30 minutes, or until the juices run clear. Season the sauce to taste with salt and pepper.

To Serve: Arrange the chicken pieces on a serving dish and spoon the sauce over them.

SERVING SUGGESTIONS: Start with Braised Baby Artichokes, Broiled Sweet Peppers, Chicken Soup with Arugula or Watercress. Serve accompanied by Plain Boiled Rice, Orzo with Parsley or Kasha.

Baked Chicken with Sun-Dried Tomatoes

8 SERVINGS

As its ingredients are not seasonal, this well-seasoned dish can be served year round.

2 ounces sun-dried tomatoes
2 roasting chickens (approximately 3 pounds each), cut into 10 small serving pieces each
2 tablespoons unsalted margarine
4 tablespoons olive oil
Kosher salt
Freshly ground black pepper

2 medium onions, coarsely chopped
3 cloves garlic, coarsely chopped
20 black (Kalamata) olives, pitted
1 cup tightly packed Italian parsley, coarsely chopped
Juice of 1½ lemons
1 cup dry white wine

Place the sun-dried tomatoes in a bowl and cover with boiling water. Let soften for 5 minutes, then squeeze dry. Set aside.

Pat the chicken pieces dry and discard excess fat and skin. In a large skillet heat 1 tablespoon of the margarine and 1 tablespoon of the olive oil. In it sauté the chicken pieces over medium heat, a few at a time, until lightly golden. Season lightly with salt and pepper. As they are browned, transfer all of the pieces, except the breasts, to a roasting pan just large enough to hold them in a single layer, placing the pieces skin side down.

Preheat the oven to 400° F.

Add another tablespoon margarine and olive oil to the skillet and sauté the onions and garlic over low heat until soft. Place the sun-dried tomatoes, onions, garlic, remaining olive oil, olives, parsley, lemon juice, and wine in a food processor fitted with a steel blade, or blender, and purée finely.

Coat the chicken with half of the purée, cover the pan with heavy foil and bake for 20 minutes. Turn the chicken, add the breasts, skin side up, and coat with the remaining purée. Cover and bake for 25 to 30 minutes, or until the juices run clear.

To Serve: Arrange the chicken pieces on a serving dish and spoon the sauce over them.

SERVING SUGGESTIONS: Start with Arugula, Leek and Potato Soup, Braised Baby Artichokes or Warm Spinach Salad. Serve accompanied by Orzo with Parsley, Broiled Zucchini Strips or Roasted Shallots.

Baked Chicken with Soy Sauce and Ginger

8 SERVINGS

This is a very easy and quick dish that yields truly satisfying results.

**2 roasting chickens (approximately
3 pounds each), cut into 10
small serving pieces each**

MARINADE

**5 scallions, including green parts,
coarsely chopped**
2 cloves garlic, minced
**A 1-inch piece fresh ginger,
peeled, minced**
2 tablespoons dry white wine

2 tablespoons vegetable oil
¼ cup dark Chinese soy sauce
1½ tablespoons sugar
**2 tablespoons pure Oriental sesame
oil**

Pat the chicken pieces dry with paper towels and discard excess fat and skin. Place the chicken pieces in a single layer in a large glass or ceramic dish.

Make the Marinade: In a small bowl mix together the marinade ingredients.

Pour the marinade over the chicken and turn the pieces to coat well. Cover and refrigerate for several hours, turning once.

Preheat the oven to 375° F.

Place all of the chicken pieces, except for the breasts, skin side up, in a roasting pan just large enough to hold them in a single layer. Bake in the middle rack of the oven for 20 minutes. Add the breasts, skin side up, pour the marinade over the pieces, and bake for 10 minutes more. Increase the heat to 450° F. and bake for a final 10 to 15 minutes, or until the chicken is well browned.

To Serve: Arrange the chicken pieces on a serving dish and pour the juices over them.

SERVING SUGGESTIONS: Start with Chicken Soup with Arugula or Watercress, Stir-fried *Shiitake* Mushrooms or either of the salmon tartare recipes. Serve accompanied by Kasha, Orzo with Parsley or Steamed Cabbage.

Broiled Chicken Breasts with Mustard and Thyme

2 TO 4 SERVINGS

Easy, quick, and low in calories.

Juice of 1 lemon
2 tablespoons vegetable oil
2 tablespoons Dijon-style mustard
2 sprigs fresh thyme or 1 teaspoon
  dried

Kosher salt
Freshly ground black pepper
4 medium chicken breast halves,
  skinned and boned

In a small bowl mix together the lemon juice, oil, mustard, thyme and salt and pepper. Place the chicken breasts in a glass or ceramic dish. Coat them with the marinade, cover and refrigerate for several hours.

Preheat the broiler. Line the rack of a broiling pan with foil and place the chicken in it.

Broil the chicken very close to the heat (approximately 4 inches from it) for about 7 minutes, without turning, or until the inside of the chicken has just turned pale pink. Be careful not to overcook the chicken or it will taste dry.

To Serve: Cut the breasts on the diagonal, across the grain, into 3 pieces.

SERVING SUGGESTIONS: Start with Warm Spinach Salad, Braised Baby Artichokes or Vegetable Medley. Serve accompanied by Stir-fried Rice, Rice with Saffron and Pine Nuts or Red Cabbage.

Baked Chicken Breasts with Lemon and Mustard

8 SERVINGS

If you are looking for a simple yet elegant dish, you may like to try this one. The chicken breasts are marinated for a number of hours, then baked. The chicken has a lovely pale color and the distinct taste of lemon and mustard.

12 medium chicken breast halves, skinned and boned
1 medium onion, quartered
2 cloves garlic, quartered
Scant ¾ cup lemon juice
2 tablespoons dry mustard

1½ teaspoons kosher salt
¼ teaspoon freshly ground white pepper
¼ cup olive oil
Fresh tarragon, fresh chives, or scallions for garnish

Arrange the chicken breasts in a single layer in a glass or ceramic baking dish, approximately 10 by 17 inches.

Purée the onion, garlic, lemon juice, mustard, salt, pepper and olive oil in a food processor or blender until smooth. Pour this marinade over the breasts and coat them well. Cover and refrigerate for about 8 hours, turning once.

Preheat the oven to 400° F.

Bake the breasts, uncovered, for 10 minutes. Turn them over, baste with the pan juices, and bake for 8 to 10 minutes more, or until the meat just turns pale pink. Be careful not to overcook the chicken or it will taste dry.

To Serve: Arrange the chicken breasts on a serving dish without the sauce and garnish with the tarragon, chives, or green parts of scallions, finely shredded.

SERVING SUGGESTIONS: Start with Gazpacho, Cold Carrot Soup or Pasta Salad with Smoked Salmon and Steamed Vegetables. Serve accompanied by Orzo with Parsley, Steamed Cabbage or Steamed Asparagus.

Steamed Chicken Breasts
with Tomato, Basil and Vinegar

2 TO 4 SERVINGS

This low-calorie dish was inspired by my dislike for eating heavy dishes on hot summer days and by my love of basil and tomatoes. The sauce can be made earlier in the day and the chicken can be wrapped and refrigerated as well, ready for steaming.

SAUCE

4 tablespoons olive oil	1 tablespoon Dijon-style mustard
4 medium shallots, finely chopped	2 to 3 tablespoons balsamic
2 cloves garlic, minced	vinegar
3 medium ripe tomatoes, peeled, seeded and coarsely chopped	1 cup tightly packed fresh basil leaves, finely snipped
4 medium chicken breast halves, skinned and boned	Freshly ground black pepper
	Unsalted margarine
Kosher salt	

Make the Sauce: In a small saucepan heat the oil. Add the shallots and the garlic and sauté over low heat until the shallots are soft. Add the tomatoes, mustard and vinegar, bring to a boil and reduce the heat. Cover and simmer for 5 minutes. Add ¾ cup of the basil, remove from heat and set aside.

Open the thin meaty fillet that is attached to one side of the breast meat and stuff with about ½ teaspoon of the remaining snipped basil. Season the pieces lightly with salt and pepper.

Lightly grease with margarine 4 pieces of plastic wrap, each large enough to enclose a piece of chicken. Place a piece of chicken in the center of each wrap, fold in the ends and roll them to seal. Set a steamer basket in a wok or pot, add water to just below the bottom of the basket and bring to a boil. Place the packages in the basket, cover and steam over high heat for about 6 to 7 minutes, or until the inside of the chicken has just turned pale pink. Turn off the heat and let stand for 1 minute.

Meanwhile, reheat the tomato sauce. Unwrap one end of each chicken package and pour the accumulated juices into the tomato sauce. Season well with more vinegar and salt and pepper.

To Serve: Arrange the chicken breasts on a serving dish or on individual plates and top with some of the sauce. Garnish with the remaining basil. Serve the remaining sauce alongside.

SERVING SUGGESTIONS: Start with Cold Carrot Soup, Pasta Salad with Smoked Salmon and Steamed Vegetables or Tuna Seviche. Serve accompanied by Orzo with Parsley, Steamed Asparagus or Steamed Cabbage.

Chicken Breasts in Tomato Mushroom Sauce

8 to 10 SERVINGS

This well-seasoned, flavorful dish is quite convenient to make—the ingredients for it are available throughout the year. You may prepare the dish in advance, and heat it through before serving.

1 ounce dried imported mushrooms (*cépes* or *porcini*)
1 cup boiling water
3 tablespoons unbleached flour
4 tablespoons unsalted margarine
4 tablespoons olive oil
14 medium chicken breast halves,
  skinned and boned
Kosher salt
Freshly ground black pepper
8 medium shallots, finely chopped

3 cloves garlic, minced
½ cup dry vermouth, or dry white
  wine
A 28-ounce can peeled tomatoes,
  drained and coarsely chopped
1 cup tightly packed Italian parsley, finely chopped
½ teaspoon crushed red pepper flakes
1 tablespoon wine vinegar

Place the dried mushrooms in a bowl and pour the boiling water over them. Let stand for approximately ½ hour. Strain the soaking liquid through a sieve lined with a paper towel, squeezing the mushrooms over the sieve to extract more liquid. Reserve the liquid. Rinse the mushrooms to remove any remaining dirt, squeezing them dry, and chop coarse. Set aside.

Spread the flour on a sheet of wax paper.

In a large skillet heat 3 tablespoons of the margarine and 3 tablespoons of the oil. Pat the chicken breasts dry with paper towels and dredge them lightly in the flour. Sauté 3 or 4 breasts at a time over medium heat, turning them once until the outside of the chicken has turned white and the inside is still pink. Transfer the chicken breasts as they are sautéed to a baking pan large enough to hold them in one layer, and season them lightly with salt and pepper.

In the same skillet heat the remaining tablespoon margarine and oil. Add the shallots and the garlic and sauté over low heat, covered, until the shallots are soft. Add the vermouth and boil it down over medium heat until the shallots are slightly moist. Add the mushroom liquid, chopped mushrooms, tomatoes, parsley, red pepper and vinegar. Bring to a boil, reduce to low heat and cook the sauce, uncovered, for 5 minutes. Season to taste with salt and pepper. Pour the sauce over the breasts and cover the pan with foil. (You can prepare this dish in advance up to this point.)

Cook the chicken through in a preheated 400° F. oven for 15 minutes on one side, turn the breasts over and cook for another 10 to 15 minutes, or until the inside of the chicken has turned white. (Do not overcook the chicken or it will become tough and dry.) Season the sauce to taste with more pepper flakes, vinegar, salt and pepper. It should be well seasoned.

SERVING SUGGESTIONS: Start with Puréed Broccoli Soup, Sherry's Jerusalem Artichoke Soup or Braised Baby Artichokes. Serve accompanied by Plain Boiled Rice, Orzo with Parsley or Steamed Asparagus.

Chicken Breasts with Lemon and Raisins

4 TO 6 SERVINGS

This is a light dish which has a lovely, delicate appearance, and a sweet-and-sour taste. The chicken and the sauce are prepared separately, then combined and heated. You may prepare the entire dish in advance and heat it through before serving. Use good chicken stock.

1 cup seedless golden raisins
½ cup cognac
4 cups strong chicken stock (see page 193)
3 tablespoons unsalted margarine
3 tablespoons olive oil
5 medium white onions, sliced into very thin rounds

Grated rind of 2 lemons
½ cup lemon juice
Kosher salt
Freshly ground black pepper
2 tablespoons unbleached flour
8 medium chicken breast halves, skinned and boned

Place the raisins in a small bowl, pour the cognac over them and let stand for approximately 1 hour. In a medium saucepan bring the stock to a brisk boil and reduce it, uncovered, to 1½ cups. Set aside.

In a medium skillet heat 1½ tablespoons of the margarine and 1½ tablespoons of the olive oil and sauté the onions over low heat, covered, until soft and transparent. Add the stock, with the raisins and cognac, lemon rind and lemon juice. Bring to a boil, reduce to low heat and cook the sauce, uncovered, for 15 minutes. Season to taste with salt and pepper and set aside.

Spread the flour on a sheet of wax paper.

In a medium skillet heat the remaining margarine and olive oil. Pat the chicken breasts dry with paper towels and dredge them lightly in the flour. Sauté 3 or 4 breasts at a time over medium heat, turning them once, until the outside of the chicken has turned white and the inside is still pink. Transfer the chicken breasts as they are sautéed to a baking pan large enough to hold them in a single layer, and season them lightly with salt and pepper. Pour the sauce over the chicken and cover the pan with foil. (You may prepare this dish in advance up to this point.)

Before serving, cook the chicken through in a preheated 400° F. oven for 15 minutes on one side, turn over, and cook for another 10 to 15 minutes, or until the inside of the chicken has turned white. (Do not overcook the chicken or it will become tough and dry.) Season the sauce to taste with salt and pepper.

SERVING SUGGESTIONS: Start with Leek and Lettuce Soup, Marinated Salmon with Green Peppercorns or either of the salmon tartare recipes. Serve accompanied by Plain Boiled Rice, Stir-fried *Shiitake* Mushrooms or Steamed Asparagus.

Stir-fried Chicken with Broccoli

2 SERVINGS

All of the ingredients for this dish can be prepared in the morning and refrigerated. The whole dish takes just a few minutes to stir-fry. It looks very pretty.

2 chicken breast halves, skinned, boned and cut across the grain into ¼-inch pieces
½ tablespoon cornstarch
2 tablespoons dry white wine
3 tablespoons peanut oil
1 bunch broccoli, tops cut into bite-size florets, stems peeled and cut into similar size pieces
1 clove garlic, cut into very thin matchstick pieces
A ½-inch piece fresh ginger, peeled and cut into very thin matchstick pieces

4 scallions, including green parts, cut into 3-inch-long thick matchstick pieces
About 1½ tablespoons dark Chinese soy sauce
½ teaspoon kosher salt
½ teaspoon sugar
1 teaspoon pure Oriental sesame oil

Place the chicken pieces in a dish and coat with cornstarch and 1 tablespoon of the wine.

Heat a wok or skillet. Add 1 tablespoon of the oil and heat the oil. Add the broccoli and 2 to 3 tablespoons cold water. Stir, cover the wok, and cook over medium heat for 2 minutes, or until the broccoli is crisply tender. Remove the broccoli to a dish. Heat the wok again, add another tablespoon of the oil and heat until hot. Add the garlic and the ginger and stir-fry for a second. Discard both. Add the scallions and sauté over low-to-medium heat until they are wilted. Add to the broccoli. Heat the wok once more and add the remaining tablespoon oil. Heat the oil, add the chicken and stir-fry it until it turns white, approximately 1 minute. Stir in the broccoli and scallion combination, the remaining 1 tablespoon wine, soy sauce, salt, sugar and sesame oil. This dish should be well seasoned.

SERVING SUGGESTIONS: Start with Warm Spinach Salad, Broiled Sweet Peppers or Tortilla. Serve accompanied by Boiled Rice Chinese Style.

Lettuce Packages Filled with Chicken

4 TO 6 SERVINGS

The combination of crunchy sweet lettuce and spicy chicken in this dish is particularly interesting. It is ideal as an unusual summer Sabbath luncheon dish, since it can be made in advance and served at room temperature. It is satisfying enough to be a meal in itself.

Each person fills a lettuce leaf with some of the chicken, folds the leaf like a package, then eats it with his fingers. Children have lots of fun with this dish.

¼ pound blanched almonds
8 dried Chinese mushrooms
6 chicken breast halves (approximately 2¼ pounds), skinned, boned and coarsely chopped

MARINADE
1 tablespoon dry white wine
1 tablespoon dark Chinese soy sauce
1 teaspoon sugar
1 teaspoon kosher salt
1 egg white, lightly beaten

⅓ cup strong chicken stock (see page 193)
2 tablespoons dry white wine

4 tablespoons peanut oil
6 scallions, including green parts, sliced into thin rounds
5 cloves garlic, minced

3 tablespoons cold water
An 8-ounce can water chestnuts, drained and finely chopped

2 tablespoons peanut oil
1 tablespoon pure Oriental sesame oil
¼ teaspoon freshly ground black pepper

About 2 tablespoons dark Chinese soy sauce

Kosher salt
Freshly ground black pepper
1 large head iceberg lettuce, leaves separated

Preheat the oven to 350° F.

Toast the almonds in a baking pan for approximately 15 minutes, or until golden. Chop them coarse and set aside. Place the mushrooms in a small bowl, cover them with boiling water and let stand for 20 minutes. Squeeze them dry, cut off and discard the stems. Dice the mushroom caps into pea-size pieces and set aside. Place the chopped chicken in a large bowl.

Make the Marinade: Combine the marinade ingredients.

Stir the marinade into the chicken and combine. Stir in the water, 1 tablespoon at a time, the mushrooms and the water chestnuts.

Combine the stock, wine and soy sauce and set aside.

Heat a wok or skillet, add 1 tablespoon of the oil and in it stir-fry the scallions and the garlic over low heat until the scallions are wilted. Remove to a plate with a slotted spoon. Heat the remaining 3 tablespoons oil in the wok, add the chicken and stir-fry over high heat until it turns white. Stir in the stock mixture, the almonds and the scallions. Mix thoroughly and season to taste with salt and pepper.

Serve with the lettuce leaves alongside, so that each person may make his own lettuce packages as described above.

SERVING SUGGESTIONS: Start with Tomato Soup, Marinated Salmon or Chinese-Style Pasta with Vegetables. Serve accompanied by Boiled Rice Chinese Style.

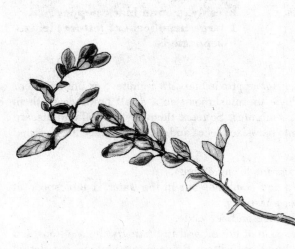

Chicken Loaf

4 TO 5 SERVINGS

This is a wonderful summer Sabbath luncheon dish that can be served at room temperature. The loaf is equally delicious made with ground turkey breast.

2 tablespoons vegetable oil, plus extra for greasing the pan
1 medium onion, finely chopped
2 cloves garlic, finely chopped
1½ pounds finely ground breast of chicken
1 medium baking potato, finely grated

2 tablespoons thin Chinese soy sauce
½ cup tightly packed Italian parsley, finely chopped
3 tablespoons ice water
Kosher salt
Freshly ground black pepper

Preheat the oven to 375° F. Line a 9- by 5-inch loaf pan with foil and brush the foil with oil.

In a small skillet heat the oil. Add the onion and garlic and sauté over medium heat until lightly golden. In a large bowl combine the onion and garlic mixture, the chicken, potato, soy sauce and parsley. Mix with your hands or a wooden spoon for a few minutes, adding the ice water gradually. Season to taste with salt and pepper and soy sauce. Spoon the mixture into the loaf pan and smooth the top with a knife. Bake for 30 minutes, then place under the broiler for a few minutes only, to brown the top.

SERVING SUGGESTIONS: Start with Hearty Vegetable Soup, Vegetable Medley or Broiled Sweet Peppers. Serve accompanied by Orzo Salad, Couscous Salad or Stir-fried Rice.

Baked Cornish Hens

4 SERVINGS

A rock Cornish hen is a small bird, a cross between a chicken and a game hen. The ¾- to 1-pounders are the right size for individual servings. These little birds cook rapidly and look very attractive.

4 rock Cornish hens, ¾ to 1 pound each
Juice of 1 lemon
1 clove garlic, minced
2 tablespoons honey
1½ tablespoons dark Chinese soy sauce

2 tablespoons vegetable oil
2 tablespoons chilled unsalted margarine, cut into 8 pieces
About 1 tablespoon wine vinegar

Wash the hens well and pat them dry inside and out with paper towels. Pull off and discard any excess fat and skin. Place the hens in a glass or ceramic dish.

In a small bowl thoroughly combine the lemon juice, garlic, honey, soy sauce and oil. Coat the hens well with the marinade. Cover and refrigerate for several hours.

Preheat the oven to 450° F.

Line a baking pan with foil and place the hens in it. Loosen their skin between the breasts and the meat and push 1 piece of margarine underneath each breast.

Bake the hens, breast sides down, in the upper third of the oven without the marinade for 15 minutes. Turn them over and bake for another 8 to 10 minutes more. The skin should be brown and the meat cooked just until the juices run clear. If you like them more brown, place them under the broiler for a minute. Sprinkle with vinegar.

SERVING SUGGESTIONS: Start with Chicken Soup with Tree Ears, Ginger and Peas, Sherry's Jerusalem Artichoke Soup or either of the salmon tartare recipes. Serve accompanied by Stir-fried Rice, Roasted Shallots or Steamed Cabbage.

Baked Cornish Hens with Chinese Flavorings

2 SERVINGS

These little birds have the distinct nutty flavor of peppercorns.

1 tablespoon dark Chinese soy
   sauce
1 tablespoon vegetable oil
1 tablespoon honey
1 tablespoon rice vinegar

2 rock Cornish hens, ¾ to 1
   pound each
½ teaspoon Szechuan peppercorns,
   crushed

Preheat the oven to 450° F. Line a baking pan with foil.

In a small bowl combine thoroughly the soy sauce, oil, honey and vinegar.

Wash the hens well and pat them dry inside and out with paper towels. Pull off and discard any excess fat and skin. Fill the cavities with peppercorns, then coat them with the soy sauce mixture. Place the hens in the baking pan.

Bake the hens, breast side down, in the upper third of the oven for 15 minutes, turn them over and bake for another 8 to 10 minutes, or until nicely browned. If the hens are not brown enough for you, place them under the broiler for a few seconds. Be careful: The honey in the coating burns quickly.

SERVING SUGGESTIONS: Start with Puréed Butternut Squash Soup, Spinach Spaghetti Primavera or Souffléed Acorn Squash. Serve accompanied by Pickled Cabbage, Roasted Shallots or Orzo with Parsley.

Broiled Cornish Hens

4 SERVINGS

This simple dish requires very little preparation and yet looks so attractive. The ingredients are readily available.

4 **rock Cornish hens, ¾ to 1 pound each**
3 **tablespoons lemon juice**
2 **tablespoons vegetable oil**
A **1-inch piece fresh ginger, peeled and minced**
1 **clove garlic, minced**

2 **tablespoons dark Chinese soy sauce**
Freshly ground black pepper
2 **tablespoons *hoisin* sauce, commercial or homemade (see page 136)**

Wash the hens and pat them dry with paper towels. With poultry shears or sturdy scissors cut away the backbone on each hen. Flatten the hens slightly with the side of a cleaver or large knife, then place them in a glass or ceramic dish.

In a small bowl combine thoroughly the lemon juice, oil, ginger, garlic, soy sauce and pepper. Coat the hens well with this marinade. Cover and refrigerate, turning the hens once, for several hours.

Preheat the broiler and line the rack of the broiler pan with foil.

Arrange the hens on the pan, breast side down. Brush with some of the marinade and broil close to the heat (about 6 inches away) for 10 minutes.

Mix the remaining marinade with the *hoisin* sauce. Turn the hens, breast side up, and brush with this mixture. Broil for another 5 minutes. The skin should be crisp and brown and the meat cooked until the juices run clear.

SERVING SUGGESTIONS: Start with Chicken Soup with Arugula or Watercress, Souffléed Acorn Squash or Stir-fried *Shiitake* Mushrooms. Serve accompanied by Acorn Squash Purée, Grated Carrots or Kasha.

Braised Soy Sauce Duck

4 SERVINGS

Braising ducks may seem like a peculiar way to cook them, but done properly, the result is a completely fat-free duck with a pungent sauce, all of which can be prepared in advance.

2 ducks, approximately 4 pounds each

6 tablespoons dark Chinese soy sauce

3 scallions, including green parts, quartered lengthwise, plus 5 scallions, including green parts, for garnish

A 1-inch piece fresh ginger, peeled and thickly sliced

3 star anise

1 cinnamon stick

4 tablespoons dark brown sugar

3 tablespoons dry white wine

⅓ cup dark Chinese soy sauce

5 cups cold water

Discard excess fat from the ducks. Wash and pat them dry inside and out with paper towels. Rub each duck inside and out with 3 tablespoons of the soy sauce. Place the ducks in a glass or ceramic dish and refrigerate overnight, uncovered.

In a large heavy pot bring the quartered scallions, ginger, star anise, cinnamon stick, 3 tablespoons of the sugar, the wine, the ⅓ cup soy sauce and water to a boil over high heat. Add the ducks, breast side down, and return to a boil. Reduce the heat, cover and cook gently for 2½ hours, turning the ducks from time to time. The ducks will be very tender. Remove the ducks to a dish and let them cool.

While the ducks are cooling add the remaining tablespoon of sugar to the sauce and boil it down, over medium heat, until it is reduced by half. Strain and skim off the surface fat. Set aside.

Slice the five scallions for garnish into 3-inch-wide and 3-inch-long matchstick pieces. Steam the scallions just to wilt them, no more than 1 minute (see page 253). Remove them from the steamer and pat dry. Set aside.

Remove the bone and skin from the duck breasts. Remove the bone and skin from the thighs, without detaching the drumsticks. (The meat should come off the bones easily.)

To Serve: Place the ducks in a roasting pan and pour a little sauce over them. Cover the pan with foil, and heat in a preheated 300° F. oven for approximately 10 minutes. Heat the sauce. Arrange the duck pieces on a serving dish, coat lightly with the hot sauce and garnish with the steamed scallions. Serve the remaining sauce separately.

SERVING SUGGESTIONS: Start with Sherry's Jerusalem Artichoke Soup, Pasta Salad with Smoked Salmon and Steamed Vegetables or Marinated Salmon with Green Peppercorns. Serve accompanied by Orzo with Parsley, Roasted Shallots or Potato and Celery Root Pie.

Broiled Duck Breasts with Ginger Sauce

2 SERVINGS

Fruit and duck are very compatible, and are traditionally served together. Once you learn to fillet a duck breast, this recipe becomes extremely easy; the fillets are simply broiled like steaks.

4 duck breast halves, skinned and
    boned
Vegetable oil
Kosher salt
Freshly ground black pepper

½ cup ginger preserves
¼ cup orange juice
1 tablespoon grated lemon rind
2 tablespoons lemon juice
2 tablespoons cognac

Preheat the broiler. Line the rack of the broiling pan with foil and place the duck fillets, smooth side up, on it.

Brush the fillets lightly with oil, and sprinkle with salt and pepper. Broil the duck breasts very close to the heat (approximately 4 inches from it) for approximately 6 minutes, without turning. The duck fillets should be medium rare.

While the ducks are broiling, mix together the ginger preserves, orange juice, lemon rind, lemon juice and cognac in a small saucepan and bring to a boil. Keep the sauce warm over low heat.

To Serve: Slice the fillets diagonally across the grain, *not* all the way through, into 1-inch pieces. Spoon the sauce onto warm plates and top with the fillets.

SERVING SUGGESTIONS: Start with Puréed Butternut Squash Soup, Chinese-Style Pasta with Vegetables or Baked Spaghetti Squash with Tomato Sauce. Serve accompanied by Rice with Saffron and Pine Nuts, Grated Carrots or Steamed Asparagus.

Duck with *Hoisin* Sauce

4 SERVINGS

Hoisin sauce, which is a thick, dark brown, sweet and slightly spicy condiment made from sugar, soya bean, vinegar, garlic, sesame seed, chili and spices, gives this dish a wonderful taste. *Hoisin* is widely available and keeps indefinitely, refrigerated in a covered jar. For those who would like to make their own *hoisin*, I include a recipe given to me by my Chinese cooking teacher, Millie Chan.

2 ducks, approximately 4 pounds each
⅓ cup dry white wine
2 tablespoons dark Chinese soy sauce
2 tablespoons pure Oriental sesame oil

4 tablespoons lemon juice
A 2-inch piece fresh ginger, peeled and minced
Freshly ground black pepper
5 tablespoons *hoisin* sauce (recipe follows), mixed with 2 tablespoons vegetable oil

Cut the ducks into quarters. Fillet the breasts and thighs without detaching the drumsticks. Discard all excess fat and skin. Wash and pat dry the pieces with paper towels. Place the duck pieces in a single layer in a large glass or ceramic dish.

In a small bowl combine the wine, soy sauce, sesame oil, lemon juice, ginger and pepper. Coat the duck pieces with the marinade, cover and refrigerate for several hours, turning them once.

Preheat the oven to 400° F.

Place the duck pieces, except the breasts, skin side down without the marinade, in a roasting pan and bake for 20 minutes. Pour off the fat and turn the duck pieces over. Add the breasts, skin side up, and baste them with some of the marinade. Bake for another 20 minutes. Remove from the oven and increase the heat to 500° F. Brush the ducks with the *hoisin* sauce and return to the oven for another 5 minutes.

SERVING SUGGESTIONS: Start with Pasta Salad with Smoked Salmon and Steamed Vegetables, Spinach Spaghetti Primavera or Salmon with Green Peppercorns. Serve accompanied by Orzo with Parsley, Steamed Cabbage or Grated Carrots.

Millie Chan's *Hoisin* Sauce

MAKES ½ CUP

2 tablespoons vegetable oil
1 clove garlic, lightly crushed
3 dried hot chili peppers
2 tablespoons water

4 tablespoons catsup
3 tablespoons dark soy sauce
4 tablespoons light brown sugar

Heat the oil in a small saucepan. Add the garlic and peppers and cook over medium heat, stirring, until the flavors are released, approximately 1 minute. Add the water, catsup, soy sauce and sugar. Simmer over low heat until the sauce is slightly thickened, about 10 minutes. Cool and store in the refrigerator in a glass jar.

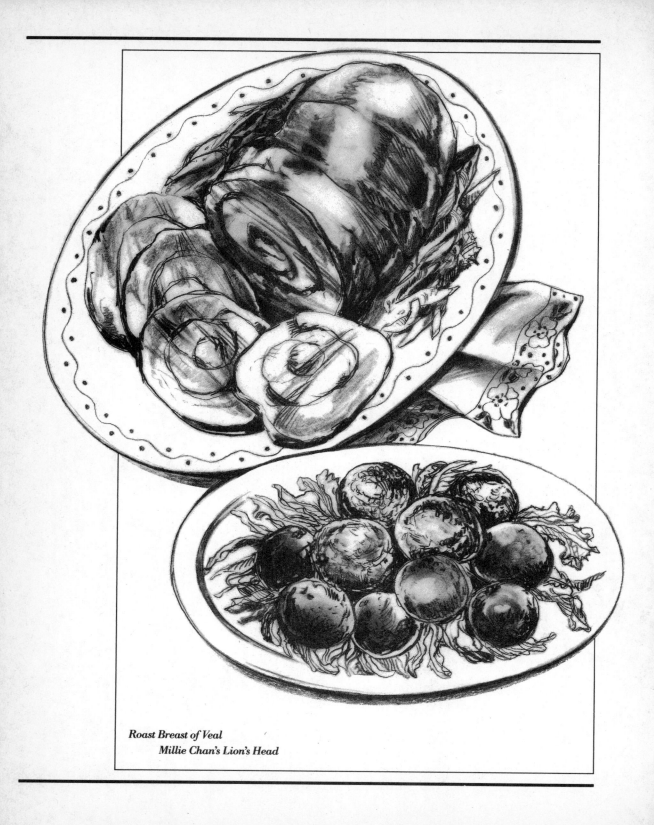

Roast Breast of Veal
    Millie Chan's Lion's Head

Meat

Broiled Veal Chops with Mustard and Mustard Seeds
Roast Breast of Veal
Braised Curried Veal
Braised Veal Shanks
Veal Stew
Beef Stew
Meat Loaf
Stir-fried Chopped Meat and Rice
Millie Chan's Lion's Head

Broiled Veal Chops with Mustard and Mustard Seeds

2 SERVINGS

Mustard seeds and mustard give these chops a wonderful pungent flavor. Mustard seeds keep indefinitely.

2 veal chops ¾ to 1 inch thick, trimmed and bone shortened
Juice of ½ lemon
Kosher salt

1 tablespoon black or yellow mustard seeds
1 tablespoon Dijon-style mustard
1 tablespoon vegetable oil

Place the veal chops in a glass or ceramic dish and sprinkle them with lemon juice and salt. Cover and refrigerate for several hours.

Preheat the broiler.

Line the rack of a broiling pan with foil and place the chops in it. In a small dish mix together the mustard seeds, mustard and oil and coat the chops. Broil the chops close to the heat (approximately 6 inches from it), without turning, for about 8 minutes, or until they are browned on top, but still pink inside.

SERVING SUGGESTIONS: Start with Spaghetti with Tomato and Crushed Red Pepper Flakes, Warm Spinach Salad or Baked Spaghetti Squash with Tomato Sauce. Serve accompanied by Crisp Potato Skins, Stir-fried Rice or Red Cabbage.

Roast Breast of Veal

10 TO 12 SERVINGS

A breast of veal will not be uniform in thickness. When sliced, the middle pieces are, normally, fairly uniform but the end pieces are so thin that they tend to fall apart. If you wish to have even slices, I recommend buying the thick center part of the breast only. For this recipe, you will need two, so the dish will be more expensive; if you prefer, use one whole breast. The meat will be delicious either way.

3 tablespoons vegetable oil
2 medium onions, finely chopped
3 cloves garlic, finely chopped
5 medium ripe tomatoes, peeled, seeded and coarsely chopped
1½ cups dry red wine
8 sprigs fresh tarragon or 2 teaspoons dried

6 pounds boned breast of veal, trimmed of all fat
Kosher salt
Freshly ground black pepper
1 tablespoon tomato paste
Extra tarragon sprigs for garnish

Preheat the oven to 375° F.

In a small skillet heat the vegetable oil. Add the onions and the garlic and sauté for a few minutes over low heat. Transfer the onion and garlic to a flameproof roasting pan large enough to hold the veal in one layer. Add the tomatoes, red wine and tarragon. Pat the veal dry, sprinkle it with salt and pepper and place it over the sauce. On top of the stove over high heat, bring to a boil, then cover the pan with heavy foil and place it in the oven. Roast for 1½ hours, uncover, turn the meat over, and continue roasting it for 1 hour more (basting it from time to time), or until tender. Let the veal cool completely, then slice it thin.

Lightly skim off the surface fat in the pan and season the pan juices to taste with the tomato paste and salt and pepper. (If the sauce is too thin, boil it down over medium-high heat, uncovered, until it reaches the desired consistency.) Return the sliced meat to the sauce, cover the pan with foil and reheat it in a 300° F. oven for approximately ½ hour.

To Serve: Arrange overlapping slices of meat on a hot serving platter with some of the sauce and garnish with the sprigs of tarragon. Serve the remaining gravy separately.

SERVING SUGGESTIONS: Start with Beet Consommé, Chicken Soup with Dilled Chicken and Beef *Piroshki* or Marinated Salmon. Serve accompanied by Kasha, Baked Spaghetti Squash or Red Kidney Beans.

Braised Curried Veal

6 TO 8 SERVINGS

In this dish the veal is braised slowly in the oven without the addition of liquid, with only vegetables. The curry does not overpower the meat, but adds a subtle flavor.

2 leeks
3 tablespoons olive oil
1 pound baby carrots, peeled
2 cloves garlic, finely chopped
8 sprigs fresh tarragon or 2 teaspoons dried
3 pounds center-cut boned shoulder of veal in one piece, rolled and tied

1¾ teaspoons curry powder
1 tablespoon unsalted margarine
Kosher salt
Freshly ground black pepper
Bouquet garni: 1 teaspoon dried thyme, 1 bay leaf and several sprigs of parsley tied in cheesecloth

Preheat the oven to 325° F.

Cut off the bottoms and most of the green tops of the leeks, and discard the tough outer leaves. Cube the remainder, place in a sieve and rinse well under cold running water. Let drain. In a small saucepan heat 2 tablespoons of the olive oil and add the leeks, carrots, garlic and tarragon. Braise the vegetables over low heat for 10 minutes.

In the meantime, pat the meat dry with paper towels and place on a sheet of wax paper. Rub the curry powder over the whole roast. In a heavy 4-quart saucepan heat the remaining 1 tablespoon olive oil and the margarine, add the roast and brown on all sides over medium heat, turning it with tongs. Sprinkle the meat with salt and pepper, add the vegetables with their juices and the bouquet garni. Cover the pan and braise the meat in the oven for 1 hour.

Remove the meat to a carving board, cut off the strings, and slice ⅛ inch thick. The center slices will be pink, but they will be cooked through and will change color once they are sliced. Arrange the meat in overlapping slices on a heated platter, cover with foil and keep warm while you are finishing the sauce. Add the juices from the carving board to the pan, and lightly skim off the surface fat. Discard the bouquet garni, bring to a boil and season to taste with salt and pepper. Garnish the meat with the vegetables and pour some of the sauce over. Serve the remaining sauce in a sauceboat.

If you wish to make this dish in advance, let the roast cool, slice it, wrap it in foil and finish the sauce. At serving time, heat the meat in the foil in a 350° F. oven for a few minutes only, and serve as above.

SERVING SUGGESTIONS: Start with Sherry's Jerusalem Artichoke Soup, Tomato Soup or Marinated Salmon with Green Peppercorns. Serve accompanied by Kasha, Orzo with Parsley or Steamed Asparagus.

Braised Veal Shanks

The shank of veal, which adjoins the breast, lends itself to braising, as in this stew with a thick sauce. If you own a food processor, you may wish to use it to chop the vegetables, but prepare each vegetable separately to preserve its distinct texture. This dish should be made in advance to allow for the flavors to blend. It also freezes very well.

4 to 6 tablespoons olive oil
3 shanks of veal (approximately 6 pounds), sawed into 12 pieces, each approximately 2 inches long
Unbleached flour for dredging
Kosher salt
Freshly ground black pepper
2 medium onions, finely chopped
3 carrots, finely chopped
4 stalks celery, peeled and finely chopped

1 large clove garlic, finely chopped
1 cup dry white wine
A 28-ounce can peeled tomatoes, drained and coarsely chopped
1 bouillon consommé cube (½ ounce), dissolved in 1½ cups boiling water
1 teaspoon dried thyme
2 bay leaves
1 cup tightly packed Italian parsley (discard the lower halves of the stems), coarsely chopped

Preheat the oven to 350° F.

In a large skillet heat the oil. Pat the veal shanks dry and dredge them lightly in the flour, shaking off the excess. Sauté several shanks at a time, on all sides (do not crowd the pan), over medium-high heat until lightly browned. As the shanks brown transfer them to a 4-quart heavy-bottomed saucepan with a tight-fitting cover, or Dutch oven, and sprinkle lightly with salt and pepper. Add the onions, carrots, celery and garlic to the skillet and sauté for a few minutes. Add the vegetables to the meat with the wine, tomatoes, bouillon, thyme, bay leaves, and parsley. Bring to a boil over medium heat on top of the stove. Cover the pan and place in the lower third of the oven. Bake for 1½ to 2 hours, turning every 20 minutes, or until the meat is tender. If the pan juices are not thick, uncover the pan, remove the meat and boil down the sauce over high heat until it reaches a thick consistency. Skim it as well if needed. Return the meat to the saucepan and season to taste with salt and pepper.

SERVING SUGGESTIONS: Start with Hearty Vegetable Soup, Puréed Broccoli Soup or Broiled Sweet Peppers. Serve accompanied by Kasha, Plain Boiled Rice or Baked Spaghetti Squash.

Veal Stew

6 SERVINGS

Again, I prefer to cook this stew in advance, to allow the flavors to blend. I also recommend using an ovenproof enameled cast-iron saucepan with a tight-fitting lid; it allows for slower, more even cooking and also enables you to serve it from or refrigerate it in the same pan. All stews freeze very well, this one included.

2 medium green bell peppers
3 tablespoons unsalted margarine
3 tablespoons olive oil
3 pounds boned shoulder of veal, trimmed of gristle and fat, cut into 2-inch cubes
Unbleached flour for dredging
Kosher salt
Freshly ground black pepper

2 medium onions, finely chopped
2 cloves garlic, finely chopped
A 28-ounce can peeled tomatoes, drained and coarsely chopped
15 pitted black olives, coarsely chopped
½ cup dry white wine
4 sprigs fresh thyme or 1 teaspoon dried

Broil the peppers (see page 254). Place the peppers in a plastic bag and let them steam. When they are cool enough to handle, peel them, remove the seeds and the ribs and cut the peppers into ½-inch cubes.

Preheat the oven to 375° F.

In a heavy skillet heat the margarine and olive oil. Pat the veal pieces dry and dredge them lightly in the flour, shaking off the excess. Sauté several pieces at a time, on all sides (do not crowd the pan), over medium heat until lightly browned. As the pieces brown, transfer them to a 4-quart heavy-bottomed saucepan with a tight-fitting lid, or Dutch oven, and sprinkle lightly with salt and pepper. Scrape the skillet to loosen the brown particles in the skillet, and add to the meat with the onions, garlic, peppers, tomatoes, olives, wine, and thyme. Bring to a boil over medium heat on top of the stove. Cover the pan and place in the oven. Bake for approximately 1 hour, or until the meat is tender but not falling apart. Skim the surface fat if needed and season to taste with salt and pepper.

SERVING SUGGESTIONS: Start with Hearty Vegetable Soup, Leek and Lettuce Soup or Braised Baby Artichokes. Serve accompanied by Kasha, Plain Boiled Rice or Baked Spaghetti Squash.

Beef Stew

All stews improve in flavor with time. It is also much easier to degrease the sauce after the stew has been refrigerated overnight. So, if you can, make this dish in advance.

4 tablespoons vegetable oil
½ teaspoon cardamom seeds
1 cinnamon stick
4 cloves
3 pounds center-cut chuck, trimmed of fat and gristle and cut into 2-inch cubes
Kosher salt
Freshly ground black pepper
2 medium onions, finely chopped

5 cloves garlic, finely chopped
A 1-inch piece fresh ginger, peeled and minced
A 28-ounce can peeled tomatoes, drained (retain the juice) and coarsely chopped
1 cup dry red wine
½ teaspoon turmeric
About 1 teaspoon chili powder
½ teaspoon ground coriander

Preheat the oven to 350° F.

In a large skillet heat 1 tablespoon of the oil. Add the cardamom seeds, cinnamon stick and cloves and sauté over medium heat for 2 minutes, or until the seasonings begin to brown. Remove to a dish. Add another tablespoon of oil to the skillet. Pat the meat dry and sauté several pieces at a time on all sides until lightly browned. As the pieces brown, transfer them to a 4-quart heavy-bottomed saucepan with a tight-fitting lid, or Dutch oven, and sprinkle lightly with salt and pepper. Add the remaining 2 tablespoons of oil to the skillet and sauté the onions, garlic and ginger for 2 minutes. Add to the meat with the cardamom seeds, cinnamon stick and cloves, the tomatoes with their juices, wine, turmeric, chili powder and coriander. Bring to a boil on top of the stove. Cover the pan and place it in the oven. Bake for 1½ to 2 hours, or until the meat is tender. Remove and discard the seasonings, skim the surface fat if necessary and season to taste with salt and pepper.

SERVING SUGGESTIONS: Start with Arugula, Leek and Potato Soup, Puréed Broccoli Soup or Warm Spinach Salad. Serve accompanied by Plain Boiled Rice, Kasha or Crisp Potato Skins.

Meat Loaf

This is an unconventional meat loaf. Instead of using bread or breadcrumbs, I add a raw grated potato, which gives the meat a light and moist texture.

2 tablespoons vegetable oil
1 medium onion, coarsely chopped
1 clove garlic, coarsely chopped
1 medium potato, quartered
1 egg
1 pound lean ground meat (½ pound veal ground together with ½ pound chuck)
1 tablespoon tomato paste

1 tablespoon catsup
About 1 tablespoon dark Chinese soy sauce
¼ cup tightly packed Italian parsley, finely chopped
A few sprigs fresh thyme or tarragon
Kosher salt
Freshly ground black pepper

Preheat the oven to 375° F. Line a 9- by 5-inch loaf pan with foil and brush the foil with vegetable oil.

In a small skillet heat the oil, add the onion and garlic and sauté over low heat until lightly golden. Place the onion and garlic with the potato and egg in a food processor fitted with a steel blade, or in a blender, and purée until very smooth. Transfer to a large bowl and add the ground meat, tomato paste, catsup, soy sauce, parsley and herbs. Mix the meat with your hands until very thoroughly combined. Season to taste with salt and pepper. Place the meat in the foil-lined pan and smooth the top. Bake for 55 minutes, then broil the meat loaf close to the heat source for approximately 3 minutes, to brown the top nicely and to allow some of the accumulated juices to be absorbed. Let the meat loaf rest for a few minutes before slicing.

NOTE: You may use only beef or only veal instead of a combination. Adjust the seasonings accordingly.

SERVING SUGGESTIONS: Start with Hearty Vegetable Soup, Puréed Beet Soup or Vegetable Medley. Serve accompanied by Bulghur Pilaf, Crisp Potato Skins or Red Cabbage.

Stir-fried Chopped Meat and Rice

4 SERVINGS

This is an attractive, easy family meal. Even the leftovers are delicious.

THE MEAT

1¼ pounds lean ground meat (¾ pound veal ground together with ¾ pound chuck)
1 teaspoon kosher salt
½ teaspoon sugar
About 3 tablespoons thin Chinese soy sauce

2 tablespoons dry white wine
½ teaspoon cornstarch
Freshly ground black pepper
¼ cup cold water
1 tablespoon peanut oil

5 tablespoons peanut oil
4 cloves garlic, minced
A ½-inch piece fresh ginger, peeled and finely chopped
1 cup cold Boiled Rice Chinese Style (see page 85), fluffed

6 scallions, including the green parts, sliced into thin rounds
8 iceberg lettuce leaves, cut in ¼-inch strips

Make the Meat Mixture: Place the meat in a large bowl, and add the salt, sugar, soy sauce, 1 tablespoon of the wine, cornstarch and black pepper. Mix in the water, 1 tablespoon at a time, stirring the mixture in one direction with your hands, until it is thoroughly combined. (Mixing the meat very well will make it fluffier.) Mix in the oil and set aside.

Heat a wok or a skillet, add 3 tablespoons of the oil and heat well. Add the garlic and ginger and sauté over medium heat for a few seconds, then add the chopped meat and stir-fry over high heat until the meat begins to change color. Stir in the remaining wine and the rice. Season the meat to taste with soy sauce and salt and pepper. Transfer it to a heated platter and keep warm.

Add the remaining 2 tablespoons of oil to the wok, add the scallions, and stir-fry over high heat until lightly wilted. Add the lettuce and stir-fry until it wilts. Scatter this mixture over the meat and serve right away.

SERVING SUGGESTIONS: Start with Chicken Soup with Arugula or Watercress, Tomato Soup or Braised Baby Artichokes. Serve accompanied by Pickled Cabbage, Beet Salad, or Stir-fried Red, Green and Yellow Peppers.

Millie Chan's Lion's Head

4 SERVINGS

I learned how to make this dish in Millie Chan's class. I am told that the large, tender meatballs served with a well-spiced sauce and crispy cabbage is called "lion's head" because each meatball is supposed to resemble the beast's head and the cabbage its mane. The original recipe calls for pork rather than veal and beef. This dish may be cooked in advance and reheated before serving.

1½ pounds lean ground meat (¾ pound veal ground together with ¾ pound chuck)
2 cups cornflakes
6 tablespoons cold water
3 tablespoons dry white wine
2 tablespoons dark Chinese soy sauce

1 tablespoon cornstarch
1 teaspoon salt
2 scallions, coarsely chopped
1½ pounds Chinese celery cabbage
1 cup vegetable oil
1 egg, lightly beaten

Place the meat in a large bowl. Place the cornflakes in a plastic bag and crush them lightly. Add them to the meat and mix well with your hands. Add 1 tablespoon of the water at a time, then mix in 1 tablespoon of the wine, 1½ tablespoons of the soy sauce, the cornstarch, ½ teaspoon of the salt and the scallions. (It is important that you mix the meat very well; it makes for a lighter and more tender meatball.) Shape the meat with your hands into thick balls, approximately 3 inches in diameter and 2 inches high. Flatten the tops of the balls slightly and set aside.

Discard the wilted outer leaves of the cabbage. Separate the rest of the leaves and wash them well. Drain the leaves and cut them crosswise into 2-inch lengths. Set aside.

Heat a wok, add the oil and heat well. Dip each meatball into the egg to coat it and place in the hot oil, 2 at a time. Brown the balls on all sides, for approximately 2 minutes, basting continuously. As they brown, transfer the meatballs with a slotted spoon to a dish. Repeat with the remaining meat mixture.

Pour off all but 3 tablespoons of oil. Heat the oil, add all the cabbage at once and stir-fry over high heat for 1 minute. Stir in the remaining 2 tablespoons of wine, ½ tablespoon soy sauce, and ½ teaspoon salt. Stir-fry the cabbage for another minute, then transfer it to a 4-quart saucepan. Place the meatballs on top of the cabbage and bring to a boil. Reduce to medium-low heat and cook, covered, for 45 minutes, turning the meat once. Serve hot.

SERVING SUGGESTIONS: Start with Hearty Vegetable Soup, Braised Baby Artichokes or Stir-fried *Shiitake* Mushrooms. Serve accompanied by Boiled Rice Chinese Style.

Steamed Cabbage
Broiled Cherry Tomatoes
Steamed Asparagus

Vegetables

DAIRY

Broiled Cherry Tomatoes
Yellow Squash au Gratin

PAREVE

Baked Spaghetti Squash
Roasted Shallots
Vegetable Medley
Potato and Celery Root Pie
Steamed Brussels Sprouts
Grated Carrots
Steamed Cabbage
Acorn Squash Purée
Red Cabbage
Stir-fried Red, Green and Yellow Peppers
Broiled Zucchini Strips
Stir-fried Red Radishes
Tzimmes (Braised Carrots)
Red Kidney Beans
Crisp Potato Skins
Steamed Asparagus

Broiled Cherry Tomatoes

4 SERVINGS

This is an easy, last-minute vegetable that complements any broiled fish dish.

**A 1-pint basket medium cherry to-
matoes (approximately 2 dozen)**
2 tablespoons olive oil
Kosher salt

Freshly ground black pepper
**2 tablespoons freshly grated Par-
mesan cheese**

Preheat the broiler.

Wipe the tomatoes clean and place them in a single layer in a foil pan. Sprinkle with the olive oil. Season with salt and pepper and sprinkle with the Parmesan cheese. Broil the tomatoes, approximately 4 inches from the heat for 2 minutes, or until lightly browned.

SERVING SUGGESTIONS: Serve alongside Broiled Fillet of Red Snapper with Pine Nut Coating, Broiled Salmon Steaks or Broiled or Barbecued Tuna Steaks.

Yellow Squash au Gratin

4 SERVINGS

3 small yellow squash (approximately 1¼ pounds)
1 tablespoon unsalted butter
1 tablespoon vegetable oil
1 small onion, minced
2 medium ripe tomatoes, peeled, seeded and coarsely chopped

3 sprigs fresh thyme or 1 teaspoon dried
Kosher salt
Freshly ground black pepper
4 ounces Gruyère cheese, grated

Preheat the oven to 450° F. Rinse the squash and pat them dry. Trim the ends and slice into ¼-inch rounds. In a large skillet heat the butter and oil. Add the onion and sauté over low heat until soft. Add the squash to the skillet with the tomatoes and the thyme and sauté rapidly over high heat, stirring, for 1 minute. Season to taste with salt and pepper. Transfer the squash mixture to a buttered 1-quart gratin dish. Sprinkle with the cheese and bake for about 10 minutes, or until crisply tender. Place under the broiler briefly to brown lightly.

SERVING SUGGESTIONS: Serve alongside Broiled Salmon Steaks or Broiled or Barbecued Tuna Steaks.

Baked Spaghetti Squash

6 TO 8 SERVINGS

This is a colorful, fun-to-prepare dish to serve with any broiled fish, poultry, meat or roasts.

1 medium spaghetti squash (approximately 3½ pounds)	Kosher salt
	Freshly ground black pepper
1 to 2 tablespoons unsalted margarine	Freshly grated nutmeg

Preheat the oven to 375° F.

Place the whole squash in a pan and bake for 45 minutes to 1 hour, turning once, until the flesh feels tender when pressed. Remove from the oven and halve at once, or the squash will continue cooking. Let cool briefly, then scoop out and discard the seeds. With a fork "comb" the strands from each half until only the shell remains.

In a medium saucepan heat the margarine, add the squash and stir until hot. Season to taste with the salt and pepper and nutmeg.

SERVING SUGGESTIONS: Serve alongside Roast Chicken, Meat Loaf or Chicken Breasts in Tomato Mushroom Sauce.

Roasted Shallots

Shallots, small-bulbed members of the onion family that are covered with papery brown skin, have a more subtle flavor than their cousins. They make an interesting winter vegetable.

24 medium shallots, uniform in size
2 tablespoons vegetable oil

Kosher salt
Freshly ground black pepper

Preheat the oven to 350° F.

Peel the shallots carefully. Place them in a glass or ceramic baking dish large enough to hold them in a single layer. Dribble the oil over them and sprinkle lightly with salt and pepper. Bake the shallots in the lowest part of the oven for approximately 1 hour and 15 minutes, turning them frequently. The shallots should be almost caramelized on the outside and soft on the inside.

SERVING SUGGESTIONS: Serve alongside any of the Cornish hen recipes, Broiled Chicken Breasts with Mustard and Thyme or Braised Soy Sauce Duck.

10 SERVINGS

I serve this dish very often, hot or at room temperature, as a first course. You can make it a day in advance.

1 medium eggplant
2 medium green bell peppers
2 medium yellow bell peppers
2 medium red bell peppers
4 tablespoons olive oil
2 medium onions, coarsely chopped
3 cloves garlic, coarsely chopped
3 medium zucchini
5 medium ripe tomatoes, peeled, seeded and coarsely chopped, or a 28-ounce can peeled tomatoes, drained and coarsely chopped

½ cup tightly packed basil leaves, coarsely chopped
½ cup tightly packed Italian parsley (discard the lower halves of the stems), coarsely chopped
3 sprigs fresh thyme or 1 teaspoon dried
About 2 tablespoons wine vinegar
Kosher salt
Freshly ground black pepper

Preheat the broiler.

Line the rack of the broiling pan with foil and place the eggplant in it. Broil the eggplant close to the heat (about 6 inches), turning on all sides until the skin is charred and the eggplant feels slightly soft to the touch, 15 to 20 minutes. (Do not overbake it.) Let the eggplant cool, remove the skin, drain off any excess juices, scrape off some of the seeds if there are many and cut the flesh into small cubes. Set aside.

Broil the peppers in the same way as the eggplant, turning them frequently until they are blistered and charred. Place them immediately in a plastic bag. (The sealed-in moisture loosens the skin.) As soon as they are cool enough to handle, peel the peppers, starting at the stem end. Discard the stems, seeds and ribs and cut into small cubes. Set aside.

In a large saucepan heat the olive oil. Add the onions and the garlic, cover and sauté over low heat until soft. Meanwhile, wash the zucchini and pat dry. Trim the ends and cut them also into small cubes. Add the zucchini to the onions and sauté for a few minutes. Add the eggplant, peppers and tomatoes and bring to a boil. Cover and cook slowly, stirring frequently, for 15 minutes. Uncover, add the basil, parsley and thyme and cook for 10 minutes more. The vegetables should still hold their shape. Season to taste with the vinegar and salt and pepper.

SERVING SUGGESTIONS: Serve alongside Roast Turkey, Roast Chicken or Broiled Salmon Steaks.

Potato and Celery Root Pie

8 SERVINGS

Despite its ungainly appearance, celery root has a wonderfully distinct flavor that complements potatoes very nicely. If you own a Mouli Julienne use the number 3 blade to save time in preparing the vegetables. And, if you wish to prepare the pie in advance, prebake it for 20 minutes, then remove from the oven. Finish baking it before serving.

Vegetable oil for greasing the pan
2 medium celery roots (approximately 1¼ pounds, without the leafy stems)
1¼ pounds baking potatoes
2 teaspoons lemon juice

3 tablespoons unsalted margarine, melted
2 tablespoons vegetable oil
Kosher salt
Freshly ground black pepper

Preheat the oven to 400° F. Grease well with oil a 10- by 1½-inch round ovenproof dish.

Peel the celery roots and the potatoes and quarter them. Place the vegetables in a bowl and cover them with cold water. Cut both vegetables into thick matchstick pieces. Toss the vegetables with lemon juice to prevent discoloration. Mix in the margarine and vegetable oil and season well with salt and pepper. Spoon the mixture into the ovenproof dish and press down to pack tightly. Bake the pie for approximately 40 minutes, or until golden brown outside and tender inside. Cut into wedges and serve hot.

SERVING SUGGESTIONS: Serve alongside Chicken with Dried and Fresh Mushrooms, Braised Soy Sauce Duck or Broiled Halibut Steaks with Tomato Coulis.

Steamed Brussels Sprouts

People who have only tasted limp, soggy Brussels sprouts will not believe that I consider them a delicious vegetable. Look for small, compact heads and do not overcook them; it's overcooking that creates a strong cabbage smell and taste.

1 pound medium Brussels sprouts	**Kosher salt**
1 tablespoon unsalted margarine	**Freshly ground black pepper**

Trim away the outside leaves and stems from the Brussels sprouts, and halve them lengthwise. Rinse well and drain. Steam the sprouts, covered, over high heat until crisply tender, approximately 5 minutes (see page 253).

In a skillet heat the margarine, add the sprouts and toss to coat well. Season to taste with salt and pepper.

SERVING SUGGESTIONS: Serve alongside Broiled Veal Chops with Mustard and Mustard Seeds, Braised Curried Veal, Baked Chicken with Soy Sauce and Ginger, Meat Loaf, Chicken Loaf or any roast.

Grated Carrots

This simple way of preparing carrots is bound to appeal to those who normally do not like cooked carrots.

5 medium carrots	**1 tablespoon honey**
2 tablespoons unsalted margarine	**Kosher salt**
Juice of 1 navel orange	**Freshly ground black pepper**

Peel the carrots and grate them coarse in a food processor or by hand.

In a medium saucepan combine the carrots with the margarine, orange juice and honey. Bring to a boil, reduce the heat, cover, and simmer for approximately 25 minutes, or until crisply tender. Season to taste with salt and pepper. Serve the carrots with or without the accumulated pan juices.

You can also prepare them in advance and reheat just before serving.

SERVING SUGGESTIONS: Serve alongside Chicken Loaf, Broiled Duck Breasts with Ginger Sauce or any baked Cornish hen recipe.

Steamed Cabbage

I prefer to steam cabbage, rather than boiling or braising it, to preserve its crunchy texture, flavor and color.

**1 medium head of white cabbage
  (approximately 2½ pounds)
2 tablespoons unsalted margarine**

**Kosher salt
Freshly ground black pepper**

Discard any discolored or limp outer leaves from the cabbage. Cut the cabbage into wedges and remove the hard core and stem. Shred the leaves fine with a knife. Steam the cabbage, covered, over high heat for about 3 minutes, or until crisply tender (see page 253).

Meanwhile, in a large skillet heat the margarine. Add the cabbage and toss to heat through. Season to taste with salt and pepper.

SERVING SUGGESTIONS: Serve alongside Steamed Salmon Steaks with Black Beans, Baked Chicken with Sun-Dried Tomatoes or Baked Chicken Breasts with Lemon and Mustard.

Acorn Squash Purée

2 OR 3 SERVINGS

This is a simple way of turning an ordinary, inexpensive vegetable into a beautiful, elegant dish.

1 medium acorn squash (approximately 1½ pounds)
1 tablespoon unsalted margarine

Freshly grated nutmeg
Kosher salt
Freshly ground black pepper

Preheat the oven to 400° F.

Halve the squash lengthwise and scoop out and discard the seeds and fibers. Place the squash, cut side down, in a baking pan and add ½ inch water. Cover the pan with foil and bake for 35 to 45 minutes, or until the flesh begins to give and feels tender when pressed. Pour off the water, turn the squash over and let cool. Carefully scoop out the cooked squash. Purée the flesh in a food processor fitted with a steel blade.

In a small saucepan heat the margarine, add the squash purée and season to taste with the nutmeg and salt and pepper.

SERVING SUGGESTIONS: Serve alongside Broiled Duck Breasts with Ginger Sauce, any of the Cornish hen recipes or Roast Turkey.

Red Cabbage

Cabbage seems to be a neglected vegetable, except when served raw in vegetable slaws and the like. I enjoy it cooked as well. This dish may be prepared a day ahead.

1 medium head red cabbage (approximately 2½ pounds)	2 bay leaves
2 tablespoons vegetable oil	½ cup water
1 medium onion, finely chopped	Kosher salt
1 Granny Smith apple, peeled, seeded and finely chopped	Freshly ground black pepper
	2 to 3 tablespoons cider vinegar
	Lemon juice

Trim off the stalk and any discolored or limp outer leaves from the cabbage. Cut the cabbage into wedges, remove the hard core and shred the leaves coarse.

In a medium saucepan heat the oil. Add the onion and the apple and sauté over low heat until soft. Add the cabbage, bay leaves and water and bring to a boil. Cover and cook very slowly until the cabbage is crisply tender, about 30 minutes. Season to taste with salt and pepper, vinegar and lemon juice.

SERVING SUGGESTIONS: Serve alongside Meat Loaf, Roast Breast of Veal or Roast Turkey.

Stir-fried Red, Green and Yellow Peppers

6 SERVINGS

2 medium red bell peppers
2 medium green bell peppers
2 medium yellow bell peppers

3 tablespoons vegetable oil
Kosher salt
Freshly ground black pepper

Rinse the peppers and pat them dry. Slice off and discard the tops and bottoms. Halve them, seed them, remove the ribs and slice them into thin matchstick pieces.

Heat a wok or a skillet. Add the oil and heat well. Add the peppers and stir-fry rapidly over medium-high heat, stirring constantly until they are slightly wilted, approximately 1 minute. Season to taste with salt and pepper.

To Serve: Remove with a slotted spoon to a serving dish.

SERVING SUGGESTIONS: Serve alongside Broiled Veal Chops with Mustard and Mustard Seeds, Broiled Chicken Breasts with Mustard and Thyme or Roast Chicken.

Broiled Zucchini Strips

I often serve a heartier version of this basic vegetable dish topped with thin slices of mozzarella, decorated with chopped basil, and chopped sun-dried tomatoes packed in oil. You may also pass extra oil and vinegar.

5 medium zucchini   **Kosher salt**
Olive oil   **Freshly ground black pepper**

Preheat the broiler.
    Line the rack of the broiling pan with foil.
    Rinse the zucchini and pat them dry. Trim the ends, then cut the zucchini lengthwise into thin strips. Each zucchini should yield 4 or 5 strips. Pat each strip dry in a dish towel. Place the zucchini strips in the pan, pour a little olive oil into a small dish and brush each slice lightly with it.
    Broil the zucchini, about 4 inches from the heat, without turning, for about 3 minutes, or until light brown. Sprinkle lightly with salt and pepper.

SERVING SUGGESTIONS: Serve alongside Broiled Salmon Steaks, Baked Chicken with Sun-Dried Tomatoes or Baked Chicken Breasts with Lemon and Mustard.

Stir-fried Red Radishes

4 SERVINGS

8 to 10 large red radishes	**Kosher salt**
1 tablespoon olive oil	**Freshly ground black pepper**

Rinse the radishes and pat them dry. Slice them thin and pat dry well in a dish towel.

Heat a wok or skillet. Add the oil and heat well. Add the radishes and stir-fry over medium-high heat, stirring all the time, until they are slightly wilted, approximately 1 minute. Season to taste with salt and pepper.

SERVING SUGGESTIONS: Serve alongside any of the Cornish hen recipes, Duck with *Hoisin* Sauce or Baked Chicken with Soy Sauce and Ginger.

Tzimmes (Braised Carrots)

Carrots are symbolic of sweetness, and when sliced into rounds they resemble coins, symbols of prosperity. They are, therefore, served frequently on Rosh Hashanah.

10 medium carrots (approximately
   1½ pounds)
2 tablespoons unsalted margarine
3 tablespoons honey
3 tablespoons brown sugar

3 tablespoons lemon juice
¼ cup orange juice
⅓ cup golden seedless raisins
Kosher salt
Freshly ground black pepper

Peel, trim and slice the carrots into thin rounds. (A food processor with a slicing attachment does this very well.) Place all the ingredients in a medium saucepan and bring to a boil over high heat. Lower the heat, cover, and cook slowly until crisply tender, about ½ hour. Uncover the pan. There will be a bit of accumulated liquid; raise the heat to high and boil it down for 5 minutes or so.

SERVING SUGGESTIONS: Serve alongside Roast Chicken, Roast Turkey or Chicken Loaf.

Red Kidney Beans

I love to serve this nutritious dish in the winter, as an accompaniment to roasts, chicken, or meat loaf. You may make it a day in advance and reheat it before serving.

1 pound (2 cups) dried kidney beans

2 medium onions

1 bay leaf

3 cloves garlic

2 sprigs Italian parsley plus ¼ cup Italian parsley, finely chopped, for garnish

4 tablespoons olive oil

A 14-ounce can peeled tomatoes, drained (retain the juice) and finely chopped

2 sprigs fresh thyme or 1 teaspoon dried

Kosher salt

Freshly ground black pepper

Place the beans in a large bowl and cover them with cold water. Let soak overnight. Drain and pick over. Place the beans in a large pot, add 8 cups cold water, 1 of the onions, whole bay leaf, the 1 whole garlic and the parsley sprigs. Bring to a boil, reduce the heat and simmer, partially covered, stirring from time to time for approximately 1 hour, or until the beans are tender but not mushy. Drain, reserving 1 cup of the cooking liquid, and discard the onion, bay leaf, garlic and parsley.

While the beans are cooking, finely chop the remaining onion and mince the remaining garlic. In a large saucepan heat the oil. Add the onion and garlic and sauté over low heat until soft. Add the tomatoes, the reserved juice and thyme and cook, uncovered, over medium heat for a few minutes. Add the beans and the reserved cooking liquid, and bring to a boil. Stir well and simmer, uncovered. Cook for 15 to 30 minutes or until almost dry. Season to taste with salt and pepper. Serve garnished with the chopped parsley.

SERVING SUGGESTIONS: Serve alongside Meat Loaf, Roast Chicken or Broiled Chicken Breasts with Mustard and Thyme.

Crisp Potato Skins

This is a delicious side dish, low in calories and nutritious, and so versatile that it can be served with fish, poultry or meat. The potatoes may be baked and scooped out early in the day; finish baking them just before serving, so that they are nice and crisp.

9 medium to large baking potatoes **Kosher salt**
Unsalted margarine

Preheat the oven to 450° F.

 Scrub the potatoes and dry them well. Rub lightly with the margarine and sprinkle lightly with salt. Place in a foil-lined pan and bake for approximately 1 hour, turning the potatoes once. Remove from the oven and cut each potato in half. Protecting your hand with a towel, grasp a potato half and scoop out most of the inside, leaving a layer of potato about ⅛ inch thick to prevent the skin from tearing. Repeat until all of the halves have been scooped out. (You can also quarter them with a scissor.) Return the skins to the pan. Increase the heat to 500° F. Bake the skins for 10 to 15 minutes, turning once, until they are crisp and brown.

SERVING SUGGESTIONS: Serve alongside Broiled Salmon Steaks, Meat Loaf, or Baked Chicken with Sun-Dried Tomatoes.

Steamed Asparagus

6 SERVINGS

Asparagus is an extremely versatile vegetable that complements almost any poultry, meat or fish. You may serve it plain as well.

36 medium asparagus spears
1 tablespoon unsalted margarine,
  melted (optional)

1 tablespoon lemon juice (optional)
1 teaspoon kosher salt
Freshly ground black pepper

Hold each asparagus spear with your hands and snap it at a point where the end breaks off easily; discard the end. Trim the spears to even them. To test if the asparagus needs peeling, cut off a piece of spear and taste it. If it is stringy, lightly peel lower part of each stalk with a vegetable peeler. Rinse and steam the asparagus in a single layer, in batches, over high heat, covered, for approximately 3 minutes or until crisply tender (see page 254).

Meanwhile combine the margarine, lemon juice, and salt and pepper. Place the asparagus in a towel to dry, then arrange on a serving dish and dress with the lemon-margarine mixture.

SERVING SUGGESTIONS: Serve alongside Broiled or Barbecued Tuna Steaks, Steamed Chicken Salad or Broiled Duck Breasts with Ginger Sauce.

Steamed Chicken Salad
Beet Salad

Salads

PAREVE
Pickled Cabbage
Couscous Salad
Orzo Salad
Beet Salad
Potato Salad
Cucumber Salad
Cherry Tomato Salad

MEAT
Steamed Chicken Salad
Chicken Salad with Fresh Herbs

Pickled Cabbage

8 SERVINGS

This is a spicy dish that whets the appetite. I like to serve it on a bed of shredded spinach leaves to cut the piquant flavor of the cabbage. This dish will keep in the refrigerator for about a week.

1 head white cabbage (approximately 2 pounds)
2 tablespoons kosher salt
3 tablespoons sugar
2 tablespoons peanut or corn oil
2 tablespoons pure Oriental sesame oil

A ½-inch piece fresh ginger, peeled and minced
2 small dried red chilis, seeds discarded, crushed
1 teaspoon Szechuan peppercorns
5 tablespoons rice vinegar

Trim off the cabbage stems and any discolored or limp outer leaves. Cut the cabbage into wedges, remove the hard core and shred the leaves fine with a knife. Place the cabbage in a large bowl, sprinkle with salt, mix well, and let stand for several hours. The cabbage will release some liquid and shrink in volume. Squeeze the cabbage, in batches, to extract all the liquid, place in a small bowl, and sprinkle with the sugar.

Heat the oil and the sesame oil in a small skillet over high heat until smoky. Remove the skillet from the heat, add the ginger, chilis and peppercorns and immediately pour over the cabbage. Add the vinegar, mix well and refrigerate for several hours.

SERVING SUGGESTIONS: Serve alongside Roast Chicken, Meat Loaf or Braised Veal Shanks.

Couscous Salad

4 TO 6 SERVINGS

Couscous, or durum semolina, is a staple prepared and eaten like rice in many Middle Eastern countries.

⅔ cup water
1 cup couscous
About 3 tablespoons olive oil
About 3 tablespoons lemon juice
3 scallions, including green parts,
   finely chopped
4 radishes, finely chopped

½ cup tightly packed Italian parsley, finely chopped
2 medium ripe tomatoes, peeled,
   seeded and coarsely chopped
3 tablespoons finely chopped mint
Kosher salt
Freshly ground black pepper

Bring the water to a boil in a small saucepan. Pour in the couscous, cover the pan and remove from the heat. Let stand for 5 minutes. Uncover the pan and stir the couscous right away with a fork. (If the grains do not separate, fluff them gently with your fingers.) Transfer the couscous to a bowl and stir in the olive oil and lemon juice. Cool for 5 minutes, then stir in the remaining ingredients. Season the salad to taste with more lemon juice and salt and pepper.

SERVING SUGGESTIONS: Serve alongside Meat Loaf, Chicken Loaf or Steamed Chicken Salad.

Orzo Salad

8 SERVINGS

2 cups orzo (rice-shaped pasta)
Scant ¼ cup olive oil
About 3 tablespoons wine vinegar
1 teaspoon Dijon-style mustard
3 scallions, including green parts,
   coarsely chopped

½ cup loosely packed Italian pars-
   ley, finely chopped
Kosher salt
Freshly ground black pepper

Bring 2 quarts of salted water to a boil in a medium saucepan. Add the orzo and boil briskly, uncovered, for approximately 7 minutes, or until the orzo is al dente, barely tender but firm to the bite. Pour into a colander, refresh with cold water, and shake vigorously to drain well.

    Place the orzo in a bowl. Combine with olive oil, vinegar, and mustard, then toss with scallions and parsley. Season the salad to taste with salt and pepper. You can also add coarsely chopped green peppers or thawed froen sweet peas.

SERVING SUGGESTIONS: Serve alongside Broiled Salmon Steaks, Whole Steamed Salmon in Foil with Ginger Vinaigrette or Chicken Breasts in Tomato Mushroom Sauce.

Beet Salad

Fresh beets seem to be an underrated vegetable, even though they are full of vitamins and minerals. I prefer to bake them rather than boil them; it enhances their flavor and the color does not bleed as it does in water. You can cut them into julienne strips, cube, or slice beets. You can also serve them dressed with olive oil and lemon juice, or with vinaigrette dressing. They are wonderful as well combined with sliced endive and watercress.

8 small to medium beets
About 2 tablespoons olive oil
Kosher salt

Freshly ground black pepper
Lemon juice or Vinaigrette Dress-
ing (page 189)

Preheat the oven to 400° F.

Trim away all but 1 inch of the leafy beet tops. Place the beets in a foil-lined baking pan and bake in the upper part of the oven for 1 to 1¼ hours, turning them occasionally, until crisply tender. (To test if the beets are cooked, pierce them with a thick sewing needle.) Let cool, peel and cut into any shape you like.

Toss the beets with the olive oil. Just before serving (or they will discolor), toss them with salt and pepper and lemon juice or the vinaigrette. Serve the salad at room temperature.

NOTE: Avoid buying large beets or those without leafy green tops; the beets may be woody, flavorless and colorless.

SERVING SUGGESTIONS: Serve alongside Chicken Loaf, Meat Loaf or Chicken Salad with Fresh Herbs.

Potato Salad

**2½ pounds baby red-skinned pota-
toes, uniform in size**

VINAIGRETTE DRESSING

2 tablespoons wine vinegar
1 teaspoon Dijon-style mustard
1½ teaspoons kosher salt

Freshly ground black pepper
⅓ cup olive oil

**4 scallions, including green parts,
coarsely chopped**

**½ cup loosely packed Italian pars-
ley, finely chopped**

Scrub the potatoes well. Steam them in a single layer over high heat, covered, for approximately 20 minutes, or until just tender (see page 254). To test if the potatoes are ready, insert a sewing needle in the middle. Lift out the steaming basket with the potatoes in it and cover it loosely with a towel until the potatoes are cool enough to handle.

Make the Vinaigrette Dressing: Place the vinegar, mustard, salt and pepper in a blender. With the motor on, pour the olive oil slowly through the opening in the lid and blend well.

As soon as the potatoes are cool enough to handle, cut them into eighths and place them in a large bowl. Toss with the scallions, parsley and the dressing. Season to taste with salt and pepper.

SERVING SUGGESTIONS: Serve alongside Tuna Seviche, any of the chicken salad recipes or Meat Loaf.

Cucumber Salad

3 SERVINGS

6 medium cucumbers, or 10
  Kirbys
3 tablespoons olive oil
3 tablespoons wine vinegar

Kosher salt
Freshly ground white pepper
10 sprigs dill, finely snipped

Peel the cucumbers, trim the ends, and halve them lengthwise. Scoop out the seeds with a spoon and slice into thin half-rounds. Place in a sieve and sprinkle with 1 tablespoon kosher salt. Leave to drain for 15 to 30 minutes. (Salt drains some of the cucumber juices, leaving the cucumbers crisp.)

Pat the cucumbers dry with paper towels and place them in a bowl. Toss with the oil, vinegar, salt, pepper and dill.

SERVING SUGGESTIONS: Serve alongside Tuna Seviche, Broiled or Barbecued Tuna Steaks or Chicken Loaf.

Cherry Tomato Salad

4 SERVINGS

**2 pints cherry tomatoes (approxi-
mately 4 dozen)**
3 tablespoons olive oil
3 tablespoons wine vinegar

**4 scallions, including green parts,
or chives, coarsely chopped**
Kosher salt
Freshly ground black pepper

Wipe the tomatoes clean, halve them crosswise and place them in a bowl. Toss with oil, vinegar and scallions. Season to taste with salt and pepper.

SERVING SUGGESTIONS: Serve alongside Marinated Salmon, any of the chicken salad recipes or Roast Chicken.

Meat

Steamed Chicken Salad

8 TO 10 SERVINGS AS A MAIN COURSE

This is not a traditional chicken salad. In this dish the chicken breasts are steamed to bring out their delicate flavor and texture. They are then sliced against the grain, and marinated overnight in dressing pungent with curry powder. The result is as attractive and tasty as it is easy. I serve the salad at room temperature on a bed of alfalfa sprouts, watercress or arugula, surrounded with steamed vegetables or raw vegetables such as asparagus, green beans, sliced cherry tomatoes and seeded cucumbers.

12 medium chicken breast halves, skinned and boned
Juice of 1 lemon
DRESSING
2 tablespoons wine vinegar
1 teaspoon Dijon-style mustard
¼ teaspoon curry powder

Creamy Vinaigrette Dressing (see page 189)

Kosher salt
Freshly ground black pepper

About 1 teaspoon kosher salt
Freshly ground black pepper
½ cup olive oil

5 sprigs fresh tarragon, chervil or rosemary for garnish

Steam the Chicken: Unscrew the middle ring of a folding steamer basket and line it with foil, making sure to pull up the edges of the foil so that the juices do not spill out. Place chicken in it in a single layer and sprinkle with lemon juice and salt and pepper. Steam, without turning, for 8 minutes, or until the chicken has turned white all the way through (see page 253). Uncover and allow to cool.

Meanwhile, make the dressing: Place all the dressing ingredients except the oil, herb, and vinaigrette in a blender or a food processor fitted with a steel blade. With the motor running, slowly pour the oil in through the opening in the lid or the feed tube.

Slice the chicken diagonally across the grain into 1-inch pieces. Arrange in the original fillet shape in a glass or ceramic dish and pour the dressing over them. Cover with foil and refrigerate overnight.

To Serve: Place salad greens on a platter. Arrange the chicken on top and drizzle with the dressing left in the dish and garnish with the herbs. Decorate each corner of the platter with a different steamed or raw vegetable drizzled with the creamy vinaigrette.

SERVING SUGGESTIONS: Start with Tomato Soup, Gazpacho or Cold Carrot Soup.

Chicken Salad with Fresh Herbs

2 OR 3 SERVINGS AS A MAIN COURSE

This is not a traditional salad where the chicken is steamed or boiled and then tossed with a dressing. In this recipe the chicken is sautéed briefly, sliced attractively, placed on a bed of lettuce leaves and drizzled with dressing, so that the natural flavor of the chicken comes through. Dried tarragon cannot be substituted for fresh, but other fresh herbs of your choice can. This dish may be prepared earlier in the day and served at room temperature.

4 medium chicken breast halves, skinned and boned
1 tablespoon unsalted margarine
1 tablespoon olive oil
HERB VINAIGRETTE DRESSING
8 chives, cut into 1-inch pieces, plus extra for garnish
8 sprigs fresh tarragon, chervil or rosemary
1 clove garlic, peeled and quartered
1 shallot, quartered

2 cloves garlic, crushed
1 tablespoon wine vinegar
Kosher salt
Freshly ground black pepper

2 tablespoons Dijon-style mustard
1 tablespoon cognac
2 tablespoons wine vinegar
¼ cup olive oil
Kosher salt
Freshly ground black pepper

Salad greens, such as arugula, watercress, *mâche*, or Bibb lettuce

Pat the chicken pieces dry with paper towels. In a large skillet heat the margarine and olive oil. Add the garlic and the chicken and sauté over medium-to-low heat, turning once, until the chicken has turned white all the way through. Sprinkle with vinegar and salt and pepper. Set aside and allow to cool.

Make the Herb Vinaigrette: Place all the vinaigrette ingredients in a food processor fitted with a steel blade or in a blender and process until smooth. Season to taste with salt and pepper.

To Serve: Slice the fillets diagonally against the grain into 1-inch pieces. Arrange the greens on a platter and place the chicken slices on top, keeping the breasts in their original shape. Top the fillets and the greens with the dressing and garnish with snipped chives.

SERVING SUGGESTIONS: Start with Tomato Soup, Gazpacho or Cold Carrot Soup. Serve accompanied by Couscous Salad, Orzo Salad or Beet Salad.

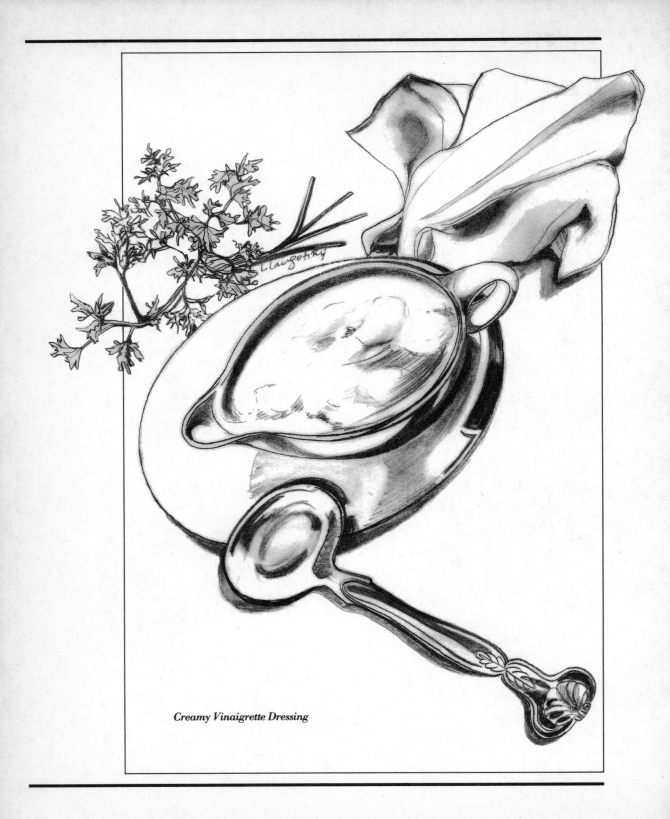

Creamy Vinaigrette Dressing

Sauces & Stocks

PAREVE
Creamy Vinaigrette Dressing
Fish Stock
Vegetable Stock
Tomato Sauce
Mayonnaise

MEAT
Strong Chicken Stock
Light Chicken Stock

Creamy Vinaigrette Dressing

ABOUT ½ CUP DRESSING, ENOUGH FOR A GREEN SALAD SERVING 6 TO 8

This is a traditional vinaigrette with one difference—the addition of the Middle Eastern spice cumin. If you do not like the distinctive taste of cumin, the dressing is equally good plain, or made with fresh herbs.

2 tablespoons wine vinegar
2 teaspoons lemon juice
½ teaspoon dry mustard
1 teaspoon Dijon-style mustard
Kosher salt
Freshly ground black pepper

½ teaspoon ground cumin
  (optional)
½ cup olive oil
Fresh mixed herbs (such as chervil,
  tarragon and chives), coarsely
  chopped (optional)

Place all the ingredients, except for the oil and herbs, in a blender. With the motor running, pour the oil slowly through the opening in the lid and blend well. Add the fresh herbs, if desired, and season the dressing to taste.

NOTE: I like to make the dressing in a blender in order to combine the ingredients thoroughly, and to make it creamy, but you may also whisk it by hand.

The dressing keeps very well, stored in a covered glass jar and refrigerated; do not add the fresh herbs until just before serving.

Fish Stock

This is a flavorful, aromatic stock that freezes very well and makes an excellent base for sauces and soups. If you have a good fish store you should be able to get bones, heads and trimmings from a variety of fresh fish. If not, buy whiting or other bony, nonoily fish.

4 pounds fresh fish bones, heads and trimmings, or 4 pounds bony, nonoily fish	2 onions, quartered
	2 bay leaves
	1 teaspoon dried thyme
6 cups cold water	Several parsley sprigs
1 cup dry white wine	7 black peppercorns
1 carrot, quartered	1 teaspoon kosher salt

Rinse the fish well and place it in a large stockpot with the water, wine, and the remaining ingredients. Bring to a boil over high heat. Lower the heat and skim the froth as it rises to the surface. Simmer the stock, partially covered, for 45 minutes. Let cool a bit.

Wet a cotton cloth with cold water, wring it dry and drape it over a large bowl. Strain the stock through the cloth. Wring the cloth to obtain all the liquid and flavor from the bones and the vegetables. Season the stock to taste. If you need a more concentrated stock, boil it down over high heat, uncovered, to the consistency you want.

NOTE: If you have refrigerated the stock for 3 to 4 days and then change your mind and wish to freeze it, bring it to a boil first and let it cool. This kills any bacteria that may have developed.

Vegetable Stock

This is a delicately flavored vegetable stock. Don't season it with salt until after cooking, as the vegetables contain their own sodium.

2 leeks, including green parts
3 carrots, quartered
2 medium onions, quartered
¼ pound string beans
½ pound mushrooms, quartered

1 parsnip, quartered
1 bay leaf
½ cup loosely packed Italian parsley with stems
Kosher salt

Trim off the ends of the leeks and discard. Slice the leeks thin. Place the leeks in a strainer, and wash very well to remove all sand. In a large stockpot combine all the ingredients and 3 quarts of cold water. Bring to a boil, then reduce the heat, cover, and simmer for approximately 2 hours. Strain the stock, discard the vegetables, and season to taste with salt.

Tomato Sauce

ABOUT 3½ CUPS

This is a thick all-purpose tomato sauce that I make with canned tomatoes since fresh flavorful tomatoes are available for only a brief season. This sauce freezes very well.

4 tablespoons olive oil
2 medium onions, coarsely chopped
4 cloves garlic, coarsely chopped
A 28-ounce can crushed tomatoes with added purée

½ cup tightly packed fresh basil leaves
5 sprigs Italian parsley
Pinch of crushed red pepper
Kosher salt
Freshly ground black pepper

In a medium saucepan heat the oil. Add the onions and garlic and sauté for 1 minute. Add the tomatoes, basil, parsley and red pepper and bring to a boil. Reduce the heat and simmer the sauce, covered, for 30 minutes. Cool slightly and purée, in batches, until smooth in a blender. Season to taste with salt and pepper.

NOTE: This sauce may be served with pasta dishes, broiled fish or chicken, or with vegetables such as spaghetti squash.

Mayonnaise

1 egg, at room temperature
¼ teaspoon dried mustard (Cole-
man's brand)
½ teaspoon kosher salt

½ cup vegetable oil
½ cup olive oil
1 tablespoon wine vinegar

Place, egg, mustard and salt in a blender. Combine vegetable and olive oils in a measuring cup. Turn motor to highest setting and do not shut it off until all the oil has been added. With motor on, add vinegar through opening in the lid, then dribble in combined oil in a very slow stream. As the mixture begins to thicken, add oil faster until finished. The thickness of the mayonnaise will depend on how quickly the oil has been incorporated into the egg. Transfer to a glass container.

NOTE: It is easier to pour in the oil from a measuring cup. The spout makes the pouring easier to control.

The mayonnaise keeps for weeks refrigerated in a tightly closed container.

Meat

Strong Chicken Stock

9 OR 10 CUPS

This strong, flavorful chicken stock is the base for many soups. Simmer the stock gently to ensure a crystal-clear broth, and strain it to make it absolutely fat free. Freeze it in jars to have on hand.

6 pounds chicken parts (carcasses, necks, wings, legs or gizzards)
4 ice cubes

1 carrot
1 onion
Several sprigs parsley

Rinse the chicken parts very well to get rid of any salt and discard excess fat. Place the parts in a large stockpot with enough cold water to almost cover the chicken. Bring to a boil over high heat. Add the ice cubes, lower the heat, and skim the scum as it rises to the surface. Add the vegetables and simmer the stock, partially covered, for approximately 2 hours. Remove the chicken parts and vegetables to a bowl.

Wet a clean finely woven cotton cloth, such as an old pillowcase, with cold water. Drape it over a large bowl or measuring pitcher, and strain the stock. (This takes a little while.) Do not wring the cloth at the end, or droplets of fat will go through. (Unlike a cheesecloth, the cloth strains the stock fat free and particle free.)

NOTE: If you have refrigerated the stock for 3 or 4 days and then decide to freeze it, bring it to a boil first and let cool again before freezing. This kills any bacteria that may have developed.

Light Chicken Stock

10 OR 11 CUPS

I use this stock as a base for soups. It is quite light and does not overpower the flavor of the soup.

5 pounds chicken parts (carcasses, necks, wings, legs, gizzards)
4 ice cubes

1 carrot
1 onion
2 cloves garlic

Rinse the chicken parts very well to get rid of any excess salt and discard any excess fat. Place the parts in a large stockpot with enough cold water to cover the chicken parts by about 1 inch. Bring to a boil over high heat. Add the ice cubes, lower the heat, and skim the scum as it rises to the surface. Add the vegetables and simmer the stock, partially covered, for approximately 2 hours. Remove the chicken parts and the vegetables to a bowl.

Follow the instructions for Strong Chicken Stock on how to skim and strain the stock.

Poached Pears
Pineapple Sorbet
Frozen Raspberry Mousse

Ice Creams, Sorbets, Mousses & Fruits

DAIRY

Banana Ice Cream

Lemon Ice Cream

Coffee Chocolate-Chip Ice Cream

Vanilla Ice Cream

Cinnamon Apple Ice Cream Chez Panisse

PAREVE

Poached Peaches with Raspberry Sauce

Poached Pears

Pears in Red Wine

Broiled Apple Rounds

Apple Crisp

Applesauce

Frozen Raspberry Mousse

Dione Lucas's Chocolate Mousse

Mango Sorbet

Pear Sorbet

Pineapple Sorbet

Banana Ice Cream

MAKES 1¼ QUARTS

If you are fond of bananas, you will love this refreshing dessert.

1½ cups heavy cream
½ cup sugar
3 egg yolks

5 medium ripe bananas (approximately 2 pounds)
2 teaspoons lemon juice

Place the heavy cream and the sugar in an enameled or glass saucepan and heat, stirring, until the sugar is dissolved. In a small bowl whisk the egg yolks lightly. Whisk in a little of the cream to warm them, then return the mixture to the saucepan and whisk the custard continuously over medium-low heat until it is thick enough to heavily coat a metal spoon. Remove from heat and transfer to a bowl.

Purée the bananas with the lemon juice in a blender until smooth. Combine thoroughly with the custard and let cool. (If you are in a hurry, chill in the freezer.) Freeze in an electric ice cream maker, following the manufacturer's instructions. Serve the ice cream right away or freeze it in an airtight container.

Lemon Ice Cream

This is a wonderful, refreshing, not overly rich ice cream—and what fun it is to make!

4 egg yolks
1 cup sugar
⅔ cup strained lemon juice (the
   juice of 3 or 4 lemons)

Grated rind of 3 lemons
2 cups half-and-half
½ cup heavy cream

In the top of a double boiler whisk together the egg yolks, sugar, and lemon juice. Place over simmering water and whisk continuously until the custard is thick enough to heavily coat a metal spoon. Remove the top of the double boiler from the heat and mix in the lemon rind, half-and-half and heavy cream. Freeze in an electric ice cream maker, following the manufacturer's instructions. Serve the ice cream right away or freeze it in an airtight container.

Coffee Chocolate-Chip Ice Cream

ABOUT 1 QUART

1 cup half-and-half
2 cups heavy cream
Scant ¾ cup sugar
4 tablespoons not too finely ground
   strong coffee beans (such as Es-
   presso or Colombian)

5 egg yolks
3 ounces semisweet chocolate, broken into small pieces

In an enameled or glass saucepan warm the half-and-half, heavy cream, sugar and the ground coffee.

In a small bowl whisk the egg yolks lightly. Whisk in a little of the coffee mixture to warm them, then add this mixture to the saucepan and whisk the custard continuously over medium-low heat until it is thick enough to heavily coat a metal spoon. Remove from heat and let cool. (If you are in a hurry, transfer the custard to another dish and chill it in the freezer.) Strain the cooled custard through a thin cotton towel to remove the coffee grounds. Wring the towel to obtain all the liquid and stir in the chocolate pieces. Freeze in an electric ice cream maker, following the manufacturer's instructions. Serve the ice cream right away or freeze it in an airtight container.

Vanilla Ice Cream

MAKES 1 SCANT QUART

A 4-inch piece vanilla bean   ⅔ cup sugar
1 cup half-and-half   5 egg yolks
2 cups heavy cream

Split the vanilla bean lengthwise and scrape out the fine black seeds. Place the seeds and the pod in an enameled or glass saucepan and mix in the half-and-half, heavy cream and sugar. Heat the mixture, stirring, until the sugar is dissolved.

In a small bowl whisk the egg yolks lightly. Whisk in a little of the vanilla mixture to warm them and return this mixture to the saucepan. Whisk the custard continuously over medium-low heat until it is thick enough to heavily coat a metal spoon. (It may take approximately 15 minutes.)

Remove and discard the pod and let the custard cool. (If you are in a hurry, transfer the custard to another dish and chill it in the freezer.) Freeze in an electric ice cream maker, following the manufacturer's instructions. Serve the ice cream right away or freeze it in an airtight container.

Cinnamon Apple Ice Cream Chez Panisse

MAKES 1 GENEROUS QUART

I am grateful to Lindsey Remolif Shere for inventing this recipe. It makes use of a popular combination—apples and cinnamon.

1½ pounds McIntosh apples, peeled, quartered and thinly sliced
3 tablespoons cold water
¼ teaspoon ground cinnamon

¾ cup sugar
3 egg yolks
1⅔ cups heavy cream
1 teaspoon vanilla extract
1 tablespoon cognac

Place the sliced apples in a heavy-bottomed saucepan and add the water and cinnamon. Bring to a gentle boil, cover and simmer over low heat, stirring frequently with a wooden spoon, until the apples are very tender, approximately 15 minutes. Mash the apples with a spoon into a coarse purée and stir in the sugar. Remove from heat.

In a small bowl beat the egg yolks lightly. Heat the cream in an enameled or glass saucepan and whisk a little of it into the yolks just to warm them. Return this mixture to the saucepan and whisk it continuously over medium-low heat, until the custard is thick enough to heavily coat a metal spoon. Add it to the apple purée, along with the vanilla extract and cognac. Allow to cool. (If you are in a hurry, transfer the custard to another dish and chill it in the freezer.) Freeze in an electric ice cream maker, following the manufacturer's instructions. Serve the ice cream right away or freeze it in an airtight container.

Poached Peaches with Raspberry Sauce

6 SERVINGS

This is a lovely, refreshing fruit dessert that can be prepared in advance and assembled just before serving. The peaches and the raspberry sauce contrast one another colorfully. You may substitute nectarines for the peaches, if you like.

2 teaspoons sugar
½ cup dry white wine
6 ripe peaches, peeled, halved and
   pitted

A 10-ounce package frozen raspberries, thawed
Fresh mint for garnish

Place the sugar and wine in an enameled saucepan large enough to hold the peaches in a single layer. (Or use two saucepans.) Bring to a boil, reduce the heat and add the peaches, cut side down. Cover the pan with heavy foil and simmer for approximately 5 minutes, or until almost tender; the exact timing will depend on the ripeness of the peaches. Transfer the peaches with a slotted spoon to a platter. Reduce the poaching liquid over high heat, uncovered, until syrupy. Allow the peaches and the syrup to cool.

Pour off all but 2 tablespoons of syrup from the raspberries and purée them in a blender until smooth. Strain the purée through a mesh sieve, pushing on the solids with the back of a spoon to extract all the juice. Discard the seeds.

Divide the sauce among individual dessert plates, top with the peaches and spoon the reduced poaching liquid over them. Serve at room temperature decorated with the mint.

Poached Pears

This is one of my favorite festive fruit desserts for fall and winter, and one that looks like a still life.

6 medium unblemished ripe but firm Bosc pears with stems	2 navel oranges
Juice of ½ lemon	½ teaspoon ground cinnamon
1 to 2 quarts orange juice	½ cup Grand Marnier or cognac
	Fresh mint for garnish

With a melon ball cutter scoop out the cores from the bottoms of the whole pears and peel them, leaving the stems intact. As you peel the pears, place in a bowl of cold water to which the lemon juice has been added. (This prevents the pears from discoloring.) Lay the pears on their sides in an enameled saucepan large enough to hold them in a single layer, and pour over just enough orange juice to cover them. Bring to a boil over medium heat, then reduce the heat, cover, and simmer, turning the pears once, for approximately 5 minutes; they should be not quite tender (insert a sewing needle to test) as they will continue to cook slightly while cooling. Uncover the pears and turn them from time to time as they are cooling to prevent discoloration.

With a vegetable peeler remove the peel from the oranges in very thin layers (being careful not to remove the white pith) and cut the peel into very thin strips. Place the strips in a small saucepan with the cinnamon, Grand Marnier or cognac and 1 cup of the poaching liquid. Bring to a boil, reduce the heat and simmer, uncovered, until the sauce is reduced by half. Allow to cool.

To Serve: Stand the pears (stem end up) on individual dessert plates, coat them with the sauce and decorate with mint. Serve at room temperature. (If a pear will not stand up, cut a very thin slice from the bottom to steady it.)

Pears in Red Wine

6 SERVICES

1 bottle dry red wine
⅓ cup sugar
A 3-inch piece cinnamon stick

6 medium unblemished ripe but
firm Bosc pears with stems
¼ cup cognac

Bring the wine, sugar and cinnamon to a boil in an enameled saucepan large enough to hold the pears in a single layer on their sides.

With a melon ball cutter scoop out the cores from the bottoms of the pears and peel the pears, leaving the stems intact. Lay the pears on their sides in the saucepan and return to a boil over medium heat. Reduce the heat to low, cover, and simmer for approximately 5 minutes, turning the pears once; they should be almost tender. (Insert a sewing needle to test.) Gently transfer the pears to a serving dish, standing them upright. (If a pear will not stand up, cut a very thin slice from the bottom to steady it.)

Add the cognac to the saucepan and boil the sauce down briskly, uncovered, until it is reduced by half, approximately 30 minutes. Remove and discard the cinnamon stick and let the sauce cool. Pour the sauce over the pears and serve them at room temperature.

Broiled Apple Rounds

If you are looking for a last-minute dessert that has few calories and is attractive, I recommend this one.

Unsalted margarine for greasing pan
4 medium to large Granny Smith apples

2 teaspoons ground cinnamon
¼ cup confectioner's sugar
9 tablespoons cold unsalted margarine cut into pea-size pieces

Preheat the broiler. Grease a jelly-roll pan.

Core the apples with a melon ball cutter, then peel them and slice into ½-inch rounds. Place the rounds in a single layer in the pan. Combine the cinnamon and sugar and place in a sifter. Sift over the apple rounds and dot them with the margarine. Broil the apples without turning them at approximately 4 inches from the heat for 3 minutes, or until crisply tender and caramelized.

NOTE: Apple rounds may be broiled earlier in the day for 2 minutes only, covered with foil and reheated in a 400° F. oven before serving.

Apple Crisp

10 TO 12 SERVINGS

A simple, easy, delicious dessert. I love to serve it in the fall or winter when the selection of fruits, in general, is limited.

1 cup walnuts
1½ cups unbleached flour
⅔ cup brown sugar, tightly packed
1½ teaspoons ground cinnamon
8 tablespoons (1 stick) unsalted
  margarine, chilled and cut into
  small pieces

8 large McIntosh apples, peeled,
  cored and cut into 12 wedges
2 tablespoons cognac

Preheat the oven to 375° F. Toast the walnuts in a baking pan for 10 minutes. Cool and chop coarse.

In a large bowl combine the flour, sugar and ½ teaspoon of the cinnamon. Add the margarine and work with a pastry blender or your fingertips until the mixture resembles cornmeal. Mix in the walnuts and set aside. Place the apples in an ungreased 9- by 14-inch glass or ceramic dish. Sprinkle them with the remaining cinnamon and cognac and mix well. Cover the apples with the nut topping. Bake in the upper third of the oven for 30 to 35 minutes, or until the topping is brown and the apples are tender. (If the topping browns before the apples are tender, cover the dish with foil.) Serve warm or at room temperature.

Applesauce

I include this recipe for those times when a cook wishes for a very simple yet refreshing dessert.

5 medium McIntosh apples (approximately 2 pounds), peeled, cored and cut into small pieces

¼ teaspoon ground cinnamon

Place the apples and the cinnamon in a heavy-bottomed saucepan. Cover and cook slowly, stirring frequently with a wooden spoon, until the apples are soft but not completely smooth, approximately 25 minutes. Be sure that the apples do not burn. Serve applesauce chilled.

Frozen Raspberry Mousse

10 TO 12 SERVINGS

The beauty of this light and pretty-to-look-at dessert is that the ingredients are available all year round, that it not only can, but *must* be made a day ahead and that it is easy to prepare. If you wish a more elaborate presentation, serve it with raspberry sauce.

RASPBERRY MOUSSE

Three 10-ounce packages frozen raspberries, thawed

4 tablespoons sugar

2 egg whites, at room temperature

2 tablespoons *framboise* (raspberry liqueur)

RASPBERRY SAUCE

A 10-ounce package frozen raspberries, thawed

1 tablespoon superfine sugar

1 tablespoon *framboise*

Make the Raspberry Mousse: Drain the raspberries over a 1-quart measuring cup. You should have about 2 cups of raspberry juice. Pour this juice into a medium saucepan, add the sugar and bring to a boil. Cook briskly, uncovered, to the thread stage (240° F. on a candy thermometer); this will take approximately 45 minutes.

In the meantime, purée the drained raspberries in a blender. Strain the purée in batches through a mesh sieve, pushing the solids through with the back of a wooden spoon to obtain as much purée as possible. Discard the seeds. You should have about 1 cup of strained puree.

Just before the raspberry syrup reaches the right temperature, beat the egg whites with an electric mixer at low speed until foamy, then increase the heat to high and beat until stiff. Still beating, dribble in the raspberry syrup. Continue beating until the outside of the bowl feels lukewarm to the touch. Add the strained purée and the *framboise* and combine thoroughly with a rubber spatula. Place the mousse in a soufflé dish, cover it with plastic wrap and freeze overnight.

Make the Raspberry Sauce: Purée the raspberries in a blender until smooth. Strain the purée through a mesh sieve, pushing with the back of a wooden spoon to obtain as much purée as possible. Discard the seeds. Transfer the sauce to a serving dish, stir in the sugar and liqueur and chill until serving.

To Serve: If you wish you can serve the mousse plain from the soufflé dish, or with the raspberry sauce.

NOTE: If you do not have a candy thermometer, you can test whether the raspberry syrup has reached the thread stage by dipping a spoon into the syrup and then dipping it into a glass of cold water. If the syrup sticks to the spoon and forms a light coat, it is ready.

Dione Lucas's Chocolate Mousse

I found this chocolate dessert so delightful and easy to make that I could not resist including it in my book. Dione Lucas recommends serving it in little *pot de crème* dishes or very small custard cups. That is certainly very appealing, but you can also present it in a beautiful glass or crystal serving dish, garnished with coarsely grated chocolate.

½ pound imported semisweet chocolate, broken into small pieces,
  plus additional semisweet chocolate, grated, for garnish
6 tablespoons cold water

Pinch of salt
5 eggs, separated, at room
  temperature
2 tablespoons dark rum

Combine the chocolate with the water and salt in the top of a double boiler. Cover and set over simmering water until the chocolate is melted.

Remove from heat, allow to cool for a minute and stir in the egg yolks, 1 at a time, and the rum.

In the bowl of an electric mixer beat the egg whites at high speed until soft peaks form. Add the chocolate mixture and beat at medium speed until thoroughly combined.

If you wish to serve the mousse in individual dishes, it is easier to pour it first into a measuring cup and then into dishes. Or you can pour the mousse into a serving dish. Freeze the mousse for 2 hours, or refrigerate it overnight. Garnish with the grated chocolate.

Mango Sorbet

MAKES ABOUT 1 QUART

This is one of my favorite desserts. It is a very creamy sorbet with the texture of ice cream.

4 to 5 medium ripe mangos   **3 tablespoons lemon juice**
1¼ cups sugar   **1 tablespoon cognac**

Peel the mangos, remove the pits and cut them into large pieces. Purée in a blender, in batches, until smooth. Strain the purée in batches through a mesh sieve, pushing with the back of a wooden spoon to obtain as much purée as possible. (You should have 3 cups strained purée.) Stir in the sugar, lemon juice and cognac. Freeze in an electric ice cream maker, following the manufacturer's instructions. Serve the sorbet right away or freeze it in an airtight container. (Mango sorbet does not freeze very hard, so you can serve it straight from the freezer.)

Pear Sorbet

MAKES 1¼ QUARTS

This is a refreshing fall or winter dessert with a pronounced pear flavor and a smooth texture.

6 medium ripe pears, Bartlett, Bosc or d'Anjou (approximately 3½ pounds)
¾ cup sugar

2 tablespoons lemon juice
1 tablespoon Poire William or cognac

Peel the pears, core them and cut into large pieces. Place them in an enameled or glass saucepan, cover, and cook over medium heat for 10 minutes, stirring frequently. They should not be mushy. While the pears are still hot (to prevent discoloration) purée in batches in a blender until very smooth. Transfer the purée to a bowl and immediately stir in the sugar, lemon juice and liqueur. Mix well, until the sugar is dissolved, then let the purée cool. (If you are in a hurry, chill it in the freezer.) Freeze in an electric ice cream maker, following the manufacturer's instructions.

Serve the sorbet right away or freeze it in an airtight container. (Pear sorbet does not freeze very hard, so you can serve it from the freezer.)

Pineapple Sorbet

MAKES ABOUT 1 QUART

This is a perfect dessert for winter, when not too many exciting fruits are available.

1 medium to large ripe pineapple	**3 tablespoons lemon juice**
1¼ cups sugar	**2 tablespoons kirsch**

Peel the pineapple, remove the core, and cut the pineapple into large pieces. Purée in a blender, in batches, until smooth. Strain the purée in batches through a mesh sieve, pushing with the back of a wooden spoon to obtain as much purée as possible. (You should have 3 cups strained purée.) Stir in the sugar, lemon juice and kirsch. Freeze in an electric ice cream maker, following the manufacturer's instructions. Serve the sorbet or freeze it in an airtight container. (Pineapple sorbet does not freeze very hard, so you can serve it straight from the freezer.)

BLUEBERRY SORBET: Substitute 2 to 2½ pints fresh blueberries for the pineapple. Rinse them first, purée, strain and proceed as above. (Blueberry sorbet freezes very hard, so I suggest that you transfer the sorbet from the freezer to the refrigerator ½ hour before serving.)

Challah
Lemon Almond Cake
Rugelach

Cookies, Cakes, Confections & Bread

DAIRY

Rugelach

Large Rugelach

Hazelnut Balls

Butter Almond Cookies

Butter Cookies

Scones

Chocolate Walnut Meringue Squares

Cheese Torte

Lemon Almond Cake

Lemon Almond Loaf

Sour Cream Coffee Cake

Chocolate Soufflé Cake

Walnut Roll

PAREVE

Mandelbrot

Brownie Thins

Almond Cookies

Chocolate Nut Clusters

Lemon Pecan Squares

Honey Date Loaf

Apple Tart with Walnut Crust

Chocolate Mousse Cake

Chocolate Almond Cakes

Chocolate Walnut Torte

Chocolate Almond Truffles

Challah

Rugelach

64 MINIATURE PASTRIES

This Eastern European specialty looks like a miniature croissant. It can be made with various doughs and fillings. This version is my favorite, with a very flaky dough and a filling rich with chocolate. The dough should be made the day before. Rugelach freeze very well.

DOUGH

2 cups unbleached flour

Pinch of salt

16 tablespoons (8 ounces) unsalted butter, chilled and cut into small pieces

1 cup sour cream

FILLING

1¼ cups walnuts, coarsely chopped

5 ounces semisweet chocolate, coarsely chopped

Scant ⅔ cup sugar

2 teaspoons ground cinnamon

Make the Dough: In a large bowl, combine the flour and salt. Add the butter and work with a pastry blender until the mixture resembles cornmeal. Add the sour cream and continue blending until the dough begins to stick together. In the bowl work the dough with your hands until you can form it into a smooth ball. Divide the dough into 4 equal balls and flatten them slightly. Dust with flour and wrap individually in wax paper. Refrigerate the dough overnight.

Make the Filling: Mix together all the filling ingredients.
  Preheat the oven to 350° F.

Form the Rugelach: Roll out each ball of dough on a floured pastry board with a floured rolling pin, on both sides, into an approximately 12-inch circle. (The dough may still show some particles of butter.) From time to time dust with the flour if the dough sticks. Cut the circle into 16 wedges and sprinkle the dough evenly with ¼ of the filling. Roll each wedge tightly from the widest part to the tip and curve it slightly into a crescent. Continue to cut, fill, and form pastries with the remaining dough in the same fashion. Place the rugelach on 2 or 3 unbuttered cookie sheets.

Bake the pastries for 25 minutes, or until golden. Cool on a wire rack.

To Freeze: Place the baked rugelach in a foil pan, cover with foil and enclose in a plastic bag.

NOTE: If you wish, you may chop the walnuts and the chocolate in a food processor fitted with a steel blade. Be sure to chop them separately and in batches, and to break the chocolate into small pieces first.

Large Rugelach

These rugelach resemble mini-croissants in shape and can be filled with either of the following two fillings. They are wonderful to have on hand for breakfast or brunch. The dough should be made the day before. They also freeze very well.

DOUGH

3 cups unbleached flour

1 envelope active dry yeast (approximately 1 tablespoon)

16 tablespoons (8 ounces) unsalted butter, chilled and cut into small pieces

3 egg yolks

1 cup sour cream

RAISIN WALNUT FILLING

2 cups walnuts, coarsely chopped

1 cup sugar

2 teaspoons ground cinnamon

1 cup golden seedless raisins

APRICOT WALNUT FILLING

2 cups walnuts, coarsely chopped

11 ounces apricot butter

6 tablespoons superfine sugar

Make the Dough: In a large bowl combine the flour and yeast. Add the butter and work with a pastry blender until the mixture resembles cornmeal. Add the egg yolks and sour cream and combine with a wooden spoon until the mixture begins to stick together. Turn the dough out on a lightly floured board and work it with your hands until you can form a smooth ball. Divide the dough into 4 equal balls and flatten each slightly. Dust lightly with flour, wrap individually in wax paper and place in a plastic bag. Refrigerate the dough overnight.

Make the Filling(s): Mix together the filling ingredients; if you are making the apricot filling, reserve 4 tablespoons of the sugar.

Preheat the oven to 350° F.

Form the Rugelach: Roll out each ball of dough on a floured pastry board with a floured rolling pin, on both sides, into an approximately 14-inch round. If the dough shows too many particles of butter and sticks to the board dust it with flour, form it into a ball and roll out again. Cut the circle into 8 wedges. If you are using the raisin filling, sprinkle the dough evenly with ¼ of the filling. If you are using the apricot filling, place 1 teaspoon filling at the widest end of each wedge. Roll each wedge tightly from the widest part to the tip and curve it slightly into a crescent. Continue to cut, fill, and form pastries with the remaining dough in the same fashion.

Place the rugelach on 2 or 3 unbuttered cookie sheets. Sprinkle the apricot rugelach with the reserved sugar. Bake for 30 minutes, or until golden. Cool on a wire rack.

To Freeze: Place the baked rugelach in a foil pan, cover with foil and enclose in a plastic bag.

Hazelnut Balls

These cookies have a distinct taste of roasted nuts. They are easy to make and freeze very well.

1 cup shelled hazelnuts (approximately 6 ounces)
1 cup sifted unbleached flour
3 tablespoons sugar

½ teaspoon vanilla extract
8 tablespoons (4 ounces) unsalted butter, chilled and cut into small pieces

Preheat the oven to 350° F. Roast the hazelnuts in a baking pan for approximately 15 minutes. While the nuts are still hot, rub them in a dish towel to remove most of their skin. (Some skin will remain.) Cool.

Lower the oven temperature to 325° F.

Place all the ingredients, including the nuts, in a food processor fitted with a steel blade and process until the dough combines well. Transfer the mixture to a pastry board and work with your hands. Place level teaspoonfuls of the dough between the palms of your hands and roll into smooth balls. Place slightly apart on 2 unbuttered cookie sheets. Refrigerate for 10 minutes. Bake for approximately 15 minutes, or until the bottoms are golden. Let cool briefly before transferring to wire racks to cool completely.

To Freeze: Place the balls in a foil pan, cover them with foil and place the pan in a plastic bag.

Butter Almond Cookies

These butter cookies are extremely easy to make. They are not too sweet and are versatile enough to serve with ice cream, tea or fruit.

8 tablespoons (4 ounces) unsalted butter, quartered, at room temperature
Scant ½ cup sugar
2 hard-boiled egg yolks
1 egg yolk
¼ teaspoon almond extract
½ teaspoon vanilla extract
1½ cups unbleached flour
1 egg white, lightly beaten
½ cup plus 2 tablespoons blanched almonds, finely chopped

In a food processor fitted with a steel blade cream the butter, adding the sugar gradually until the mixture is light and fluffy. Add the hard-boiled yolks and the raw yolk and the extracts and mix well. Add the flour and process until the dough just begins to stick to the blade. Transfer the dough to a piece of wax paper and, with the help of the paper, work until it is smooth. Wrap the dough in wax paper and refrigerate for 1 hour.

Preheat the oven to 325° F.

Work with ¼ of the dough at a time. Place the dough between two sheets of wax paper and roll it out approximately ⅛ inch thick. Cut into shapes with 1¾- to 2-inch cookie cutters and place on wax paper. Gather the scraps of dough with the help of the wax paper and roll them out as well. Brush the cookies lightly with egg white, dip the tops in the almonds, then transfer to 3 or 4 unbuttered cookie sheets. (Brushing the cookies on wax paper before placing them on cookie sheets prevents any spilled egg white from causing the cookies to burn.) Bake for 13 to 15 minutes, or until light golden. Remove right away to wire racks to cool. These cookies keep very well, stored in an airtight tin in a cool place. They also freeze very well, placed in a foil pan with wax paper between the layers. Cover with foil and place the pan in a plastic bag.

Butter Cookies

1 generous cup unbleached flour
⅓ cup superfine sugar
8 tablespoons (4 ounces) unsalted
    butter, chilled and cut into small
    pieces

1 egg yolk
1 egg white, lightly beaten
½ cup blanched sliced almonds

Mix the flour and the sugar together in a bowl. Add the butter and the egg yolk and work with the pastry blender until the mixture resembles cornmeal. Turn out the mixture on a pastry board and work with your hands to form a smooth ball of dough. Divide the dough into 2 equal parts. Shape each into a smooth rope, approximately 7 inches long and 1¼ inches in diameter. Wrap each rope in wax paper and refrigerate for several hours or overnight. The dough should be firm.

Preheat the oven to 375° F.

Spread the almonds on a sheet of wax paper. Cut each rope of dough into rounds ¼ inch thick and place them on wax paper. Brush the rounds with egg white and sprinkle with the almonds. Transfer to unbuttered cookie sheets. (Brushing the cookies on wax paper before placing them on cookie sheets prevents any spilled egg white from causing the cookies to burn.) Bake for 8 to 10 minutes, or until the edges are golden. Cool very briefly, then transfer the cookies to a wire rack to cool completely. These cookies keep very well, stored in an airtight tin in a cool place. They also freeze very well, placed in a foil pan with wax paper between the layers. Cover with foil and place the pan in a plastic bag.

These scones are dainty, light, and not too sweet.

2 cups unbleached flour
1 tablespoon baking powder
½ teaspoon salt
1 tablespoon sugar, plus additional for dusting
12 tablespoons (6 ounces) unsalted butter, chilled and cut into small pieces

2 eggs, lightly beaten
Scant ½ cup heavy cream
⅓ cup currants or raisins combined with ½ teaspoon flour
1 egg yolk mixed with 1 tablespoon water

Preheat the oven to 450° F.

Combine the flour, baking powder, salt and sugar in a food processor fitted with a steel blade. Add the butter and process until mixture resembles cornmeal. Add the eggs and pour the heavy cream through the feed tube with the motor running. Process until the dough just begins to stick to the blade. (It should not form a ball.) Transfer the dough to a bowl and mix in the currants or raisins.

Divide the dough into 4 pieces. Place each piece of dough on a well-floured surface and pat it into a round ½ inch thick. With a round floured 1¾-inch cookie or biscuit cutter, cut out rounds and place them on a piece of wax paper. Use the scraps of dough as well. Brush the scones with the egg yolk mixture, sprinkle with sugar and place on 2 unbuttered cookie sheets. Bake the scones for approximately 8 minutes or until light golden. Serve warm, on a cloth napkin, with butter and preserves. Scones freeze very well wrapped in foil and placed in a plastic bag.

Chocolate Walnut Meringue Squares

If you are looking for an easy, quick and delicious cookie that serves many, try this one. Should you have a food processor, you can use it to grind the walnuts and the chocolate separately, in batches. Be sure to cut the chocolate into small pieces first.

DOUGH

1⅔ cups unbleached flour

Scant ⅓ cup sugar

10 tablespoons (5 ounces) unsalted butter, chilled and cut into small pieces, plus additional for greasing pan

4 egg yolks

½ cup strained apricot preserves

MERINGUE

½ pound walnuts, finely ground

4 ounces semisweet chocolate, finely ground

4 egg whites

Scant ½ cup sugar

Preheat the oven to 375° F.

Make the Dough: Combine the flour with the sugar in a medium bowl. Add the butter, and work with a pastry blender until the mixture resembles cornmeal. Add 1 yolk at a time and continue working the dough with the pastry blender until it begins to stick together. Now work the dough with your hands in the bowl until you can form it into a smooth ball. Place the dough between two sheets of wax paper and roll it out on both sides into a 12- by 14-inch rectangle. (Do not worry if the rectangle is uneven or if the dough crumbles; you will be able to fix it easily in the pan.) Peel off the wax paper and wrap the dough very loosely over the rolling pin. Unroll it over a buttered 13- by 9- by 2-inch pan. Fit it firmly into the pan, fixing any cracks with your fingers, and form an even border, approximately ½ inch high. Bake the dough for 20 minutes, or until the edges are light golden. Remove from the oven and spread the dough with the apricot preserves.

Make the Meringue: Combine the walnuts and the chocolate. In the clean dry bowl of an electric mixer beat the egg whites at high speed, adding the sugar gradually until the whites are very stiff. With a rubber spatula gently fold in the chocolate-nut mixture. Spread the meringue evenly over the preserves.

Return the pan to the oven and bake for 25 minutes, or until lightly firm to the touch. Remove and let cool on a wire rack. Loosen the sides with a knife and cut into 1½-inch squares. These cookies freeze very well, placed in a foil pan with wax paper between the layers. Cover with foil and place the pan in a plastic bag.

Cheese Torte

This is a light, almost soufflélike cheesecake in a pastry shell that requires no prebaking. The torte is equally delicious the following day, but be sure to refrigerate it, then serve it at room temperature.

DOUGH

1⅓ cups unbleached flour

Scant ¼ cup sugar

8 tablespoons (4 ounces) unsalted butter, chilled and cut into small pieces

1 egg yolk

1½ tablespoons prepared orange juice

FILLING

3 egg yolks

½ cup less 1 tablespoon sugar

½ teaspoon vanilla extract

Grated rind of 1 lemon

½ pound farmer cheese

1 cup (8 ounces) sour cream

2 tablespoons unbleached flour

4 egg whites

Make the Dough: Combine the flour and sugar in a bowl. Add the butter and work with a pastry blender until the mixture resembles cornmeal. Mix the egg yolk with the orange juice and sprinkle over the dough. Continue working the mixture with a pastry blender until it begins to stick together. Turn the dough out on a pastry board and work it with your hands until you can form it into a smooth ball. Flatten the ball, wrap it in wax paper and refrigerate it overnight.

Remove the dough from the refrigerator and let it rest until it is malleable. Place the dough between two sheets of wax paper and roll it out on both sides into a 12- to 13-inch round. (Do not worry if the circle is uneven or if the dough crumbles; you will be able to fix it easily in the pan.) Peel off the wax paper and wrap the dough very loosely over the rolling pin. Unroll it over a 9-inch springform pan. Fit the dough firmly into the pan, fixing any cracks with your fingers, and form an even border, approximately 2 inches high. Refrigerate while you prepare the filling.

Preheat the oven to 350° F.

Make the Filling: In the bowl of an electric mixer beat the egg yolks at medium speed, adding the sugar gradually until the mixture is pale and bubbles appear on the surface, approximately 10 minutes. With a rubber spatula mix in the vanilla extract and the lemon rind.

Strain the farmer cheese through a mesh sieve (or a potato ricer), pushing it through with a wooden spoon. Add to the sugar-egg mixture with the sour cream and flour and mix well.

In a clean dry bowl beat the egg whites at high speed until stiff. With a spatula fold the whites into the cheese mixture until no whites are visible.

Pour the filling into the prepared pan and smooth the surface. Bake the torte on the lowest rack of the oven for 30 minutes. Transfer the cake to the center rack and bake for 20 to 25 minutes more, or until the top is golden. Remove the pan from the oven and let cool on a wire rack. Loosen the sides of the cake with a knife and remove the sides of the pan. When the cake is completely cool, loosen the bottom with a knife and slide it onto a serving platter.

NOTE: You can also prebake the pastry shell for 15 to 20 minutes in a preheated 350° F oven. But be sure to prick the dough with a fork and brush it lightly with beaten egg white beforehand.

Lemon Almond Cake

This cake is made like *génoise*—the eggs are beaten over hot water to increase their volume and then the remainder of the ingredients are folded in gently. I love the contrasting flavors of lemon and almond.

Unsalted butter for greasing pan
Unbleached flour for dusting pan
3½ ounces almond paste
2 egg yolks
Grated rind of 2 lemons
¼ cup lemon juice
8 tablespoons (4 ounces) unsalted butter, melted

4 eggs
Scant ¾ cup sugar
¼ cup cornstarch
½ cup blanched almonds, finely ground
3 tablespoons apricot preserves
¼ cup blanched almonds, sliced and lightly toasted

Preheat the oven to 350° F. Butter a 9-inch springform pan and dust it with flour. Invert the pan and tap to shake out the excess.

In a large bowl mash the almond paste with 1 of the egg yolks, the lemon rind and the lemon juice until the mixture is smooth. Mix in the melted butter.

Place the whole eggs plus the remaining yolk and the sugar in the top part of a double boiler. Set over simmering water and beat by hand or with an electric hand mixer until the mixture is very pale and has doubled in volume. Remove the top of the double boiler from the water. With a large rubber spatula fold ¼ of the egg mixture into the almond paste mixture until thoroughly combined, then gently fold in the rest of the egg mixture.

Place the cornstarch in a sieve. Sprinkle ½ of the cornstarch and all of the ground almonds over the batter and fold in gently, then sprinkle on the remainder of the cornstarch and fold quickly, until no traces of cornstarch are visible. Work fast, so as not to deflate the eggs.

Pour batter into the prepared pan and bake for approximately 35 minutes. (If the cake begins to brown too quickly, cover it with foil.) The cake is done when a cake tester or toothpick inserted in the center comes out clean. Place the cake on a wire rack to cool briefly, then loosen the sides with a knife and remove the sides of the pan. Loosen the bottom of the cake with a knife and let cool. Invert the cake onto a cake platter.

Warm the apricot preserves in a small saucepan over low heat. Strain through a mesh sieve, pushing the solids through with the back of a spoon. Spread the apricot preserves evenly around the sides of the cake with a knife and pat the sliced almonds evenly over the preserves. Sprinkle the top of the cake with the remaining almonds.

Lemon Almond Loaf

10 TO 12 SERVINGS

I love to serve this cake with tea. It is moist, lemony and keeps very well, refrigerated or frozen.

Unsalted butter for greasing pan
Unbleached flour for dusting pan
1 cup sifted unbleached flour
¾ teaspoon baking powder
1 cup finely ground blanched almonds (¾ cup whole)
GLAZE
3 tablespoons lemon juice

12 tablespoons (6 ounces) unsalted butter at room temperature
¾ cup sugar
3 eggs at room temperature
Grated rind of 2 lemons

1½ tablespoons confectioner's sugar

Preheat the oven to 350° F. Butter a 9- by 5-inch loaf pan. Dust it lightly with flour. Invert the pan and tap it to shake out the excess.

Sift the flour and the baking powder directly into a measuring cup. Combine it with the ground almonds and set aside. In the bowl of an electric mixer cream the butter at medium speed, adding the sugar gradually until fluffy, approximately 10 minutes. Still beating, add 1 egg at a time, then the lemon rind. Mix until thoroughly combined. With a rubber spatula fold the flour-almond mixture thoroughly into the batter. Pour the batter into the prepared pan and smooth the surface. Bake the cake for about 40 minutes. It is done when a cake tester or a wooden match inserted in the center comes out dry and the top is golden. Let cool in the pan on a wire rack for 5 minutes.

Make the Glaze: Thoroughly combine the lemon juice and sugar. Loosen the sides of the cake with a knife and invert the cake onto a wire rack.

Place a piece of wax paper under the rack to catch any drippings. Glaze the bottom of the loaf right away while still warm. Stir the glaze and slowly spoon it over the cake. Let cool completely.

Sour Cream Coffee Cake

This is a lovely, easy-to-make cake to have on hand for breakfast, tea, or snacks. And it freezes very well.

Unsalted butter for greasing pan
Unbleached flour for dusting pan
12 tablespoons (6 ounces) unsalted butter at room temperature
Generous 1⅓ cups sugar
2 eggs
1 cup sour cream at room temperature

½ teaspoon vanilla extract
2 cups sifted unbleached flour
1 teaspoon baking powder
¼ teaspoon salt
1 cup coarsely chopped pecans or walnuts
1 teaspoon ground cinnamon

Preheat the oven to 350° F. Butter a 9-inch Bundt pan and dust it lightly with flour. Invert the pan and tap to shake out the excess.

In the bowl of an electric mixer cream the butter at medium speed, adding the sugar gradually until the mixture is fluffy and pale, approximately 10 minutes. Still beating, add 1 egg at a time. With a large rubber spatula fold in the sour cream and vanilla. Sift the flour with the baking powder and the salt directly into a measuring cup. Fold the flour gradually into the butter mixture until well combined. Combine the nuts and the cinnamon. Sprinkle half of the nut mixture in the bottom of the prepared pan, spoon half of the batter over, then sprinkle wtih the remaining nuts. Top with the remaining batter. Bake the cake for approximately 1 hour, or until a cake tester or toothpick inserted in the center comes out dry. Cool on a wire rack before inverting.

Chocolate Soufflé Cake

ONE 9-INCH CAKE, TO SERVE 10 TO 12

This chocolate cake is very light and moist. It is one of my favorites. Its center will appear undercooked. Don't worry, that's how it is meant to be. Do serve it with crème Chantilly.

Unsalted butter for greasing pan
Unbleached flour for dusting pan
9 ounces imported extra bitter-sweet chocolate, broken into pieces
9 tablespoons (4½ ounces) un-salted butter, melted

6 eggs, separated, at room temperature
Scant ½ cup sugar
6 tablespoons cornstarch

Preheat the oven to 350° F.

Butter a 9- by 2½-inch springform pan. Dust it lightly with flour. Invert the pan and tap to shake out the excess.

Melt the chocolate, covered, in the top of a double boiler set over simmering water. Remove top, let the chocolate cool a bit, and stir in the butter. In the clean dry bowl of an electric mixer beat the egg whites at high speed until soft peaks form. Add 1 tablespoon of the sugar at a time and continue to beat until all the sugar is incorporated. In a small bowl beat the egg yolks lightly with a fork. Add the egg yolks to the whites and continue to beat at high speed for 4 minutes more. Place the cornstarch in a sifter and sift half of it over the egg mixture. Add half the chocolate mixture and fold together with a large rubber spatula, making a figure eight motion and scraping the batter from the bottom and sides of the bowl. Repeat with the remaining cornstarch and chocolate. Be sure that the batter is well combined. Pour the batter into the prepared pan, distributing it evenly all around the sides. Bake the cake in the center of the oven for 25 to 30 minutes. The inside of the cake will be moist and the center will not be fully set. Let cool on a wire rack for 10 minutes.

To Serve: Loosen the sides of the cake with a knife and remove the rim of the pan. When the cake is completely cool, loosen the bottom of the cake and invert it onto a serving dish. The bottom, which is now the top, will have a moist, soufflélike texture. Cut in small wedges and serve with crème Chantilly.

Crème Chantilly

ABOUT 1 CUP

Try to buy cream that is no more than one or two days old, not the super- or ultra-pasteurized variety. Day-old cream whips easily, since it thickens naturally as it stands in the refrigerator. If you wish, make crème Chantilly several hours in advance; you might have to whisk it again just before serving, as it may separate slightly.

1 cup heavy cream, chilled
1 tablespoon confectioner's sugar

1 tablespoon cognac or another liqueur

Place a small metal mixing bowl in the freezer for 30 minutes or so. (The colder the bowl and cream, the lighter the crème Chantilly will be.) Place the cream in the bowl and beat with an electric mixer at low speed, rotating the beater around the bowl. As the cream begins to hold a shape, add the sugar and continue beating at high speed until it holds almost firm, not stiff, peaks. With a rubber spatula, fold in the liqueur. Transfer the cream to a glass bowl and refrigerate it until ready to serve.

Walnut Roll

This is a foolproof, flourless soufflé made in a jelly-roll pan. It is a beautiful and delicious dessert that can be made early in the day, refrigerated and served at room temperature. It is extremely light.

Vegetable oil for greasing pan
6 eggs, at room temperature,
   separated
¾ cup sugar
1 teaspoon baking powder
¼ teaspoon almond extract
4 ounces walnuts (approximately
   1½ cups), finely ground

1¼ cups heavy cream
2 tablespoons confectioner's sugar,
   plus additional for dusting
1 tablespoon powdered instant
   coffee

Preheat the oven to 350° F. Brush the bottom and the sides of an 11- by 16-inch jelly-roll pan with oil. Line the pan with a 21-inch sheet of wax paper. (It will extend several inches beyond the short ends of the pan.) Brush the paper with oil.

In the bowl of an electric mixer beat the egg yolks at medium speed, adding the sugar gradually until the mixture is pale and bubbles appear, approximately 10 minutes. Beat in the baking powder and almond extract. In a clean dry bowl beat the egg whites at high speed until stiff. With a large rubber spatula fold a quarter of the whites and half the walnuts into the yolk mixture. Repeat with another quarter of the whites and the remaining walnuts. Now reverse the process: Pour the nut mixture over the whites, gently folding the two mixtures together, with a motion like a figure eight, until all the whites have disappeared.

Pour the batter into the pan and tip the pan to spread the batter evenly. Smooth the surface. Bake for 15 to 20 minutes, or until the cake is springy to the touch and the top is golden. Let the cake cool completely on a rack covered with a dry towel.

Meanwhile, whip the cream in a well-chilled bowl until it begins to hold a shape. Add the sugar and continue beating until stiff. With a rubber spatula, fold in the powdered coffee.

Invert the pan onto a double layer of wax paper, about 12 inches long. Gently peel off the top sheet of wax paper. Spread the whipped cream evenly over the roll. With the help of the paper, lift the long side of the roll, and roll the cake up loosely, like a jelly roll. Adjust the log shape with the paper to even it (don't worry if it cracks) and sift confectioner's sugar over the top.

To Serve: Slide a wide metal spatula under each short end of the roll and lift it from the wax paper to a serving platter. Or lift the roll with the wax paper onto the platter then slide the wax paper out from under it.

Mandelbrot

ABOUT 4 DOZEN COOKIES

In German, *mandelbrot* means almond bread. It is the combination of nuts and long slow baking that gives these cookies their wonderful crunch. They keep indefinitely without loosing their crispness, and are very convenient to have on hand.

Unsalted margarine for greasing pans
Unbleached flour for dusting pans
6 ounces shelled hazelnuts
6 ounces shelled almonds
8 ounces dark raisins

8 tablespoons unbleached flour
8 tablespoons sugar
1½ teaspoons ground cinnamon
½ teaspoon powdered ginger
2½ to 3 eggs, lightly beaten

Preheat the oven to 325° F. Grease two 9- by 5-inch loaf pans and dust them lightly with flour. Invert the pans and tap to shake out the excess.

Chop the hazelnuts very coarse in a food processor fitted with a steel blade and transfer them to a large bowl. Chop the almonds coarse and add to the bowl. Mix in the raisins, flour, sugar, cinnamon and ginger. Add 2 eggs and combine thoroughly, using a wooden spoon. If the mixture does not hold together add the extra ½ egg. Divide the dough equally between the two pans and press down to pack very firmly. Place the pans side by side in the oven, reduce the heat to 300° F. and bake for 1 hour.

Place the pans on wire racks to cool, then loosen the edges of the *mandelbrot* with a knife. Turn the pans over and bang the pans to release the bottoms. With a serrated knife cut the *mandelbrot* into ¼-inch slices and arrange them on a cookie sheet. Dry them in a preheated 200° F. oven for 45 minutes, then turn over and toast for 45 minutes more. The *mandelbrot* should be very dry. Let cool completely on racks. *Mandelbrot* will keep indefinitely, stored in an airtight tin in a cool place.

Brownie Thins

These are thin, crunchy chocolate cookies that happen to freeze very well.

4 ounces shelled hazelnuts (approximately ¾ cup)
Unsalted margarine for greasing pan, plus 5 tablespoons
Unbleached flour for dusting pan
¼ cup unsweetened cocoa powder

1 tablespoon powdered instant coffee
½ cup sugar
1 egg, lightly beaten
¼ cup unbleached flour
½ teaspoon vanilla extract

Preheat the oven to 350° F. Toast the hazelnuts in a baking pan for approximately 15 minutes, or until the brown skin darkens and cracks slightly. While the nuts are still hot, rub them in a dish towel to remove most of their skins. (Some skin will remain.) Cool and chop coarse. Grease an 8- or 9-inch square baking pan with margarine and line it with wax paper. (The wax paper may extend over the edges.) Grease the wax paper and dust it with flour. Invert the pan and tap it to shake out the excess.

In the top of a double boiler set over simmering water melt the margarine with the cocoa and coffee. Stir with a wooden spoon until the mixture is smooth, then remove from heat and stir in the sugar, egg, flour and vanilla. Fold in the hazelnuts. Spread the dough evenly in the pan, but not all the way to the sides. Straighten the edges of the dough with a knife so that it is of uniform size. Bake for 12 or 13 minutes, or until the top is firm to the touch. Remove from the oven and let rest for 1 minute only. Carefully invert the pan onto a wire rack and gently peel off the wax paper. Leave to cool. Transfer the brownies to a cutting board. With a serrated knife cut the brownies into 1-inch strips. Make diagonal cuts in each strip 1½ to 2 inches apart. Each strip will yield 4 cracker-thin diamond-shaped brownie thins.

To Freeze: Place the thins in a foil pan with wax paper between the layers. Cover with foil and place the pan in a plastic bag.

Almond Cookies

These cookies are light, crisp, and easy to make. They also freeze very well.

Unsalted margarine for greasing pans plus 6 tablespoons (3 ounces) unsalted margarine at room temperature
6 tablespoons sugar

½ teaspoon almond extract
½ cup sifted unbleached flour
¾ cup blanched thinly sliced almonds

Preheat the oven to 400° F. Grease 2 cookie sheets with margarine.

In the bowl of an electric mixer cream the margarine at medium speed, adding the sugar gradually until the mixture is pale and fluffy, approximately 5 minutes. Lower the speed and mix in the almond extract and flour. With a rubber spatula fold in the almonds.

Drop level teaspoons of the batter 1 inch apart onto the cookie sheets and flatten them slightly with a knife. Bake one sheet at a time in the upper third of the oven for approximately 7 minutes, or until the cookies are light golden. Let the cookies cool for a few seconds, then remove them to a wire rack to cool completely.

To Freeze: Place the cookies in a foil pan with wax paper between the layers. Cover with foil and place the pan in a plastic bag.

Chocolate Nut Clusters

ABOUT 10 DOZEN COOKIES

These are fun to make with children of any age.

Unsalted margarine for greasing
   cookie sheets, plus 16 tablespoons (8 ounces) at room
   temperature
½ pound shelled almonds
⅔ cup dark brown sugar
1 tablespoon powdered instant
   coffee

1 egg, lightly beaten
1¾ cups unbleached flour
⅛ teaspoon salt
½ cup unsweetened cocoa powder
8 ounces semisweet chocolate in
   small pieces

Preheat the oven to 350° F. Grease approximately 4 cookie sheets. Toast the almonds in a baking pan for 15 minutes. Cool and chop coarse.

In the bowl of an electric mixer cream the margarine at medium speed, adding the sugar gradually until the mixture is pale and fluffy, about 5 minutes. Add the coffee and the egg and mix well. In a large bowl mix together the flour, salt, cocoa powder, and the almonds. Add to the creamed margarine mixture and mix thoroughly with a wooden spoon. Fold in the chocolate. Drop level teaspoons of the batter onto the cookie sheets and bake for approximately 8 minutes, or until the tops of the cookies feel firm. Let rest for a minute, then transfer the cookies to a wire rack to cool. These cookies freeze very well.

NOTE: If you like, you may chop the almonds and the chocolate in a food processor fitted with a steel blade. Be sure to break the chocolate into small pieces first.

Lemon Pecan Squares

FORTY-EIGHT 1½-INCH SQUARES

These delicious cookies have a distinct lemony flavor and a nutty texture.

**Unsalted margarine for greasing
  pan, plus 8 tablespoons (4
  ounces) at room temperature**
Unbleached flour for dusting pan
¾ cup sugar
3 eggs, separated

1½ cups sifted flour
¼ teaspoon baking powder
½ cup confectioner's sugar
Grated rind of 2 lemons
⅓ cup lemon juice
1 cup pecans, coarsely chopped

Preheat oven to 350° F. Grease a 13- by 9- by 2-inch pan. Dust lightly with flour. Invert the pan and tap to shake out the excess.

In the bowl of an electric mixer, beat the margarine at medium speed, for 5 minutes, gradually adding the sugar. Add 1 egg yolk at a time and set aside. Sift together the flour and the baking powder and set aside. In a clean dry bowl beat the egg whites at high speed until foamy. Gradually add the confectioner's sugar and continue beating until very stiff. With a rubber spatula gently fold the flour, alternating with the lemon rind, lemon juice and the pecans, into the margarine-yolk mixture. Then gently fold in the whites. Pour the batter into the prepared pan and smooth the surface. Bake the squares for 15 to 20 minutes, or until the top is firm, when a cake tester or a toothpick inserted in the center comes out dry. Remove and let cool on a wire rack. Loosen the sides with a knife and cut into 1½-inch squares. These cookies freeze very well stored in a foil pan with wax paper between the layers. Cover with foil and place the pan in a plastic bag.

Honey Date Loaf

Unsalted margarine for greasing
    pan, plus, 8 tablespoons (4 table-
    spoons), chilled and cut into
    small pieces
Unbleached flour for dusting pan
½ pound pitted dates, cut into
    small pieces
¾ cup water

½ teaspoon baking soda
2½ cups unbleached flour
½ teaspoon baking powder
½ teaspoon salt
1 egg, lightly beaten
½ cup honey
1 cup walnuts, coarsely chopped

Preheat the oven to 300° F. Grease a 9- by 5-inch loaf pan and dust it lightly with flour. Invert and tap the pan to shake out the excess.

Place the dates in a small saucepan, add the water and slowly bring to a boil. Remove from the heat and stir in the baking soda. (It will bubble up.) Leave to cool completely.

Sift together the flour, baking powder and salt directly into a measuring cup. Place the flour in a large bowl, add the margarine and work with a pastry blender until the mixture resembles cornmeal. With a wooden spoon mix in the egg, honey, walnuts, and dates and combine thoroughly. The dough will be slightly wet. Spoon the dough into the loaf pan, smooth the top with a knife and bake for approximately 1 hour and 15 minutes, or until a cake tester or a toothpick inserted in the center of the cake comes out dry. Cool on a wire rack briefly, then loosen the sides with a knife, invert onto a rack and leave to cool completely. This cake freezes very well.

Apple Tart with Walnut Crust

This is an apple tart with an unusually fine walnut crust. If you wish, you may roll out the dough, place it in a tart pan, cover it with foil and refrigerate it. The following day fill it and bake it.

CRUST

1½ cups unbleached flour
4 tablespoons sugar
¾ cup finely ground walnuts
8 tablespoons (4 ounces) unsalted margarine, chilled and cut into small pieces

½ teaspoon vanilla extract
3 tablespoons ice water
1 egg white, lightly beaten

FILLING

5 medium Cortland or Golden Delicious apples (approximately 2½ pounds), peeled, cored and cut into approximately ¼-inch wedges

1½ tablespoons dark brown sugar
½ teaspoon ground cinnamon
3 tablespoons (1½ ounces) unsalted margarine
¼ cup apricot preserves

Make the Crust: In a medium bowl combine the flour, sugar and walnuts. Add the margarine and work with a pastry blender until the mixture resembles cornmeal. Add the vanilla and 1 tablespoon of the water at a time and continue blending until the dough begins to stick together. In the bowl work the dough with your hands until you can form a smooth ball. Flatten the ball, then wrap it in wax paper and refrigerate for 1 hour.

Place the dough between two lightly floured sheets of wax paper and roll it out into a 12- to 13-inch round. Peel off the wax paper and wrap the dough very loosely over the rolling pin. Unroll over an ungreased 11-inch tart pan with a removable fluted rim. Pat the dough gently into the sides of the pan and up the sides. (Do not be afraid if the dough cracks; you can easily patch it.) Roll the rolling pin over the top to trim off the excess dough. Refrigerate the shell for 30 minutes or longer.

Preheat the oven to 400° F.

Prick the crust lightly with a fork (to prevent air bubbles from forming) and brush with the egg white. Bake for approximately 20 minutes, or until light golden.

Prepare the Filling: Arrange the apples attractively in the tart shell. Combine the sugar and cinnamon and sprinkle over the apples. Melt the margarine in a small saucepan, add the apricot preserves and heat slowly, mixing well. Spoon over the apples and bake for approximately 30 minutes, or until the apples are tender but not falling apart. Serve at room temperature.

To Serve: Place the tart on a coffee can or other round object of a similar size and remove the rim. Loosen the bottom of the tart with a knife and slide it onto a serving platter.

Chocolate Mousse Cake

This delicious sugarless and flourless dessert has an underbaked middle, which is the secret to its lightness. Please make it a day in advance and refrigerate it until serving. It is wonderful for Passover.

Unsalted margarine for greasing pan, plus 7 tablespoons (3½ ounces), quartered
Unbleached flour for dusting pan
9 ounces imported semisweet chocolate, broken into small pieces
6 eggs, separated, plus 2 whites, at room temperature

2 tablespoons cognac
Pinch of salt
½ cup minus 1 tablespoon lukewarm water
Unsweetened cocoa powder (optional)

Preheat the oven to 325° F. Grease a 9-inch springform pan and dust it lightly with flour. Invert the pan and tap to shake out the excess.

In the top of a double boiler set over simmering water melt the chocolate and margarine, uncovered, stirring until smooth. In a large bowl lightly whisk together the egg yolks, cognac and salt. Whisk in the melted chocolate until thoroughly combined, add the water and mix again.

In a clean dry bowl beat the egg whites at high speed until stiff. With a large rubber spatula fold ⅓ of the whites into the chocolate mixture until they are well combined. Repeat with another ⅓ of the whites, then pour the chocolate mixture over the remaining whites and fold the two mixtures together gently, making a motion like a figure eight, until all the whites have disappeared. Do not overfold. Pour the batter into the pan, distributing it evenly, and bake for 30 to 35 minutes; the center should be barely set and still moist inside. Let cool on a wire rack. (The cake will shrink slightly.) Loosen the sides of the cake with a knife and remove the sides of the pan. Cover the cake with foil and refrigerate it overnight.

To Serve: Loosen the bottom of the cake with a knife and slide it onto a serving platter, or cut it into small wedges and serve on individual plates. Sprinkle with cocoa, if desired.

Chocolate Almond Cake

These cakes are ideal for a large party, or for Passover. Since they are flourless and quite moist, it is best to refrigerate them to facilitate slicing. They also freeze very well.

Unsalted margarine for greasing pans, plus ½ pound (8 ounces) at room temperature

Unbleached flour or Passover potato starch for dusting pans

9 ounces imported semisweet chocolate, broken into small pieces

Scant 1¼ cups sugar

6 eggs, separated, at room temperature

¼ cup strained freshly squeezed orange juice

1 tablespoon unsweetened cocoa powder

2 teaspoons cognac

1½ teaspoons unbleached flour or potato starch

1 teaspoon grated lemon rind

1 teaspoon grated orange rind

¼ teaspoon vanilla extract

9 ounces blanched almonds, finely ground

Unsweetened cocoa powder or powdered sugar for dusting cakes

Preheat the oven to 300° F. Grease the bottoms and sides of two 9- by 1½-inch round pans. Line the pans with wax paper (paper should extend beyond the rims) and grease the wax paper. Dust with flour or potato starch, then invert the pans and tap to shake out the excess.

Place the chocolate in the top of a double boiler, cover, and set over simmering water until it is melted. Let cool.

In the bowl of an electric mixer cream the margarine at medium speed, adding the sugar gradually until the mixture is pale and bubbles appear, approximately 10 minutes. Still beating, add 1 egg yolk at a time, beating well after each addition. Lower the speed and beat in the cooled chocolate and the orange juice. With a large rubber spatula mix in the cocoa powder, cognac, flour or potato starch, lemon rind, orange rind, vanilla extract and almonds.

In a clean dry bowl beat the egg whites at high speed, until stiff. Fold ½ of the whites into the batter with a rubber spatula. Repeat with another ¼ of the whites, then reverse the process, pouring the batter over the whites. Gradually fold the two batters together, making a motion like a figure eight, until all the whites have disappeared. Divide the batter equally between the two pans and smooth the tops. Bake both cakes on the center rack of the oven, not touching, for 40 to 45 minutes. (A cake tester or toothpick inserted in the center of the cake should come out clean.) Let the cakes cool for 10 minutes on wire racks, then invert the cakes onto the racks, gently peel off the wax paper and let cool completely. Refrigerate.

To Serve: Sprinkle with cocoa powder or confectioner's sugar and slide the cakes onto a serving platter.

Chocolate Walnut Torte

12 TO 14 SERVINGS

This is a chocolatey, moist cake that is easy to make. It is ideal for Passover or for any other large party. It stays fresh for several days refrigerated, or you may freeze it.

Unsalted margarine for greasing
   pan
Unbleached flour or potato starch
   for Passover for dusting pan
6 ounces imported semisweet chocolate, broken into small pieces

8 eggs, separated
¾ cup plus 2 tablespoons sugar
1 tablespoon dark rum
12 ounces walnuts, semifinely
   ground

Preheat the oven to 350° F. Grease the sides and the bottom of a 10- by 2½-inch springform pan. Dust with flour or potato starch, then invert the pan and tap to shake out the excess.

Place the chocolate in the top of a double broiler, cover and set over simmering water until melted. Let cool.

In a bowl of an electric mixer beat the egg yolks at medium speed for 5 minutes, gradually adding ½ cup of sugar. Beat in the chocolate and the rum. Set aside.

In a clean dry bowl beat the egg whites at high speed until they are barely foamy; gradually add the remaining sugar and beat until stiff. With a large rubber spatula fold half of the walnuts and ¼ of the whites into the batter. Repeat with the remaining walnuts and another ¼ of the whites. Then reverse the process, pouring the batter over the whites. Gradually fold the two batters together, making a motion like a figure eight, until all the whites have disappeared. Pour the batter into the prepared pan and smooth the top. Bake for 40 to 45 minutes, or until a cake tester or a toothpick inserted in the center of the cake comes out clean. Cool on a wire rack. Loosen the sides of the cake with a knife and remove the rim of the pan.

To Serve: Loosen the bottom of the cake with a knife and invert the cake onto a serving platter.

Chocolate Almond Truffles

These truffles improve with time, so do make them in advance and refrigerate them to have on hand; or freeze them. Allow just a few minutes for defrosting.

1 cup (6 ounces) shelled almonds
¼ pound imported semisweet chocolate, broken into small pieces
½ cup sugar

2 egg yolks (reserve the whites)
1¼ tablespoons dark rum
3 tablespoons unsweetened imported cocoa powder

Preheat the oven to 350° F. Toast the almonds in a baking pan for approximately 15 minutes. Allow to cool.

Place the almonds, the chocolate and the sugar in a food processor fitted with a steel blade and chop coarse. Add the yolks and rum and continue processing until the mixture is fine. (To test if the nut mixture is fine enough and moist enough, roll a spoonful into a ball; if it is too dry add a few drops of the egg white and process again for a second.)

Spread the cocoa on a sheet of wax paper.

Roll level teaspoonfuls of the chocolate-almond mixture into balls in the palm of your hand, then roll them in the cocoa to coat well. (If hands get too sticky, rinse them.)

To Freeze: Place the truffles in a small foil pan, sprinkle them with the leftover cocoa, cover with foil, and place the pan in a plastic bag.

Challah

Challah is one of the delights of a Friday night or holiday meal. Once you familiarize yourself with this recipe, you will see how easy it is to make. Challah freezes very well.

2¼ cups warm water (100° F.–115° F.)
2 envelopes active dry yeast (approximately 2 tablespoons)
1 tablespoon sugar
¼ cup honey
2 eggs plus 1 yolk, at room temperature

GLAZE
1 egg yolk mixed with 1 tablespoon water

1¼ tablespoons salt
¼ cup vegetable oil
2 tablespoons (1 ounce) unsalted margarine at room temperature
About 8 cups unbleached flour

Pour the warm water into the bowl of an electric mixer; add the yeast and sugar. Stir lightly, cover the bowl with a towel and leave in a draft-free place for 10 to 15 minutes, or until bubbles appear on the surface. (This is called proofing the yeast to make sure it is still active.)

In a small bowl mix together the honey, eggs, egg yolk, salt, vegetable oil and margarine. Add this to the yeast mixture along with 7½ cups of the flour and knead with a dough hook at low-medium speed for approximately 10 minutes, adding more flour as needed to make a dough that no longer sticks to the sides of the bowl. Turn the dough out on a pastry board and knead further with the heel of your hand, adding more flour as needed until the dough no longer sticks to the board or your hands and is smooth and elastic.

Wash and dry the mixer bowl. Grease it lightly and place the dough in it, turning to coat all the sides. Cover the bowl with a towel and leave the dough to rise in a warm, draft-free place (80° F.–100° F.) such as a food warmer or a slightly warm oven, for approximately 1 hour, or until double in bulk.

Punch the dough down and divide it into 12 equal pieces. Working with 3 pieces of dough at a time, roll each out on a floured surface into 10- to 12-inch-long strands thinner at the ends than in the middle. Let them rest for a few minutes, then braid: Pinch the ends of the three strands together, braid them loosely to the other end and pinch again. Repeat with the remaining pieces of dough.

Place the challahs on baking sheets. Cover the loaves with a towel and leave in a warm, draft-free place for the final rise, approximately 30 minutes.

Preheat the oven to 350° F.

Brush the challahs with the glaze. Bake in the center of the oven for approximately 35 minutes, or until they are golden and sound hollow when tapped on the bottoms. Remove and let cool on wire racks. This challah will stay fresh for several days without freezing. But if you wish to freeze the loaves, cool them completely, wrap them in plastic wrap, then in foil, and place in a plastic bag.

To Serve: Remove the wrapping and place the challah directly on a rack in a preheated 350° F. oven for approximately 20 minutes, or until heated through.

NOTE: For smaller challahs, divide the dough into more pieces and make more loaves. For variety, you can sprinkle the challahs with poppy seeds.

To Make Round Challahs: On Rosh Hashanah, Yom Kippur and Sukkot you may wish to bake special round challahs with raisins. Add ¾ cup golden raisins to the dough after the first rising. Shape the dough into 4 equal pieces. Working with one piece of dough at a time, divide it into two pieces. Roll them into 10- to 11-inch strands. Form the first strand into a circle, then wind the second strand around it.

Notes on Ingredients

BLACK BEANS are fermented whole soy beans preserved in salt. They have a pungent flavor that lends a wonderful taste to poultry and fish dishes. After opening, you can refrigerate them indefinitely. They are found in Oriental markets and in some specialty food shops.

WASABI (POWDERED JAPANESE HORSERADISH) has a pungent flavor of horseradish. It comes in small can and has a long shelf life. It can be found in Oriental markets.

PURE ORIENTAL SESAME OIL is made from roasted sesame seeds. It has a thick, nutty flavor and is light brown in color. Do not confuse it with the cold-pressed Middle Eastern sesame oil, which is light in color and not as aromatic. Chinese sesame oil is used more as a flavoring then in cooking. It comes in various bottle sizes and keeps indefinitely, refrigerated or in a cool place. It is imported from China and you can find it in Oriental markets and specialty stores.

CHINESE SOY SAUCE is an ancient condiment made from soy beans fermented with other grains. It comes in two varieties: One is the dark (also known as thick) soy sauce, and the other, thin (also known as light). The dark soy sauce has a thicker consistency, darker color and sweeter taste than the thin sauce.

Even though there is a considerable amount of sodium in soy sauce, there are low sodium brands available. I use it in small quantities in marinating or in seasonings. These imported Chinese soy sauces come in various size bottles and are available in Oriental and other markets. Soy sauce keeps indefinitely.

SZECHUAN PEPPERCORNS are tiny whole dark reddish brown peppercorns that have a stronger aroma than black or white peppercorns. They keep indefinitely.

HOISIN SAUCE is a thick brown-red paste. It is both a sweet and spicy condiment made from soy beans, wheat flour, red beans, ginger, garlic and spices. It comes in jars or cans. Once opened it keeps indefinitely, refrigerated. It is imported from China and is available in most Oriental stores.

TREE EARS, also known as cloud ears, are edible fungi. They are curled, shriveled, black-gray and dried. Thin and brittle when dry, they expand when soaked in boiling water. They do not have a flavor of their own but take on the flavor of other ingredients, and have a crunchy and chewy texture. They keep on a pantry shelf indefinitely and are available in Oriental markets.

CHINESE DRIED BLACK MUSHROOMS are edible tree fungi. The caps have striated indentations on the surface which curl under. (European dried mushrooms are not a good substitute, since they have a different taste.) They are sold by weight, packaged in cellophane bags. They keep indefinitely, stored in a container with a tight-fitting lid.

DRIED *PORCINI*, MORELS OR POLISH MUSHROOMS are wild mushrooms imported from Europe with totally different tastes from cultivated mushrooms. They are soaked in boiling water and add a wealth of taste to soups, sauces, stews and pasta. Fresh *porcini* and morels are available, in season, in specialty stores.

FRESH *SHIITAKE* MUSHROOMS are rich and meaty in taste. They have over 2-inch caps and lend themselves to broiling or stir-frying over high heat. Chanterelles are a good substitute. These mushrooms are easily available in specialty supermarkets.

STAR ANISE is a dry, brown, licorice-flavored spice that looks like a 1-inch star with eight points. It is available in Oriental markets and keeps indefinitely.

WONTON WRAPPERS are thin, 3-inch squares of dough made from wheat flour, egg and water. They are found fresh or frozen in Oriental or specialty stores.

SESAME SEEDS are tiny flat seeds that come either white or dark; the white ones are hulled. They are sold by weight, they freeze very well and are available in specialty and health food stores.

GINGER is spicy and hot in taste. Look for plump pieces, light tan in color, with a tight skin. If the ginger looks gray inside and shriveled, it is old. It keeps well for several weeks, wrapped in foil and refrigerated.

KOSHER OR COARSE SALT is a coarse salt without any preservatives. It tastes less salty than regular salt.

RICE VINEGAR, a light amber-colored vinegar, is neither as sharp nor as sour as malt vinegar. It keeps indefinitely. It is found in most stores.

KASHA is roasted buckwheat groats. The grains of kasha can be whole, medium ground or finely ground. I prefer the medium grind as it is more delicate.

DAIKON is a long Japanese white radish. It is a wonderful garnish.

ORZO is rice-shaped pasta.

EGGS: All of the recipes in this book have been tested with large eggs, not medium or extra large. I freeze leftover egg whites in small jars either individually or collected. It's best to beat egg whites that are at room temperature; they contain more air and make the dish so much lighter.

DRIED BEANS AND LENTILS: Try to buy them in health food stores, as they seem to be fresher there. Dried beans last a long time and it is hard to distinguish long-stored ones from newer ones.

BULGHUR is a ground wheat that is available in three textures: coarse, medium coarse and fine. I like the medium grain. It is a wonderful alternative to rice. It is found in health food and other specialty stores.

CHILI PASTE WITH GARLIC is made from hot peppers, salt and garlic. It is sold in small jars and keeps indefinitely, refrigerated. It can be found in Oriental markets.

GREEN PEPPERCORNS are undried peppercorns. They come in jars or in cans. You can find them in most specialty stores.

PHYLLO is very thin, strudel-like sheets of dough that comes in one-pound packages, fresh or frozen. If you buy them frozen, defrost them in the refrigerator. You can find them in supermarkets and specialty shops.

SUN-DRIED TOMATOES come plain or packed in oil. They are sold by weight and have a wonderful concentrated tomato flavor. They are spicy and salty and add extra flavor to any dish. They keep very well, refrigerated. They can be found in specialty stores and some supermarkets.

TOMATOES: Unless tomatoes are fully ripe, canned peeled Italian plum tomatoes are preferable in cooking. They come in many sizes. If you can, buy imported ones.

HERBS: Herb growing has become quite popular. Most supermarkets and specialty stores carry cilantro, dill, chives, basil, tarragon, thyme, parsley and mint. If not, you may like to grow your own. Dried herbs are not too good a substitute, but when using them try to rub them between your hands to release more flavor.

BOUQUET GARNI is a small bundle of herbs, such as bay leaf, thyme and parsley, tied in a small piece of cheesecloth. It is used to flavor soups and stews. When the dish is ready remove the cheesecloth.

CILANTRO, also known as Chinese parsley or coriander, has a pungent aromatic flavor. It is sold like parsley, in bunches, and is used as a seasoning or garnish.

DILL: Do not wash dill. Try to keep it dry by wrapping it in a paper towel, placing it in a plastic bag and refrigerating it. Snip it with scissors when needed. It is a wonderful herb used in soups, salads, sauces, fish and vegetables. It is available all year. It freezes well, snipped and placed in a plastic container.

CHIVES are slender green shoots of the onion family. They do not require washing, just keeping dry. Wonderful as a flavoring or garnish for soups, salads, vegetables, sauces and fish. Snip with scissors when using.

BASIL is a versatile herb for cooking and garnishing. It is excellent in sauces, stews, soups, salads and roasts. Basil leaves require rinsing and spin drying. If you wish to keep basil for a few days, make sure that the leaves are completely dry. After spin drying I spread them on a piece of paper towel to expose them to the air for a few minutes. Then I wrap them in a paper towel and place them in a plastic bag and refrigerate.

TARRAGON is one of my favorite herbs. The pointed leaves have a delicate flavor of anise. It's a wonderful herb used with poultry, roasts, fish, eggs, sauces and salads. It requires no washing; just keeping dry.

THYME: Next to parsley this is the most popular herb for stocks, stews, bouquet garni, soups, roasts and braised dishes. It also requires no washing, just keeping dry.

PARSLEY: There are two kinds of parsley, the familiar curly kind used in garnishes, and the Italian flat-leaf kind. I prefer the Italian kind in cooking, as it has a subtler, more refined flavor. It is not great as a garnish; it wilts easily. Italian parsley keeps for several days, refrigerated. Be sure to wash it first, dry it thoroughly, wrap it in paper towel, then foil, and refrigerate it.

MINT is used more for flavoring and as a garnish than in cooking. It is very good in soups, salads and sauces, and makes a lovely garnish for desserts and sorbets. You do not have to wash it; just keep it dry.

NUTS: Today most nuts sold for cooking purposes come shelled. I prefer to buy them in health food or specialty stores, as they seem to be fresher. All nuts freeze very well but should be brought to room temperature before using.

Nuts keep better whole. If you need them chopped or ground, process only the amount you need. For fine nut grinding I recommend using a nut grinder with a drum or a Mouli grinder. For coarser grinding or chopping, use a food processor fitted with a steel blade. Chop the nuts in batches, removing each batch before placing in the next one.

TO BLANCH ALMONDS: Drop them into boiling water, return the water to a boil and drain right away. While the almonds are still hot, slip off their skins by pressing them between the thumb and index finger. Dry them on paper towels before using.

TO BLANCH HAZELNUTS: Spread them in a baking pan and place them in a preheated 350° F. oven for 10 to 15 minutes; the skin will be blistered. Right away wrap the nuts in a coarse towel and rub the towel against a hard surface such as a table. Most of the skin will come off; don't worry if some skin remains on the nuts.

CHOCOLATE: Whenever possible, buy imported chocolate of the best quality. You can grind it fine in a nut grinder or a Mouli grinder. If you wish to chop it or grind it coarse, you can do so in a food processor fitted with a steel blade, but be sure to break the chocolate into small pieces first, and do it in batches, removing each one before adding the next.

SPICES such as turmeric, ground coriander, cumin and cardamom seeds are ground commercially. They can be found in most supermarkets.

FRISÉ, also known as French chicory, is a light-green, faintly bitter salad green that works very well as a garnish or combined with other greens.

TO KEEP SALAD GREENS, PARSLEY, BASIL OR SPINACH wash the leaves, spin dry, and spread them on paper towels exposed to air for 5 to 10 minutes to dry thoroughly. Wrap them in paper towels, place them in a plastic bag and refrigerate them. The leaves should remain crisp for several days. The exceptions are arugula and watercress, which will only keep overnight.

TO PEEL AND SEED TOMATOES AND OTHER FRUITS drop the tomatoes into boiling water. Return the water to a boil and drain. Loosen the tomato skin and pull it off. Core the tomatoes, halve them crosswise and, holding each half cut side down, gently press with your hand, making the seeds fall out.

TO PEEL PEPPERS: Line a rack of a broiling pan with foil and place the peppers in it. Broil them close to the heat (about 6 inches away) for 15 to 20 minutes, turning on all the sides, until charred and blistered. Place the hot peppers in a plastic bag and let steam until they are cool enough to handle. Peel them and remove the seeds and the ribs. They are now ready for using.

STEAMING VEGETABLES: Boil just enough water in a wok or in a pot to cover the bottom of a steamer basket without touching the holes. Place the vegetables in the basket. Cover the wok or pot and steam over high heat as specified. Remove the basket from the heat right away. Refresh the vegetables with cold water to stop the cooking, then dry them in a towel.

Chicken or certain kinds of fish that have little moisture may also be steamed in a steamer basket. Line the basket with foil, oil the foil and steam as specified. Remove from heat right away. For steaming fish or vegetables that have moisture, I suggest filling a wok or pot with water to a depth of 1½ to 2 inches and bringing it to a boil. Place a trivet in the water. Arrange the chicken or fish in a heatproof dish and set it on the trivet. Cover and steam over high heat as specified. Remove the dish from the heat right away.

Notes on Equipment

CANDY THERMOMETER is a thermometer that registers the range of temperatures for deep-frying, for proofing yeast, for making sugar syrup and for caramelizing sugar. Taylor is the brand that I recommend.

FOOD MILL: This is a simple hand-operated metal or plastic device that comes with three discs. It is good for puréeing, for ricing potatoes or farmer or pot cheese, or for straining tomato sauce.

MOULI JULIENNE is a simple hand-operated device with five discs. It is ideal for fine, medium or superfine chopping, slicing and shredding vegetables and fruits. It is a small, inexpensive and very useful device.

MOULI GRATER is a small hand-grater with a drum that is perfect for grating small amounts of nuts, chocolate or even cheese.

NUT GRATER is a drum grater that comes in various sizes and is wonderful for finely grating nuts.

ICE CREAM MAKERS: I have tried a number of ice cream machines and found the electric ones to be the easiest to use. The Oster Ice Cream Maker or the Waring Ice Cream Parlor is an inexpensive electric model that uses salt and ice and produces silky ice creams and sorbets. Also available are electric machines that do not require any salt or ice. They are expensive but well worth the investment. I do not like the hand-cracked nonelectric machines that do not use ice or salt.

ELECTRIC MIXER: I find the Kitchen Aid Mixer made by Hobart to be a very useful device. I have had mine for many, many years. It comes in a larger and smaller model and with many attachments. You can also get extra bowls and parts for it.

STEAMERS: There are many steamers available. The easiest and least expensive are stainless steel folding baskets with 3 legs that fit into a wok or the pot of your choice. They come in two sizes and can be found in hardware stores.

OVENS: Learn to use your oven. I have an electric one and find it very accurate for baking and convenient for broiling. I still use an oven thermometer from time to time to check if the oven temperature is accurate; many a cake has been ruined without checking. The Taylor brand is the thermometer I recommend.

SALAD SPIN DRYER: A wonderful gadget that makes drying salad greens, spinach, parsley, or basil very easy. The greens are placed in an inner slotted basket, which is set in a plastic bowl. When the basket spins, the water on the leaves is thrown into the outer bowl. Do not pack too many greens at one time, and empty the water each time. To make sure that the leaves are very dry after spinning, place them on paper towels for a few minutes to dry them even more. If you are using the salad right away, place it in a bowl and refrigerate it, uncovered, until needed. If you are using the greens the following day, wrap them in paper towels and place them in a plastic bag. Most greens will remain very crisp for several days, except arugula, watercress and *mâche*, which should be used the same day.

WOK: I find the wok to be the most useful of all cooking vessels. I use it for stir-frying, frying and steaming. It heats very quickly and is easy to clean. I like the simple variety made of carbon steel with a rounded bottom and fitted lid, allowing for the heat to spread evenly and rapidly. I also prefer those with one wooden handle instead of two metal ones. The wooden handle is easier to grasp and does not get as hot. Buy a metal rack that fits into it so that you can rest a heatproof dish on it for steaming.

Notes on Techniques

BLANCH means to drop foods such as tomatoes, peaches or nuts into boiling water, bring the water back to a boil, then drain the food immediately. Blanching loosens the skin and facilitates peeling.

Cutting foods into **MATCHSTICK** pieces usually means cutting them into ⅛- to ¼-inch-wide sticks, with the length designated by the respective recipe.

DICE means to cut food into ¼-inch squares.

DEEP-FRY means to cook food in enough hot fat or oil to cover it completely. (Adjust the temperature of the fat according to the food.) The finished food should be crisp on the outside and just cooked through.

MINCE means to chop very fine.

JULIENNE refers to cutting food into matchstick pieces, usually ⅛ to ¼ inch wide and whatever length the recipe calls for.

PURÉE means to reduce the food to a smooth mixture. Depending on the consistency you want, it may be done in a blender, food processor, or food mill, or by forcing the food through a sieve.

SAUTÉ refers to cooking food for a very short time in a small amount of hot fat, such as butter, oil or margarine.

SIFT means to put dry ingredients such as flour, baking powder, baking soda, cornstarch and salt through a sieve in order to remove lumps and to make the ingredients light and airy. A cup of unsifted flour is heavier and contains more flour than a cup of sifted flour.

STEAM means to cook foods in the steam rising from water boiling in the pan beneath it. The food may be set in a separate steaming basket or on a heatproof dish set in a steamer.

STIR-FRY means to cook very quickly in a small amount of hot oil, stirring and tossing the food continuously as it cooks. Stir-frying may be done in a skillet, but the best utensil is a wok because it heats very quickly and the rounded surface makes stirring easy.

Wine...and Food

Stephen H. Anchin
Kosher Wine Consultant
Yorkville Wine & Liquor

Many people still believe in the rigid rules of mating wine and food—that red wine goes with beef and white wine with chicken and fish. But just as red wine is now frequently served with fish, many chefs are pairing red-wine sauces with salmon, tuna and other fish, as well as with veal, chicken and eggs.

CRAIG CLAIBORNE *with* PIERRE FRANEY,
The New York Times Magazine
Sunday, September 20, 1987

Wine and food: Once there were rules, rules, rules; now there are no rules at all. That is the current state of affairs in the ever evolving styles of American dining, a situation likely to continue for a long time. For the kosher/American way of cooking—and dining—it is an absolutely perfect development at precisely the right time! A revolution is under way in the life-style of the American Jewish community that has left behind much of the heavy East European food and replaced it with lighter, healthier and more elegant kosher cuisine, paralleling the preference for light new foods among nonkosher American cooks. Similarly, the taste for wine as the ideal beverage to serve with the new foods has caused the rapid expansion of the selection of wine available to consumers and raised Americans' consciousness of that selection. This, too, has occurred in the last few years for the kosher consumer. And therein lies the rub: What wine does one serve with what—and how—and why? It's a whole new world out there.

If beautiful dishes and fine wines are marks of civilization, then pairing the right wine and food should be a creative challenge, not a pretension. There are no longer "right" and "wrong"—only personal preferences. Experience and knowledge, however, should be our guides. For me, choices are based on circumstances. At home, if I plan to serve truly fine quality wines with a meal, and the wines are the main focus, I use recipes that complement the wines rather than overwhelm them. If, however, my wife is intent on demonstrating her gastronomic expertise, I diplomatically choose wines that enhance the pleasure of the meal but do not steal the show. Whatever the final choice, there are basic principles that should be followed.

At this point, most cookbooks dealing with wine would begin to outline a guide on how to serve wine, which wines to serve and, perhaps, a short description of various types and categories of wine. This, however, is a chapter about wine in a "kosher" cookbook, albeit fine cuisine that happens to follow the rules of kashrut. Therefore, a short layman's explanation (without being rabbinic, for I am not a rabbi) of what makes a wine kosher follows.

Basically, from the moment the harvested grape is crushed to the moment it is bottled, it may only be physically handled by Sabbath-observant Jews. Period. For example, a young nonobservant Jew from California who was the wine maker at an ultramodern high-tech winery in Israel's Golan Heights was not allowed to touch the wine he was making. He told me that to test (and taste) the wine, a Sabbath-observant member of the local kibbutz would draw off samples from the vats and barrels and hand them to him. He was not even allowed to have keys to the winery! And speaking of keys, it is interesting to note that during the fermentation period of the Beaujolais produced in France in 1985 there was a small quantity under rabbinical supervision. Something went wrong during the Sabbath and the locked winery could not be opened until after sundown. By then, the wine was ruined and the entire vintage had to be destroyed. But the rules had not been broken—or even bent.

There are a few other rules as well. Because of the prohibition against the "mixing of species," grapes used for wine making cannot be grown in a vineyard where other types of fruits (olives, apples, etc.) are grown between the rows of vines. In Israel the grapes must be allowed to drop to the ground once every seven years (which encourages segmentation of the vineyards). Many who do not understand the reasons for kashrut are under the misconception that some rabbi "blesses" the wine and therefore it is kosher. Nothing could be further from the truth! Although this book deals with modern methods of cuisine and dining—with or without wine—wine is by religious standards an instrument for making kiddush. It is sacramental and therefore must be handled in terms of sacramental law.

There is one other rule applying to kosher wine, having to do with whether or not it is "mevushal." This term literally means that a wine has been boiled. In the past that is exactly what was done! Today, through modern technology, a wine can be "flash pasteurized" at high temperatures for a short period of time so as to satisfy this rule. The religious reason for flash pasteurization has to do with the physical handling of a sacramental product by non-Sabbath-observant people, Jewish or Gentile. If a non-observant person opens or pours a nonmevushal wine—be it at home, in a restaurant or at a catered affair (Bar or Bat Mitzvah, wedding, etc.)—it immediately loses its kashrut. If it has been "boiled," however, it is no longer officially considered "wine" and therefore may be handled by nonobservant persons. (This is especially important to caterers, who have problems locating Sabbath-observant wine stewards.)

And that's it. From this point forward, we may deal with the basics of serving and enjoying wine. Well-prepared foods deserve wines chosen with the same care.

Basic Principles of Serving Wine

ORDER OF SERVICE

Aperitif wines are served before a meal. I personally prefer them to hard liquor, which tends to reduce one's appreciation of the meal to come. Aperitifs usually are white, rosé or blush wines—all served cold—but my favorite and the most elegant aperitif is champagne from France. There are many sparkling kosher wines from all over the world, but true champagne is French.

If the occasion calls for a kiddush over wine and a sweet sacramental wine is to be used, provide an extra wine glass for each person having the sweet wine.

Pouring a dry wine into a glass with sweet wine residue may ruin its character. A glass or crystal goblet should *always* be used when serving *any* dry or semidry (non-kiddush) wine.

Serve dry white (or rosé and blush) table wines before red table wines. They are called table wines because they are ideal with food. They are called "dry" table wines because they are not sweet, although they may be "fruity."

Cold wines are served before those at "room temperature." Nonchilled wines are generally red, although with today's new flexibility, even some reds are served slightly chilled, or at "cellar temperature."

Serve dry wines before sweet wines, which generally come at the end of a meal, with dessert. Serving sweet wine before dry wine will make the dry wine taste sour.

What to Serve

WHITE WINES

Many people prefer white wine to any other with a meal or hors d'oeuvres. Choosing wine to complement food is not difficult if you know the style of the food.

Fish, poultry, lamb, goat cheese and low-fat cheese should generally be accompanied by white wine, although I will suggest some red and pink wines that work as well.

CHARDONNAY is the name of a grape that produces the most prestigious dry white wines—and champagnes—throughout the world. Chardonnay wines have many subtle differences—depending upon where the grape is grown and who makes a wine with it—but their character is basically the same. In the Burgundy region of France the Chardonnay grape is legally the only white wine grape that may be used (with one exception, of course). There the wine is called by the name of the village or region where it is made: Chablis, Mâcon-Villages, Pouilly-Fuissé, Chassagne-Montrachet. Not all these places produce kosher wines yet, but they are beginning to appear. There are kosher Chablis and Mâcon-Villages and soon there will be Montrachets and Mersaults.

California is currently the region providing the greatest number of kosher Chardonnay wines. There wine is named by vineyard rather than by town or region. Vineyards like Hagafen, Weinstock, Gan Eden and Baron Jaquab de Herzog produce excellent examples of California Chardonnay which have won awards in competition with their nonkosher brethren.

Chardonnay is generally a dry, smooth, white wine, often with hints of the flavor of butter and apples and a rich creamy texture, although not heavy. If aged in oak barrels it develops a complexity that allows it to be savored by itself or with cheese and bread or crackers. It is wonderful with nearly all poultry and fish dishes, especially those with sauces or gravies.

SAUVIGNON BLANC is the next most important white wine grape, one which provides perhaps the greatest variety of kosher wines, in styles ranging from crisp and dry to quite fruity and soft. The Sauvignon Blanc grape is successfully grown in Israel, France and California, and is sometimes blended with other grapes to make more complex wines. This grape produces wines that are often described as "earthy," "grassy," "puckery," or "tart."

The New York Times has called Yarden Sauvignon Blanc (from the Golan Heights in Israel) "one of the best under $10 bottles of wine from around the world." This wine is composed partly of another grape called Semillion which takes away some of the grassiness and tartness of the Sauvignon Blanc grape. It gives the wine "roundness," meaning a softer, more subtle flavor that goes well with poultry and sauced fish. All French white Bordeaux are made in this manner as well, whether they are called "semidry" or "dry" or "sec." These wines are also lovely by themselves and make terrific aperitif wines.

The Sauvignon Blanc grape is also used to make another excellent French wine from the Loire Valley called Sancerre. This wine is tart, dry, crisp and slightly citric. It has to be one of the best wines to serve, with grilled fish or as an aperitif. It may be hard to find, but it's worth it. California Sauvignon Blanc is often made in this style although it is usually more "grassy" and is also well worth seeking out. These wines also tend to be a little fruitier and less tart than their French cousins.

GEWÜRZTRAMINER is another grape used to produce white wine. It used to be used only in Alsace, France, but now is growing quite popular with California wine makers. It has a wonderful fragrant bouquet (or, in wine jargon, "nose") that smells like flowers and orchards. Gewürztraminer wine is usually quite dry when made in the French style but in California it is often quite fruity. Gan Eden vineyard makes a sweet nectarlike Gewürztraminer in California (it has 4 percent residual grape sugar after fermentation) that is superb as a dessert wine with fruits and cakes. The dry Gewürztraminer wines go well with strongly flavored or spiced foods.

CHENIN BLANC is an often underrated grape that produces a "blending" wine for simple aperitif use or fruity "jug" wines. In France, however, it is used in the Loire Valley near Paris to produce superb demi-sec (slightly sweet) wines called Vouvray. You can now find the first kosher Vouvray on the market. They are wonderful with cheese and fruit or raisiny sauces used on some fish or crepe recipes. This grape is also used to make a sparkling wine (Sparkling Vouvray) that is dry, crisp, "clean" (meaning it leaves your mouth refreshed without a sugar or grape aftertaste) and a great alternative to Champagne, often at half the price.

JOHANNISBERG RIESLING and some of its hybrids like Emerald Riesling produce soft, fruity and fragrant wines that are best suited for those who like white wines to be "not too dry" and yet not really sweet. Today the best kosher Rieslings are being produced in a fruity style in both California and upstate New York and in a crisp, dry style in Alsace, France. Barbecued chicken in a sweet and sour sauce (or any other dish that is sweet and sour) and kosher Chinese recipes are well suited for Riesling wines.

RED WINES

Although I have found during my years as a retail wine merchant that the majority of Americans, whether kosher or not, prefer white wine, as time passes and experience is gained their taste for dry red wine grows. It would not be incorrect to say that most of the world's great wines are red. Unfortunately, red wines in the kosher category have a way to go—but the process has begun. As this is being written the very first kosher red Bordeaux produced at a vineyard owned by the renowned Rothschild family (Château Clarke, Haut-Médoc) is arriving on American shores. The first Chianti Classico arrived but weeks ago from Italy. In due time there are certain to be great personal kosher cellars filled with old vintages of great kosher red wine.

But what to serve now? There are, in fact, many good quality red wines to be found in the kosher selection at your wine shop. Red wines seem to go best with lamb or hearty poultry dishes as well as many veal dishes and stews. Red wines also go well with strong or full-flavored hard cheeses and substantial soft cheeses like Brie. The following will list some red wines by grape type (as in the white section) and others by place of origin.

CABERNET SAUVIGNON   is one of the world's two great red wine grapes which, like Chardonnay, produces subtly different wines depending where the grape is grown and who the wine maker is. (The other great grape is called PINOT NOIR, the main red wine grape of Burgundy and now also grown in California and the Northwest part of the U.S., but there have yet to arrive any kosher red wines made from it. I have heard rumors that this may change, but again, check with your wine merchant.)

The Cabernet Sauvignon grape is the base for almost all fine dry red kosher wines. Nothing complements a steak, prime ribs, rack of lamb, brisket or veal in a cabernet sauce better than this variety of wine.

The place of origin is the Bordeaux region of France. Wines produced here are often blended with other grapes like Merlot and Cabernet Franc to achieve various textural and flavor characteristics. These wines are not labeled by the grape name but by the name of the vineyard, usually beginning with the word "Château." Usually on the label, under the name of the vineyard—or Château—the French will tell you where in Bordeaux the wine originated. Kosher Bordeaux that I have seen have come from the following areas; Médoc, Haut-Médoc, St.-Estèphe, St.-Émilion or just regional Bordeaux or Bordeaux Supérieur. All are similar in style but differ widely in quality.

Try to find wines that are at least three or four years old, as aging time in the bottle is needed for the wine to develop the proper character. It's also a good idea to open it fifteen to twenty minutes before serving, as a little aeration brings out the wine's flavors and bouquet. Do not chill the wine. It is meant to be served at room temperature or slightly cooler ("cellar temperature").

Fine kosher Cabernet Sauvignon grapes are also grown in Israel, originally planted there in the 1890's by the Rothschild family. Some of the cuttings of the original vines are still producing the highest quality grapes. Carmel recently released an all-new Carmel Vineyard Cabernet Sauvignon that is excellent, and Yarden/Gamla vineyards in the cool Napa Valley–like Golan Heights are producing top-flight wines from this grape.

Excellent Cabernets have long been produced in California. At Hagafen Vineyards in the Napa Valley they made the first kosher wine of this type served at the White House. Baron Jaquab de Herzog (Kedem) has released the best mevushal Cabernet on the market. I have tasted kosher Cabernet from Hungary that was served a couple of Passovers ago at Tavern on the Green in Central Park, New York City. It was dry, lovely smooth red wine, ideal with roasted meats.

GAMAY   also produces good red wines that are much lighter in body and flavor than Cabernet Sauvignon and tend to be fruitier (not sweeter). This red may be lightly chilled—not cold—and is a perfect accompaniment to lighter meat dishes. It's great with hamburger or meat loaf, a barbecued steak, veal chops or stews that have slightly sweet gravies.

Most Gamay wines are labeled as Beaujolais from the southern section of Burgundy, France. They are country wines whose chief charm is youth. Do not buy any that are more than three years old. They are not meant to be aged. Recently some Gamay wines have arrived from California. They are similar to their French counterparts, but six thousand miles make a difference. If you can, try a Beaujolais and a California Gamay at the same meal—you'll see the difference.

LOIRE VALLEY, FRANCE   Red wines produced in this lush agricultural region of France are made from a number of grapes, but it is more important to know their style, not origins. They are called names like Gigondas, Côtes du Rhone and Coteaux du Tricistan. These true dry red French wines are often hearty, rich and smooth (sometimes velvety). Similar types of hearty dishes are best served with them. A hearty Gigondas and a rich wine-based beef stew on a cold winter's day is a pleasure to be experienced! If you can get kosher venison, it is ideal with the wines of this region.

ITALIAN RED WINES   are generally lighter than French and California reds. As of this date there are only two kosher Italian reds: Valpolicella and Chianti Classico. The Valpolicella is a simple light dry red that is inexpensive and all purpose. The Chianti is more interesting. It is slightly tart and rough in a pleasant sort of way, with a bright cherrylike color. It is perfect with any pasta or red meat dish—or served with pizza and salad during the Sunday afternoon football game. It is also good with hard cheeses.

ROSÉS AND BLUSH WINES

Kosher rosés and the new category of rosés called "blush wines" tend to be simple, light, fruity (sometimes semidry), enjoyable wines. Although I never found rosés very interesting, the blush wines are an exciting recent development and great fun for everyone. Whether you are sipping one on a patio, at the beach or in your living room or serving it with salad and cheese, chicken or fish, hot dogs from the grill or poached salmon, these wines are all purpose and adaptable to almost any occasion. They are also excellent as introductory wines for young or new wine drinkers.

Blush wines are made from red grapes, are usually called "white" or "blanc" and are pink to salmonlike in color. The two most popular are WHITE ZINFANDEL from California and CABERNET BLANC from Israel. A number of different vineyards produce these wines under various brand names (Weinstock, Baron Jaquab de Herzog, Hagafen, Carmel, Yarden, Gamla).

CHAMPAGNES AND SPARKLING WINES

These are nature's most festive beverages. The perfect aperitif, the ideal dinner wine, dessert's best friend, bubbly wine ranges from bone dry (usually called "Brut") to somewhat fruity (usually called "Demi-Sec" or "extra dry") to rather sweet (usually from Italy and called Asti Spumante or Moscato Spumante). It should always be served icy cold in tall thin glasses called flutes (not flat round sherbet dishes that let all the bubbles escape) or tulipes. Champagne or sparkling wine adds a touch of elegance to any occasion.

Kosher Champagnes (only from France) and sparkling wines (from everywhere else in the world but France) have also come a long way. They are as well made and elegant as any nonkosher sparkler—or as cheap and poorly made as any nonkosher bubble-infused wine. Your taste and the knowledge of a reputable wine merchant should help you in choosing the right price and quality for the occasion. Just remember, no matter what the occasion, Champagne is always correct—and always appreciated.

Menus

NOTE: Many of these menus suggest a mixed green salad. I am not referring to a particular recipe, but to your favorite salad greens—you may choose from arugula, *mâche*, endive, Bibb, radicchio, among others—tossed with a vinaigrette dressing.

BUFFET BRUNCH
Spinach Roll, Feta
Cheese Strudel
Tortilla
Smoked Whitefish Pâté
Marinated Salmon
Mixed Green Salad with Vinaigrette Dressing
Fresh Fruit
Scones
Large Rugelach
Lemon Almond Loaf
Chardonnay (California) or
Cabernet Blanc (Israel)

CASUAL
SUMMER LUNCHEON
Cucumber Soup
Bow Ties with Green Beans and Basil
Mixed Green Salad
Fresh Berries
Butter Cookies
White Zinfandel or
Pinot Noir Blanc

ELEGANT
SUMMER LUNCHEON
Tomato Soup
Tuna Seviche
Cucumber Salad
Cherry Tomato Salad
Potato Salad
Lemon Ice Cream
Rugelach
French Sancerre or
California Sauvignon Blanc

CASUAL
WINTER LUNCHEON
Puréed Beet Soup
Steamed Chicken Salad
Seasonal Fruits
Mandelbrot
White Bordeaux or
French Beaujolais

ELEGANT
WINTER LUNCHEON
Puréed Vegetable Soup
Whole Steamed Salmon in Foil with Ginger Vinaigrette Dressing
Orzo Salad
Cheese Torte
Alsace or California Gewürztraminer (dry)

CASUAL
SUMMER DINNER
Gazpacho
Broiled or Barbecued Tuna Steaks
Mixed Green Salad
Vanilla Ice Cream
Hazelnut Balls
Italian Pinot Grigio or
Pinot Noir Blanc

ELEGANT
SUMMER DINNER
Carrot Soup
Steamed Salmon with Tomato Sauce and Julienne Vegetables
Mixed Green Salad
Mango Sorbet
Chocolate Walnut Meringue Squares
Mâcon-Villages or
Chablis Grand Cru

CASUAL
WINTER DINNER
Latkes
Hearty Vegetable Soup
Chicken with Capers and Olives
Plain Boiled Rice
Mixed Green Salad
Broiled Apple Rounds
Brownie Thins
Red Côtes du Rhone (France)
or California Gamay Beaujolais

ELEGANT
WINTER DINNER
Crunchy Chicken Tidbits
Souffléed Acorn Squash
Chicken Breasts with Lemon and Raisins
Plain Boiled Rice
Steamed Asparagus
Assorted Winter Fruits
Chocolate Mousse Cake
Rosé de Clarice

SUMMER
SABBATH LUNCHEON
Challah
Cold Carrot Soup
Cold Chinese-Style Linguine with Chicken and Vegetables
Mixed Green Salad
Fresh Berries
Almond Cookies
Italian Chianti or
Italian Soave

WINTER
SABBATH LUNCHEON
Challah
Marinated Salmon
Cholent
Beet Salad
Apple Tart with Walnut Crust
Israeli or
California Cabernet Sauvignon

FRIDAY NIGHT DINNER
Marinated Salmon with Green Peppercorns
Beet Consommé with Dilled Chicken or Beef Piroshki
Baked Chicken with Soy Sauce and Ginger
Baked Spaghetti Squash
Pears in Red Wine
Lemon Pecan Squares
French Vouvray

THANKSGIVING
Smoked Whitefish Pâté
Sherry's Jerusalem Artichoke Soup
Roast Turkey
Bulghur Pilaf
Acorn Squash Purée
Apple Crisp
Beaujolais-Villages (Nouveau if available) or
California Chardonnay

ROSH HASHANAH
Round Challah
Gefilte Fish
Chicken Soup with Dilled Chicken or Beef Piroshki
Roast Breast of Veal
Kasha
Tzimmes
Pineapple Sorbet
Chocolate Almond Cake
French Red Bordeaux from St.-Estèphe,
Haut-Médoc, Médoc, Margaux or St.-Émilion

NEW YEAR'S EVE

Salmon Tartare I or II

Duck with Hoisin Sauce

Roasted Shallots

Stir-fried Shiitake Mushrooms

Orzo with Parsley

Poached Pears

Chocolate Almond Truffles

French Brut Champagne

Index

Daikon, 250
Dairy foods, xiv, xv
  see also Cake, dairy; Cocktail
    food, dairy; Cookies, dairy;
    Desserts, dairy; Fish, dairy;
    Fruits, dairy; Ice cream, dairy;
    Pasta, dairy; Pâtés, dairy;
    Salad, dairy; Sauces, dairy;
    Soufflé, dairy; Soups, dairy;
    Vegetables, dairy
Dates:
  Honey Date Loaf, 240
Deep-frying, 257
  Crunchy Chicken Tidbits, 31
  Curried Wontons, 32–33
  Sole in Seaweed Batter, 14
Desserts, dairy, 199–203
  Banana Ice Cream, 199
  Butter Almond Cookies, 223
  Butter Cookies, 224
  Cheese Torte, 227–28
  Chocolate Soufflé Cake, 232
  Chocolate Walnut Meringue
    Squares, 226
  Cinnamon Apple Ice Cream Chez
    Panisse, 203
  Coffee Chocolate-Chip Ice
    Cream, 201
  Hazelnut Balls, 222
  Large Rugelach, 221
  Lemon Almond Cake, 229
  Lemon Almond Loaf, 230
  Lemon Ice Cream, 200
  Rugelach, 219–20
  Scones, 225
  Sour Cream Coffee Cake, 231
  Vanilla Ice Cream, 202
  Walnut Roll, 234
Desserts, pareve, 204–14
  Almond Cookies, 237
  Apple Crisp, 208
  Applesauce, 209
  Apple Tart with Walnut Crust,
    241
  Blueberry Sorbet, 214
  Broiled Apple Rounds, 207
  Brownie Thins, 236
  Chocolate Almond Cake, 243
  Chocolate Almond Truffles, 245

Chocolate Mousse Cake, 242
Chocolate Nut Clusters, 238
Chocolate Walnut Torte, 244
Dione Lucas's Chocolate Mousse,
  211
Frozen Raspberry Mousse, 210
Honey Date Loaf, 240
Lemon Pecan Squares, 239
Mandelbrot, 235
Mango Sorbet, 212
Pear Sorbet, 213
Pears in Red Wine, 206
Pineapple Sorbet, 214
Poached Peaches with Raspberry
  Sauce, 204
Poached Pears, 205
Detergents, kosher, xvi
Dicing, 257
Dill, 251
Dilled Chicken or Beef *Piroshki*, 94
Dinner, Friday night, menu for, 270
Dinner, summer (menus):
  casual, 268
  elegant, 269
Dinner, winter (menus):
  casual, 269
  elegant, 269
Dione Lucas's Chocolate Mousse,
  211
Dip:
  for Crunchy Chicken Tidbits, 31
  Pepper-Salt Dip, for Sole in
    Seaweed Batter, 14
  Strips of Crisp Potato Skins with
    Sour Cream Dip, 7
Dish drainers, xvi
Dishes, separating, xv–xvi
Dishwasher racks, xvi
Dishwashers, separating, xv–xvi
Domestic birds, *see* Poultry
Dough:
  for Cheese Torte, 227
  for Chocolate Walnut Meringue
    Squares, 226
  for Large Rugelach, 221
  for Potato Cheese *Piroshki*, 71–
    72
  for Rugelach, 219
Dressing:

for Chicken Salad with Fresh
  Herbs, 184
for Chinese-Style Pasta with Veg-
  etables, 83
for Cold Chinese-Style Linguine
  with Chicken and Vegetables,
  92, 93
Creamy Vinaigrette Dressing, 189
for Potato Salad, 179
for Spinach Spaghetti Primavera,
  82
see also Vinaigrette dressing
Dried beans, xv, 251
Dried herbs, 251
Dryer, salad spin, 256
Dry white table wine, 261
Dry wine, 261
Duck:
  Braised Soy Sauce Duck, 133
  Broiled Duck Breasts with Ginger
    Sauce, 134
  Duck with *Hoisin* Sauce, 135

Eggplant:
  Spaghetti with Eggplant, Peppers
    and Ricotta, 67
Eggs, 250
  consumption of blood forbidden
    for, xiv
  see also Omelets, pareve
Egg whites, 250
Electric ice cream makers, vs. non-
  electric ice cream makers, 255
Electric mixer, 255
Electric ovens, 256
Emerald Riesling white wine, 262
Equipment, kitchen, 255–56
European dried mushrooms, 250

Feta Cheese Strudel, 11
Fillets of Grey Sole en Papillote,
  100
Filling:
  for Apple Tart with Walnut
    Crust, 241
  for Cheese Torte, 227–28
  for Curried Wontons, 32

About the Author

HELEN NASH was born in Cracow, Poland, and comes from an old rabbinical family. Having spent the war years in the Soviet Union and Asia, she moved to New York, where she studied with such famous cooks as Michael Field and Lydie Marshall. Determined to prove that kosher cooking could be as varied, light, elegant and exciting as any other style of cooking, she published *Kosher Cuisine* in 1984 to great acclaim. *Helen Nash's Kosher Kitchen* is her second book. Helen Nash lives in New York City with her husband, Jack.